N. H. VOCATIONAL-TECHN

WHEELS WITHIN WHEELS

Boyhood sweetheart—the family physician's Model A Ford
(Photo taken with a Brownie camera by the author at the age of nine)

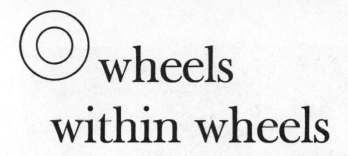

wheels within wheels

A Short History of American
Motor Car Manufacturing

Second Edition, Revised

PHILIP HILLYER SMITH

FUNK & WAGNALLS   New York

To my son, Philip

preface

This book is the outcome of an early love affair with the automobile.

The romance began when a 1904 Premier blundered down our dead-end street to the delight of us small fry and to the consternation of our parents. It became passionate when an intimate relationship was established with the family physician's Model A Ford (Henry's firstborn) and Mitchell, and when a one-mile ride in a Pope-Toledo could be purchased for ten cents at the annual church picnic, courtesy of the wealthiest man in town.

The Pope-Toledo suffered an early death; the Mitchell followed it into oblivion two decades later, but always there were new cars appearing to catch and hold the affections of the horseless vehicle fan.

Youngsters of my generation would stand at a main road intersection, not to watch the Fords go by, but to see and distinguish a Matheson, a Chadwick, or a Grout steamer, and to catch a glimpse of license plates from far-off states. They came there for a vision of a larger world, much as boys of an earlier generation visited the docks to see clippers arrive from foreign ports, or more recent generations have been lured to airports to watch transports wing in from countries not to be found in old geographies.

Out of an interest in cars grew an interest in the lives of the companies building them. There have been hundreds of scattered factories putting their horseless vehicles at the mercy of the market place. They came and went, only a few surviving for long, yet the industry expanded and grew fatter.

Watching the cycle of birth and death of individual companies, which seemed to lead to increasing vitality, I came to think of the industry as a living organism composed of individual cells. Some cells divided, some came together, some were replaced by new ones, but the vast majority simply died. All of them fought for survival and through that struggle, even though it ended in defeat, they accelerated the development of the automobile and public acceptance of it.

The struggle and what those who took part in it contributed to the industry is the substance of this book. Presenting the industry as a living organism brings to light events and activities the significance of which has become obscured by the passage of time and the blinding success of the survivors. In doing this it has been necessary to shatter a few myths.

Basic to this study is a listing of passenger cars and their manufacturers which have constituted the industry since its inception. This list is to be found at the end of the book with an explanatory introduction. All statistical data regarding companies have been derived from this compilation; total production or factory sales figures are those published by the Automobile Manufacturers Association. For those who enjoy seeing history portrayed in chart form, a turn to the back of the book may be rewarding.

What this story covers, then, is the period of experimentation from 1895 to 1900, and the period 1900 to 1966, the years which saw the industry crawl, get up on its feet, sow its wild oats, and finally become tame, respectable, and obese.

PHILIP HILLYER SMITH

Sherman, Connecticut

contents

WHEELS WITHIN WHEELS

1
age of innocence:
1895–1899

Chronicles of the Gay Nineties recall gaslight, extreme fashion, and a hybrid architecture. Far more important and rarely mentioned was the laying of the foundation for America's most cherished industry—the manufacture of automobiles.

It is difficult to pinpoint the exact date and place of birth of the industry to everyone's satisfaction. Between 1895 and 1900, scores of men were building rigs that ran after a fashion and occasionally selling their handiwork, or a duplicate, to a venturesome spirit, but few had reached the state of commercialization.

Nevertheless, a historian surveying the industry of today sees an aggregation of companies producing vehicles powered by internal-combustion engines and, reaching back to see when and where such vehicles were first produced for commerce, comes up with the date 1895 and the birthplace New England. Perhaps 1900 is a more meaningful date, but let us not quibble.

If by some trick one could obliterate the seventy-three years that have passed since 1895 and ask a knowledgeable person of that era what he thought about the automobile industry, he might well ask, "What industry?" He would be aware only of electric vehicles, a few steam-propelled cars that scared him half to death, and an occasional gas buggy that stank to high heaven and was noisy as well. He would know little or nothing about the manufacturers.

If it were possibilities for investment that prompted the query and it was addressed to a substantial citizen, he would most likely advise looking into the bicycle business, which was then profiting from the enormous popularity of the newly introduced "safety" bicycle—a bicycle with two equal-size wheels rather than a single large wheel and small trailing wheel.

The "safety" was giving urban residents a mobility never before experienced. The craze was "doing a century," pedaling one hundred miles in one day, a feat much less debilitating to a man in good physical condition than piloting a horseless carriage an equal distance.

The year 1895 is generally accepted as the birth year of the industry and New England as the cradle because of the brothers Charles and J. Frank Duryea. In that year they won the Chicago *Times-Herald*-sponsored race in Jackson Park, Chicago. By covering fifty-two miles in the elapsed time of ten hours, twenty-three minutes, which figures out to about five miles per hour, they beat all competitors, in particular a Benz car, pride of Germany, and captured the prize of $2,000. This whirlwind feat made headlines in the press and attracted attention to the horseless vehicle as never before. And because the Duryeas went on to build more and better vehicles and sold some, they were in business and the impression was given that there was more to the automobile than met the eye.

Two years later, the Electric Vehicle Co. was formed by some traction magnates, using as a nucleus the Electric Carriage & Wagon Co. of Philadelphia. In addition to putting a fleet of electric taxicabs on the streets of New York City, its promoters unloaded a large amount of stock on the public. The whole business was more manipulative than constructive and it was relatively short-lived.

But let us assume for the moment that such pioneers as the Duryeas, Henry Ford, Elwood Haynes, Charles King, and Alexander Winton had become discouraged with their gasoline-powered vehicles and, further, that the Electric Vehicle Co. and others producing electric cars had gone on to great achievement. Would they now be considered the founders of the industry? No one in 1895, or even in 1899, could have given an assured forecast of things to come. Few people saw an industry in the making and fewer still were venturing a prophecy. All the more unusual, therefore, is this editorial which appeared in *The Horseless Age* in November, 1895:

> Those who have taken the pains to search below the surface of the great tendencies of the age, know what a giant industry is struggling into being there. All signs point to the motor vehicle as the necessary sequence of methods of locomotion already established and approved. The growing

needs of our civilization demand it; the public believes in it, and await with lively interest its practical application to the daily business of the world.

Given the year 1895 as the founding year, the birthplace was New England because the Duryea brothers manufactured in Springfield, Massachusetts. But this raises the question why New England rather than some other section of the country. Two reasons are generally advanced—accumulated wealth and manpower. There were many wealthy New Englanders, but few channeled their wealth in the direction of automobile manufacture. They adopted the horseless vehicle because it was new, exciting, and sporting. The rich man purchased electric vehicles or foreign cars, mainly French, because they had a better reputation. Also, he could afford a chauffeur, and a chauffeur was really indispensable if the owner wished to arrive at his destination and, if he reached it, look like a man of means rather than like a mechanic.

I am inclined to believe the factor of wealth to be overestimated as an explanation of why New England didn't sleep. What the wealthy contributed was their patronage, which raised the automobile in public esteem to give it what we now call status. And their importations brought to these shores the latest in European developments to stimulate the inventive mind.

What New England had in abundance was skilled artisans—a reservoir of men who knew how to fabricate articles from metal. Firearms and clocks were notable examples. The Yankee had always shown a marked streak of inventiveness and in his manufacturing enterprise he had already begun to use special-purpose tools and a division of labor in the production of component parts. He was a good salesman as well. If he did not actually make and sell wooden nutmegs, the claim that he did is admirably symbolic.

Searchers have turned up the names of well over one hundred individuals or companies producing a car in New England, but a close examination reveals most of the vehicles to have been purely experimental.

In December, 1899, the *Automobile Magazine* said: "Of the 300 and odd American manufacturers of automobiles, as enumerated in a recent English trade manual, barely a dozen have their products in general evidence."

From this one can conclude that a great deal of experimentation was going on, but that few tinkerers had crossed the threshold to genuine manufacture for the public. This is borne out by other statements.

In March, 1909, *Motor* published a list of companies manufacturing automobiles during the period 1895–1909. Charles E. Duryea and Julian Chase, editor of the magazine, were the chief compilers. Duryea had manufactured in Springfield, Massachusetts, Chase hailed from Pawtucket, Rhode Island, hence any bias they had might have favored New England. They put the number of producers between 1895 and 1899 at forty-two. Of these, fifteen were in New England, fifteen in the Middle Atlantic states, and twelve in the Middle West. Moreover, that proportioning among the three areas pertained from the first to the last of the period; hence it is clear that New England's leadership was neither outstanding nor lasting.

These figures are important because they refute the widely held impression that manufacture was concentrated in New England and spread slowly westward. The impression almost completely obscures one of the most astonishing and significant of phenomena. The westward sweep, far from being sluggish, was so rapid as to resemble wildfire epidemic rather than a fever transmitted slowly from person to person. The news and sight of a few strange contraptions had been sufficiently widespread to capture the attention of hundreds of men and spur them to develop the potentialities of the self-propelled vehicle.

New England may have had the money and the skilled artisans, particularly in the Connecticut River Valley, but so did New York and Pennsylvania, centering around the cities of New York and Philadelphia. The territory east of the Mississippi and north of the thirty-eighth parallel may not have contained as many wealthy people, but it had plenty of ingenious men with the entrepreneur spirit, as subsequent events showed.

As the century drew to a close, horseless vehicles were being propelled by electricity, steam, and gasoline engines. The electrics were silent but slow; steamers were quiet and fast; gasoline vehicles both raucous and slow. The electric vehicle was by far the most popular, but lost out to the steamer. Then both electricity and steam capitulated to the gasoline engine as the principal power source.

Whatever the motive power, the vehicle of that day bore a striking resemblance to its progenitor, the horse-drawn vehicle minus the shafts. It was basically a buggy with power added. Bicycle parts, such as the tubular frame and wire-spoked wheel, were often employed because they were strong and right at hand. Design had not become set and it was to take years before it did. It could not happen until the heritage of the horse-drawn vehicle had been swept from mind.

It is doubtful that anyone foresaw the ultimate dominance of the gasoline-propelled vehicle except the fanatics who were working to perfect it. Looking back from the near vantage point of 1901, the *Automobile Magazine* offered this explanation for the popularity of the electric and the steamer: "The electric carriage was the rage in this country for a short time, mainly because a rich company discovered the opportunity for disposing of thousands of storage batteries by taking advantage of the public's predisposition in favor of electricity." This sounds like a veiled reference to the Electric Vehicle Co., which was still in existence. It went on to say: "The steam vehicle subsequently gained ascendancy mostly through the fact that it could be produced on a large scale by automatic machinery already existing—and, then, because gasoline machines in those days left an odorous trail and rattled."

Development of the steam car centered in and around Boston and never did gain a foothold in the Middle West. The brothers Francis E. and Freeland O. Stanley of Newton, Massachusetts, were the most successful of the pioneers. Having developed a photographic dry plate which they later sold to Eastman Kodak, they worked on steam boilers and by 1896 they were able to put a steamer on the market. Three years later they sold their patent rights, thus giving rise to the Locomobile Co. of America at Bridgeport, Connecticut, and the Mobile Co. of America at Tarrytown, New York, and bringing about their own temporary withdrawal from the scene. The "of America" in the corporate titles imparted a grandeur not evident in the products.

The automobile was winning increasing attention from the press and the public. The popular magazines of the day were discussing the banning of cars from public parks, and the vehicles they described in their pages were predominantly of French extraction. Automobiles (it is proper to use this French-coined word because it had then come into general use) were a prime attraction at country fairs throughout the nation. But this does not mean that every vehicle displayed was a commercial product any more than were the jars of home-canned string beans exhibited by the housewife. With reference to an auto exhibition at an agricultural fair held near Providence, Rhode Island, in 1898, the *Scientific American* suggested editorially that no infant industry had been encouraged as this one and that the results to date did not indicate that the sums thus expended were warranted.

To add to the sour note struck by a periodical respected for its interpretation and evaluation of things mechanical, there were anguished cries from horse lovers and horse owners. The horse took a violent dislike to the automobile. Its reaction on meeting one of the new devil wagons was to rear on its hind legs, then bolt. To prevent such wild conduct, the driver would dismount, hold the quivering animal by its bridle, and lead it past the snorting rival. This did not add to the charm of driving, nor did it generate good will for the automobile. The flavor of the controversy between the horse lover and the motorist is eloquently conveyed in a passage-at-arms which appeared in the columns of the Boston *Transcript*. The writer, who signs himself "The Listener," said:

It is hard enough to live or work in the city even with the daily sight of strong, sweet, sensible, beautiful, patient horses all about one. Without them it would be simply impossible —not for a moment to be thought of. Neither wild horses nor any sort of self-propelled vehicle or locomotive could drag me into a horseless city.

To this praise for the horse and his contribution to the city beautiful was appended this reply:

A city without noise is the ideal of civilization, and it is towards that ideal that the automobile is bringing us. The horse is now one of the greatest drags upon the wheels of progress. It is the chief maker of the vast and overwhelming din that envelopes the modern city. It is for the horse that the stone pavements are laid, to keep his feet from slipping. And over every separate stone, set to that end, he drags bumpingly, poundingly, crashingly, with unceasing rattlety-bang, the endless procession of clamoring carriages, wagons, carts, and drays. Then at the end of the day every frequented street that meanwhile has not been constantly cleaned is literally carpeted with a warm, brown matting of comminuted horse-dropping, smelling to heaven and destined in no inconsiderable part to be scattered in fine dust in all directions, laden with countless millions of disease-bearing germs. Then what words can characterize the nuisance for hundreds of city neighborhoods caused by the stables that house the "sweet" animal, ruining the property of the unfortunate persons near whom their erection chances to be permitted by the perversity or cupidity of municipal authorities? A horseless city means a clean city, a quiet city, a wholesome city, a more odorless and beautiful city.

Since the automobiles then most common were propelled by electricity or steam and rolled on rubber, the vision of a more attractive city to be had by replacing the horse was not as silly as it sounds today. What no prophet foresaw was the reduction in the population of English sparrows, which were great contributors to the noise and dirt of the city.

Another stout defender of the automobile was one Sylvester Baxter, who had this to say in an article entitled "How the Horse Runs Amuck":

> It is particularly appropriate that some cold facts about the horse be laid before the public at the present time. These will substantiate the assertion that the horse is an animal of extraordinary little sense—using the word as synonymous with judgment. He has a remarkably delicate perception, coupled with a slight power of correlation. He is therefore subject to seizure at any moment with fits of the most violent insanity, induced at the slightest provocation. . . . It is quite natural that the horse should have a nature so unbalanced mentally.

Mr. Baxter then appended a list of accidents and runaways and ended with these prophetic words:

> And what reason will there be for keeping a horse in any part of the country when there are good roads, when a good motor vehicle can be had for the price of an ordinary horse and carriage with equipment, while the items of depreciation and of running expense on the part of the automobile are trivial in comparison?

The automobile was on trial before the bar of public opinion, and until it won its case the attitude of the horse-and-buggy owners represented potent sales resistance. These people had to be won over, for they were the logical buyers of motorcars by virtue of their financial ability to possess a horse and buggy.

While the infant industry was engaged in this struggle, an event took place which threatened to strangle that part of the industry using the gasoline engine as the motive power. In 1899, Colonel Albert A. Pope, manufacturer of the famed Columbia bicycle, who had teamed up with the Electric Vehicle Co., acquired the Selden patent from George B. Selden. The patent holders claimed coverage of any vehicle powered by a gasoline engine. Selden applied for the patent in 1879, then by delaying tactics forestalled its issuance until 1895. At no time had he made any effort to collect royalties, but in the hands of the colonel and the Electric Vehicle Co. the situation changed rapidly. Selden had sat like a spider waiting for the flies to breed; the flies were now breeding fast and the new owners of the patent were going to collect royalties and split with Selden. The element of monopoly, the legal right to prevent manufacture, did not become clearly apparent for several years.

If the future appeared ominous for the "screwballs" seeking to perfect the gasoline vehicle, the threat was not sufficient to swerve them from their purpose and the new century opened with a crescendo of popping engines.

2
trial and error:
1900–1909

There is every probability that it [the automobile] will prove the vehicle of flight for runaway lovers of the incoming century. Side by side they can sit as they speed onward, the young man's attention only being distracted from his beloved by his being obliged to keep an eye on the brake, and there is no need of a grinning, horrid coachman.

Automobile Magazine, 1900

The twentieth century dawned with hardly better prospects for a viable industry. If a concern turned out a dozen cars in a year, it was doing well. There was no Ford company, no General Motors, and no Chrysler Corporation. Henry Ford had been experimenting for several years and was trying to get under way as a producer, but there was little reason to believe he would ever build a practical machine, much less get into volume production.

Ransom E. Olds had built a steamer, become discouraged with steam as a power source, and had swung over to the internal-combustion engine. He was hard at work trying to develop a vehicle that would be salable. The automobile was still considered a fly-by-night proposition by the vast majority of the public.

The Automobile Manufacturers Association, to which one must turn for production figures, gives the output for the year 1900 as 4,195 vehicles. Since there were no more than 60 companies producing cars for sale and none of them building any great number, the total would seem to include all vehicles fabricated that year, whether purely experimental or commercial. No make of car built that year survives to this day, with the sole exception of the Oldsmobile. The Olds Motor Works was readying a car to be put into volume production in another year.

The cars attracting public attention in 1900 were the Haynes-Apperson, Locomobile steamer, Columbia electric (a Pope creation), Packard, Peerless, Stearns, and Winton. All gasoline-propelled vehicles were relatively high in price.

New York City boasted the greatest number of manufacturers (though not the largest production), followed by Chicago and Cleveland. Detroit moved into second place in 1903, and in 1905 took the lead, never to relinquish it.

1900	New York	10	Chicago	6	Cleveland	4
1901	New York	12	Chicago	5	Cleveland	5
1902	New York	7	Cleveland	7	Chicago	5
1903	Cleveland	11	Detroit	9	New York	8
1904	Cleveland	11	Detroit	11	New York	10
1905	Detroit	13	Chicago	8	Cleveland	8

In the spring of 1900, the holders of the Selden patent began preparations for battle and in July brought suits for infringement against the Buffalo Gasoline Motor Co. and the Winton Motor Carriage Co. Winton was tackled in the belief that if the best-known and largest producer could be plucked, other companies would fall like ripe apples. Very lenient terms were offered the Winton company and, hearing that other companies were capitulating, Winton gave in. However, before Winton signed up, an agreement was reached which brought into existence the Association of Licensed Automobile Manufacturers (A.L.A.M.). This drastically altered the situation.

The formation of the A.L.A.M. can be characterized as an "if you can't lick 'em, join 'em" action on the part of five unlicensed manufacturers. They proposed to the Electric Vehicle Co. that, in return for accepting the validity of the patent and paying royalties, the A.L.A.M. should be formed, to which one half of one percent of the royalties would be paid to be used for the benefit of the industry as a whole. Further, that the association would have the say as to who should be, or should not be, sued and who should, or should not be, granted a license.

The effect of this settlement was to strengthen backing for the patent. Anyone fighting the patent would now be up against a large part of the industry rather than a single concern, the E.V.C. The payment of royalties was not so onerous as to break a manufacturer, but the power to keep companies from engaging in manufacture, or to put existing companies out of business, was ominous indeed. It had all the earmarks of monopoly. If the power was exercised, A.L.A.M. members could fend off competition until the patent expired in 1912, or until their hold on the market was strong enough to make competition less troublesome.

If the suit against the Winton company and the capitulation had the effect of dissuading men from going into the business, it cannot be proved by statistics. There were thirty-five new companies organized that year and thirty-one more engaged in manufacture in 1901. The prospects may not have been of the best—vehicles were very unreliable, relatively high priced, and hard to sell. For every automobile enthusiast there were many more opposed to the horseless vehicle, yet 1900 was a year of ferment ushering in the yeastiest decade in the entire history of the automobile industry.

Ransom E. Olds introduced the curved-dash Oldsmobile in 1901. It was an immediate success with first-year sales of 425. This car is credited with being the first mass-produced vehicle—mass produced in the sense of volume production, not streamlined production as we think of it today.

Of the twenty-five companies entering the industry that year, six were to establish excellent reputations and five were to have fairly long lives. There was the E. R. Thomas Motor Co. of Buffalo, which produced the Thomas Flyer, the first car to circle the world and beat all competitors. There were the Stanley brothers of Newton, Massachusetts, back in the business of building steamers. Their little ten-horsepower vehicle won hill-climbing events so consistently as to spoil the fun for competitors with gasoline-powered cars, and attempts were made to ban them from competition. Shades of things to come—the Boston Police Department used Stanley runabouts as prowl cars. In 1906, a Stanley racing car driven by Fred Marriott established a world's record by going 127.6 mph at Daytona Beach, a record not broken until 1910. When the cigar-shaped vehicle was displayed at the Boston Automobile Show, I was amazed to see its rubber tires "paved" with pebbles, which became embedded when the tread softened from the heat of travel.

Kenneth A. Skinner, eager to exploit the French De-Dion engine, persuaded George N. Pierce, a prominent Buffalo bicycle manufacturer, to go into the automobile business. Thus the Pierce motorette appeared on the scene. Later, Pierce-Arrow cars were among the first to have bevel gears for final drive, aluminum castings for bodies, lubrication of main bearings through a hollow crankshaft, and a six-cylinder powerplant.

Three other manufacturers braving the hazards of infancy were the Bartholomew Co. of Peoria with its Glide car, produced for sixteen years; the White Sewing Machine Co. of Cleveland with a steamer, and the Elmore Manufacturing Co. of Clyde, Ohio. The Elmore was powered by a two-cycle engine which, according to advertisements, "will run on gasoline, and after warming up, on alcohol, kerosene, whiskey and a mixture of all."

The first year to see production of any single make of car climb into the thousands was 1902, when Olds built 2,500 runabouts. The Northern Manufacturing Co., too, did well for a newcomer. Formed by J. D. Maxwell, who had helped Elwood Haynes, and Jim Brady, who had been with Olds, the company produced 200 Silent Northerns in its first year. The epithet "silent" was deserved. The car was by all odds the quietest gasoline-propelled vehicle on the road. Designed by Charles B. King, who brought out a car under his own name nine years later, the Northern had engine and two-speed planetary transmission made integrally with three-point suspension. It also had running boards. By 1903, output had mounted to 750 and increased from then on until the company was purchased in 1908, together with the Wayne Automobile Co., to form the Everitt-Metzger-Flanders Co.

The Cadillac Automobile Co. brought out a "one-lunger," as single-cylinder-engine cars were then called. Henry M. Leland, a highly experienced man with devotion to precision manufacture, guided this company in the direction of quality and by the second year of operation about 2,000 Cadillacs were built. The Cadillac company was successor to the Henry Ford Co., Ford's first venture into manufacture. His vehicle never progressed past the experimental stage, and when a disagreement arose with his backers he pulled out and Leland took over the management.

In that same year of 1902, the Studebaker brothers brought out an electric vehicle. Probably the most successful and largest carriage and wagon builders, they were taking no chance on being rendered obsolete. The Holsman, Jackson, Rambler, Stevens-Duryea, Franklin, and Apperson also made their debut. The Holsman was a high-wheel, buggy-type vehicle which was marketed for eight years. In retrospect the high-wheel car seems antiquated from the very outset, but it had its merit and was bought in rural communities where the roads were at their worst. Frank Duryea, who had parted company with his brother Charles, was back in business with the J. Stevens Arms & Tool Co. at

Chicopee Falls, Massachusetts. The Stevens-Duryea quickly acquired a fine reputation. Duryea designed and built the first six-cylinder car in this country, inspired, it is said, by seeing the American version of the British Napier. One of the finest compliments to be paid Duryea was the oft-spoken comment that the Stevens-Duryea was ahead of its time.

H. H. Franklin of Syracuse, New York, brought out an air-cooled car. A firm believer in the superiority of air cooling over water cooling, he was to promote it long after water cooling had swept the field. When the Franklin company went under during the depression of the thirties, air cooling disappeared for a quarter century or until revived by General Motors for the Corvair. In that same year, the Apperson brothers parted company with Elwood Haynes in the manufacture of the Haynes-Apperson and launched their own company. The break seemed to do neither of them any harm. Both Haynes and Apperson cars were built well into the 1920's.

Colonel Albert Pope, the same Pope who joined forces with the Electric Vehicle Co. to hold the Selden patent, gave every appearance of becoming the dominant figure in the growing industry. He was the first producer to offer a number of makes to cover all price classes. By 1903, he was manufacturing the low-priced Pope-Tribune at Hagerstown, Maryland, the medium-priced Pope-Hartford at Hartford, Connecticut, the high-priced Pope-Toledo at Toledo, Ohio, and the Pope-Waverley, an electric, at Indianapolis. The Pope-Robinson, often referred to as part of this empire, was not one of the Colonel's babies. It was built by a relative at Hyde Park, Massachusetts. Four years later, the Pope empire began going bankrupt piecemeal, the Pope-Hartford alone surviving until 1914.

By 1903, the gasoline vehicle was gaining on the electric and the steamer. The electric was limited in its speed and range. Batteries were very heavy, lacked durability, and had to be recharged after a run of about thirty miles. Development appeared to have reached a dead end. Nevertheless, electric cars continued to be made by a large number of companies and a few persisted for a couple of decades. Steamers, which gave so much promise, were already on the wane.

For an on-the-spot appraisal of the steam car at this juncture, I know of none better than one made by Julian Chase in an address delivered before the Providence (Rhode Island) Association of Mechanical Engineers in 1903. Chase had been involved in the development of both gasoline and electric vehicles, but was thoroughly conversant with steam cars. He said:

> Steam power had never been applied successfully to the propulsion of a pleasure vehicle until the coming of the American light steam car in 1896 and 1897.
>
> These small cars were fairly successful; they were rather delicate and their parts extremely inaccessible, but their greatest trouble came, not from their defects so much as from the fact that they were the first automobiles to be obtained at a reasonable cost in this country and, consequently, they were called upon by indiscriminate buyers to do tasks which they were wholly unfitted to perform. Their failure to meet all demands caused public favor to turn against them as a class.
>
> The lack of economy of the steam car is one of the chief

disadvantages today, especially when gasoline is burned as a fuel. By the use of petroleum or one of the heavier oils, the cost of running can be materially cut down, but burners that will properly vaporize the oil and burn it without smoke or smell, and do these things with little or no noise are few and far between. In fact, the really good one has yet to be invented.

The steam car of that early period had no condenser. Steam passed from the engine to the atmosphere with great loss of efficiency and it was necessary to stop at frequent intervals to take on water. Boilers, or steam generators, of whatever type were extremely heavy, and it took a considerable length of time to generate enough steam to get the car on its way. In contrast, the gasoline car promised quick starting, though that promise was not always fulfilled.

Burning fuel to generate steam and then using the steam for propulsion rather than burning fuel in a cylinder and applying the power so generated directly to the wheels seemed a needlessly roundabout performance and a cogent reason for favoring the internal-combustion engine.

Gasoline cars had their troubles, too. Spark plugs had a short life, carburetors lacked finesse in mixing fuel and air, engines overheated, metals failed to withstand road impact, but the failings of the gasoline car promised to be overcome in time.

Two highly important events took place in 1903. The Ford Motor Co. and the Buick Motor Co. were organized. If this caused any excitement in Detroit and Flint, where their respective factories were located, it caused hardly a ripple elsewhere in the country. Buick produced no more than 16 cars that year and Ford only 658, nor were the cars cheap. The Buick sold for $1,200 and the Ford for $850. Had one been thinking of putting money into this highly speculative industry, there was more reason to be interested in Cadillac, which had produced to the figure of 1,895, or the Oldsmobile company, which accounted for 4,000 cars out of the industry total of 11,235.

The Ford company was not getting out of low gear when the A.L.A.M. took action. Suit was brought jointly against the Ford company and C. A. Duerr, Ford's agent in New York, in the U.S. District Court for the Southern District of New York. Other suits followed, notably against John Wanamaker, who was selling Fords in his New York department store, and against two importers of foreign cars. In all, five suits were brought but were rolled into one for trial.

After weighing the pros and cons of the situation, Ford elected to fight it out, although he had arrayed against him all the important people. While lawyers prepared their cases there ensued a battle royal in advertisements. The A.L.A.M. sought to convince the industry and the public of the patent's validity (though it had yet to be proved), and that it would be unwise to do business with unlicensed manufacturers or their dealers. Ford countered with disparaging remarks about the patent and announced his protection of both Ford dealers and car buyers.

To strengthen their position, twenty unlicensed manufacturers got together and formed the American Motor Car Manufacturers Association (A.M.C.M.A.) in 1905. Among them was Ford. The association stated its objectives to be furtherance of the industry's interests paralleling in all respects those advanced by the A.L.A.M., but without wielding any threat of suits based on patent rights. From then on, both A.L.A.M. and A.M.C.M.A. struggled to win adherents from the uncommitted members of the industry.

By 1905, with the decade half over, 183 new companies had undertaken the building of pleasure cars (the term then used to designate passenger cars) and 93 companies had ceased production. Over the same period of time, annual production had climbed from 4,192 to 22,130. Cars were still costly in relation to purchasing power, or in comparison with a horse and buggy. Ford was selling for $800, $1,000 and $2,000 according to model; the Cadillac was priced at $750, and the Century Motor Vehicle Co. of Syracuse, New York, had a steamer on the market for $750. Other makes, too, were offered in the $650–$750 range, but they were exceedingly primitive in construction.

The situation was precarious with so many entering the business and sales so hard to make, and E. H. Cutler, president of the Knox Automobile Co. in Springfield, Massachusetts, was voicing the concern of many when he said: "There will be a danger from the attempt to manufacture and sell large quantities of machines that have not been fully tested; and there is a limit to the quantity that this or any other country can absorb, and we are inclined to advise conservatism in the planning of production."

No one heeded this warning, no one applied brakes, and by the end of the decade 531 companies had been formed (more than one a week for ten years) and 346 had gone out of business, most through bankruptcy. Some producers simply called it a day and retired when the competitive heat became too intense, and a great many companies changed hands. The financial panic of 1907, which came and passed like a thunderstorm, may have contributed to the doubling of failures taking place that year, as contrasted with the previous year, but new companies doubled in number, too.

Hard on the heels of the 1907 panic came the formation of General Motors. The press paid little attention to it. In columns listing new companies organized, or corporate changes, was a brief item announcing organization of the company under the laws of the State of New Jersey. It was just one more company to the gatherers of the news and to the public at large.

Just one more company! Like an army on the attack, there were always new recruits to the industry to fill the gaps left by those who fell by the way, and their number swelled. Who were these people so eager and willing to engage in this new and highly speculative venture?

The answer is, no group in particular. The legion getting under way during the period 1900–1909 included companies established in the making of carriages and bicycles, as has been said. Also among them were producers of stationary engines, farm machinery, stoves, tacks, hardware, milling machines, locomotives, and household appliances. They saw the building of cars to offer great profit possibilities and they took it on as an adjunct to their standard line. Some of them, when matters went well and promised to go even better, made car building their primary business; others, faring less well and seeing what they thought to be the handwriting on the wall, went back to their lasts. Many more went bankrupt.

John North Willys entered the business inadvertently. While acting as sales agent for the Overland car in Elmira,

New York, he learned that the manufacturer was on the point of going out of business. This was unthinkable to Willys, who had orders calling for delivery, so he hurried to the Toledo factory to find the company deeply in debt and without cars. By methods best described as sleight-of-hand he pacified creditors, assembled as many cars as there were parts for, and gradually rebuilt the company out of virtually nothing.

The Mercer, which made its debut in 1909, had as strange an origin as any. In 1903, the American Chocolate Machinery Co. began building the Walter car in New York. Two years later, the Walter was being built in Trenton, New Jersey, by the Walter Automobile Co., which also made the Roebling-Planche. This fact suggests that the Roeblings, who made the cables for the famous Brooklyn Bridge and were located in Trenton, put money into the venture. In 1909, the name Walter went out and the name Mercer came in. Findley Robertson Porter, who designed the T-head engine for the Mercer, produced the F.R.P. on Long Island in 1914.

The Studebaker brothers entered the business with an electric vehicle of their own design. When they saw the gasoline car gaining supremacy, they acted as selling agents for the E-M-F, Flanders, and Garford. Once well established, they bought out the E-M-F company.

The American Locomotive Co. and the St. Louis Car Co. also entered the business without going through the crucial stage of designing. The locomotive company brought out the French Berliet under the name American Berliet, later Alco; the St. Louis Car Co., builders of street railway cars, launched the French Mors as the American

Mors, later Standard Six. William Steinway, the piano manufacturer, followed the same policy by acquiring rights from the German Daimler company to produce the American Mercedes.

There were men who were attracted to the business by an overwhelming interest in things mechanical. They wanted to pit their brains against the problems needing solution to make the automobile truly functional and reliable. These men did not always have a keen business sense, and when this was the case they came to grief regardless of their mechanical ability.

Many a man who helped develop the earliest cars, especially in association with such pioneers as Henry Ford and Ransom Olds, got the "I can do it, too" virus in his blood, for which the only effective antibiotic was to establish a business of his own. Thus we find Jonathan Maxwell, who aided Elwood Haynes and the Apperson brothers in the development of the Haynes-Apperson, teaming up with Benjamin Briscoe to produce the very successful Maxwell-Briscoe. Walter E. Flanders, who contributed production skills to the Ford company, joined with B. F. Everitt, a manufacturer of auto trimmings, and William Metzger, a Cadillac sales manager, to launch the E-M-F, which was a success from the start. Howard Coffin and Robert Hupp, associates of Olds, went on to manufacture the Hudson and Hupmobile, respectively.

Some men there were who dreamed of designing and manufacturing a truly superior car to bear their name. Cases in point were C. Harold Wills and Henry M. Leland. To Wills the able metallurgist goes much credit for the ruggedness of the Ford Model T. He did not realize his dream for twenty years. Leland, who did much for both Ford and Olds and was dominant in the Cadillac organization until 1917, embodied his dream in the Lincoln, which he launched in 1920.

Profits, which were generous provided a manufacturer could dispose of his product, lured many a man who was looking for dollars but had no special mechanical ability or knowledge and no interest in the automobile per se. William Crapo Durant, founder of General Motors, was an example of this breed. Another was John North Willys, who put the Overland car on the map.

In this early period it was possible to start a company with a very small capital investment and make a profit on a limited output. For example, E. H. Belden, who ran the Belden Motor Car Co. in Pittsburgh, announced to an indifferent world that his 1908 production would be limited to twenty-five cars. He continued to build cars for three years thereafter. No manufacturer undertook to fabricate every component of a vehicle. There were foundries and machine shops capable of turning out engines and transmissions to order, carriage builders ready to supply bodies, and someone, somewhere, eager and willing to make any component needed.

When F. L. Smith, secretary and treasurer of the Olds Motor Works and president of the A.L.A.M., hinted to Henry Ford that he might be denied a license under the Selden patent because he was only an assembler of parts, it was a case of the representative of the pots calling the kettle black. Every manufacturer was an assembler to some degree.

The modest capital requirements and the shoestring on

which many a manufacturer operated are suggested by this news note of 1908: "All visible assets of the Earl Motor Car Co. of Kenosha were seized by sheriff on a claim of $90."

Capital requirements were small because the manufacturer was being subsidized. The parts maker gave the auto maker thirty to ninety days' credit and the manufacturer demanded cash from his dealers. With this cash he paid off his debts to the parts makers. This system of operating on other people's capital worked fabulously well as long as there was a steady demand for the product. When sales were sluggish and cars backed up on the dealer, it was the dealer who went bankrupt if he could not raise the cash to pay for the shipment of cars. When the dealer organization was milked dry, the manufacturer was in real trouble. Assuming the plowing back of profits for expansion of plant facilities, as was common practice, there was little or no working capital to fall back on and one of four things happened: the auto maker got a bank loan to tide him over, he persuaded someone with means to advance funds, he was taken over by his creditors, or he went bankrupt.

Proverbially, the pioneer manufacturer was wary of bankers, whom he regarded as birds of prey. And bankers were generally disdainful of the auto maker because the business was so highly speculative and so often run in a slipshod manner. Affection did not grow as the business expanded and prospered. The manufacturer knew indebtedness meant some loss of control and he feared banker participation would lead to enthronement of moneymaking at the expense of production. Nevertheless, he realized the great importance of having a source of capital to tap when the going became rough.

The difficulties of raising large amounts of capital to launch a company into volume production before it had learned to crawl are indicated in a letter from an official of a company explaining to me why a certain company went out of business in 1910. The company desired to build cars as an offshoot to its buggy business. The buggy company had $400,000 capital with $200,000 surplus, and orders with deposits for five thousand cars. Directors estimated $1,000,000 in capital needed to start to meet this production demand. His letter said:

> Cincinnati bankers were approached, but at that time could not see anything but ruin for the country in the progress that the automobile was making. Failing in this, capitalists were approached, but all were afraid to venture into the automobile business, so that rather than take the chance of losing capital invested in the buggy business, it was decided that since neither capital nor banks could be interested in a large automobile production in the Cincinnati district, the company would discontinue. All debts were paid and the biggest chance that Cincinnati ever had for becoming a large automobile production center was passed up because of lack of support. Vision on the part of financial interests in this district was not equal to the vision of financial interests in the Detroit district.

Since this explanation was offered fourteen years after the company was dissolved, the figure of orders on hand and the rosiness of prospects could have become inflated in the writer's mind. The unwillingness to use capital invested in the buggy business shows an awareness of risk, and the bankers and capitalists who were approached could hardly be damned for exercising similar caution.

Steady sale of cars was essential for corporate life and many schemes were tried to assure a flow of cars from the factory. A common practice was to contract with a sales agent to take an entire year's output, thus guaranteeing a market for a fixed number of cars for a year in advance. In a few instances the sales agent affixed his own brand name to the car. The Wayne Works of Richmond, Indiana, for example, produced and sold the Richmond car, but it also contracted to supply the Herff-Brooks Corp. of Indianapolis with Richmond cars to be sold under the Herff-Brooks name.

Salesmen had to be enterprising. Prospects had to be convinced through demonstration that a car could be started with reasonable ease, could climb hills, plow through mud and sand, and would be reliable. To prove the worth of products there were many well-publicized hill-climbing contests and reliability runs over roads no sane person would attempt to traverse today in anything but a four-wheel-drive vehicle with high road clearance. Holsman tied its product to the roads very neatly and honestly in its advertisement of 1908 which said, "High wheels travel all roads because all roads are made to be traveled by high wheels."

When national automobile shows were held, demonstrating cars lined the curb outside of the exhibition hall as an adjunct to the floor show. Anyone faintly resembling a live prospect was cajoled into taking a ride and seeing for himself that all claims were facts.

The advertising of that day stressed as realities those qualities yet to be attained—quiet performance, mechanical excellence, and reliability. When these qualities became fact rather than a hope, the message changed, as we shall see. A scheme used by one auto maker to prove a reduction of engine vibration to bearable proportions was to place a wine glass of water on the hood of the car with a "See, it doesn't spill!" Public interest centered on the mechanical features of a car unless the car was a simple electric. Every show exhibitor had a chassis on display and a lecturer who expatiated on the mechanical features for the benefit of the male who was the buyer and destined sooner or later to find himself under the car. As late as 1921, the sales manager of a company distributing the expensive Locomobile was trying to overwhelm dowagers with the spoonerism "all our steels are treat-heated."

With so many manufacturers intent on building practical, reliable vehicles and design seemingly limited only by man's imagination, it is perhaps no wonder that the first decade was distinguished as no other for the variety of engineering innovations and range of design.

The earliest models were designated stanhopes, surreys, cabriolets, broughams, and victorias, all names inherited from the horse-drawn vehicle. Undoubtedly the use of long-established and familiar names eased acceptance of the motorcar. Charles Duryea, who was building a vehicle more like an overgrown baby carriage than an automobile, stressed in his 1902 advertisements that the Duryea was "A Carriage—not a Machine." To emphasize the point further, the ad read, "Why own a locomotive and be an engineer when a Duryea phaeton is a carriage in every respect, adapted to the use of any and all members of the family, over any and all kinds of roads, at any desired speed?" Perhaps the homiest touch ever imparted to a car was to place a whip socket on the dashboard.

While Duryea was using the word "carriage" to lure the horse lover, others had begun using the descriptive terms "runabout," "roadster," "touring car," and "limousine." The town car did not appear until 1909. This was called a "Go to Hell" model in some circles because the chauffeur and footman were exposed to the weather while the passengers were snugly enclosed. The tonneau, or phaeton, body carried four people, the back seat being entered from the rear. "Button up the back" was the phrase often used to describe this European importation, which was abandoned for the side entrance around 1905.

The driver's seat was at the right in imitation of the European car. Both tiller and wheel were used for steering all through the first decade, the tiller persisting longest on high-wheel and electric vehicles. Gear shift and brake levers were placed outside the body, where they effectually blocked access to the driver's seat. Windshields were nonexistent; folding tops could be purchased as extra equipment for two-seaters, but were not introduced for touring cars until 1905. Prior to this innovation, the motorist stayed indoors during rainstorms, or wore a poncho. Truly, this age produced pioneer motorists as well as pioneer manufacturers.

It is a wonder that so many people bought and continued to buy such notoriously unreliable products. Our family doctor's Model A Ford, for example, had faulty brakes. On descending a hill one day, the brakes failed to have any retarding effect and the good doctor prepared to jump rather than to crash into a stone wall at the bottom of the hill. But a moment before he jumped, a rear wheel fell off and the car dragged to a stop. Did this brush with death lead to an abandonment of the motorcar? It did not. The doctor bought a Mitchell.

Ownership of a curved-dash, merry Oldsmobile proved equally unrewarding to a prominent lawyer in my town. Here again a hill brought the downfall. Every time the lawyer returned from an outing, a horse had to be hired to drag the car up the grade to his residence. Since the Oldsmobile was acquired in a lottery for an outlay of about $5, the weakness of its performance could not have been financially disturbing. It happened this way:

A chain drugstore offered the car to the holder of a winning number in a contest. To get a number one bought a five-cent bottle of Moxie. Having bought and consumed about a hundred bottles of this renowned soft drink, the lawyer had one hundred chances and one bore the winning number. Far from being dismayed by his first experience with an automobile, the lawyer went on to purchase a Stanley steamer and then a Franklin.

Mechanical designs changed more rapidly than the design of bodies and it was fitting that they should. Cars could not be sold on the strength of appearance alone. The "one-lunger" quickly gave ground to the two-cylinder engine, which commonly was of the horizontally-opposed type located under the seat. Then came the vertical engine, placed in its own compartment in front of the driver as it is today. Soon the public had a choice of one-, two-, three-, four-, five-, and six-cylinder engines. The first sixes were built by the Automobile Co. of America at Marion, New Jersey, and by E. R. Thomas at Buffalo. Both tried hitching together two three-cylinder engines. Thomas survived this experiment; the other company went bankrupt in 1902.

Use of aluminum to lighten weight is not, as often believed, new to the automobile world. As far as is known, the first commercially-made car to employ aluminum in any form was the Berg, made in New York City in 1902. From 1903 on, aluminum was used for bodies, fenders, hoods, crankcases, transmission cases, and covers. Actually, the light-weight metal came into use long before alloy steels. Its weight relative to steel was very much in its favor, but high cost retarded its use. Ford used aluminum for the intake manifold, crankcase, and water-pump housing of his six-cylinder Model K, which preceded the Model T; otherwise no manufacturer using it prior to 1910 survives to this day.

If a customer favored air-cooled engines over water-cooled ones, there were many from which to make a choice. Some manufacturers offered both. Air-cooled systems did away with a lot of plumbing and eliminated the danger of freeze-up. Outstanding among the air-cooled cars were the Franklin, Premier, and Frayer-Miller, which appeared on the market in that order. If two-cycle engines seemed preferable to four-cycle ones, there was the Atlas hailing from Springfield, Massachusetts, and the Elmore from Clyde, Ohio, which could be had in a three- or four-cylinder model. There was something appealing about the two-cycle engine, in which every stroke of the piston was a power stroke instead of every other one as in the four-cycle engine now in general use.

Among the radical engineering designs of that era were

those of the Adams-Farwell, Compound, and Gas-au-lec. The Adams-Farwell had a five-cylinder revolving engine pancaked over the rear axle. When the company ceased production after ten years and went on to engage in other business, the revolving-cylinder engine disappeared until revived for airplane use.

The designers of the Gas-au-lec strove to overcome the nuisance of gear shifting. It was one of the earliest of such attempts. The car had a conventional gasoline engine and drive shaft to the rear axle, but geared to the shaft was an electric motor. The electric motor was used for starting and acceleration, then the gasoline engine cut in, and because the switch was made automatically, no hand shifting was required. When the foot was lifted from the throttle and the car decelerated, the gasoline engine cut out and the electric motor took over. Current was supplied by a storage battery which was kept charged by the gasoline engine.

The Compound, built by the Eisenhut Horseless Vehicle Co., had an internal-combustion engine with two high-pressure and two low-pressure cylinders. Exhaust from a high-pressure cylinder passed to a low-pressure one where the gas did more work by further expansion before passing into the atmosphere. Since the final exhaust gas issued at low pressure, it caused less noise than in the conventional engine.

A notable number of discarded innovations reappeared years later. Placing the gearshift lever on the steering column was practiced by Peerless in 1901, Ward Leonard in 1902, and Pierce in 1903. It was revived on almost all cars in 1937. Its disappearance may be traced to lack of functional value. When car bodies were narrow and accommodated running boards, the front seat could not seat three people in comfort. Moreover, some states had laws against seating three abreast. Haynes had free-wheeling in 1906; Studebaker revived it in 1930. The Sturtevant Blower Works in Hyde Park, Massachusetts, offered an automatic transmission in 1904; a fully-automatic transmission appeared on the Reo in 1930. Now it is almost standard equipment.

The Sturtevant transmission had two forward speeds and two automatic friction clutches. The clutches engaged by centrifugal masses rotating at engine speed. One clutch, engaging at relatively low speed, gave low car speed through double-reduction spur gears. The second clutch at higher speed gave direct drive by clutching the main drive shaft to crankshaft or flywheel.

The Peerless of 1902 and the Jones-Corbin of 1903 had a joint in the steering column to permit pushing the steering wheel forward and down for easy entrance and exit. That, too, did not last long. When the idea was revived in the early sixties, the steering column was made to swing sideways.

Transmission of power to wheels was always a problem. Most cars had a gear box with at least two sets of gears and took the drive first by belt, then by chain, and finally by shaft. A radical departure from the orthodox, used on the Cartercar, Lambert, Metz, and Kelsey, is worthy of special mention because it has not been seen on any car for over forty years, yet in its day it made a place for itself.

In lieu of gears, these cars had a friction drive. There was a large disk attached to the engine by shaft, and set at a right angle to it was a second disk connected to the drive shaft. When the second disk was advanced by lever so that its periphery contacted the flat surface of the first disk, which revolved with the engine, power was transmitted. Whereas gear sets offered fixed ratios, the friction drive had almost infinite ratios. For low speed and heavy pulling, the second disk was applied close to the center of the first disk so that engine revolutions were many times those of the driving wheels. Ever higher ratios were obtained by moving the second disk toward the periphery of the first. When the driver had the ratio he desired he simply locked the two disks together and regulated speed by the throttle. To reverse the car, the second disk was moved to engage the first disk on the opposite side of center.

The basic trouble with friction drive was the lack of suitable long-wearing friction material for covering the metal disks. When they wore smooth, there was slippage and loss of efficiency. Nevertheless, the Metz, in particular, scored well among higher-priced contenders in many reliability runs. In the unjelled mechanical world of the motorcar, friction drive appeared to have great possibilities. Durant purchased the Cartercar company for General Motors, explaining later that he did not know what mechanical features would prove best and he wished to be ready for any contingency. Like the two-cycle Elmore, the Cartercar was discontinued in 1915.

When General Motors was organized as a holding company it became immediately the largest manufacturer—Buick and Oldsmobile production totaling 9,542. There was nothing on the horizon to guarantee a continuation of this lead, nor any indication it might be lost, nothing, that is, but an undiscernible gleam in Henry Ford's eye. The ups and downs of car manufacture were too unpredictable to warrant betting on outcome with any more assurance than can be had with a wager on a horse race.

Durant improved his position in 1909 by acquiring the Cadillac company, which was earning good profits under Leland's direction. In that same year, the Cadillac car demonstrated to the world what Leland had accomplished in the way of precision manufacture. Three Cadillacs were shipped to England, where they were disassembled, the parts put in a scrambled heap, then reassembled by mechanics using screwdrivers and wrenches. The cars were then put to a five-hundred-mile test run and performed without a hitch. Such interchangeability of parts had never before been seen and it raised the Cadillac car as well as American manufacture in world esteem. Durant's other acquisitions of the year—the Oakland, Elmore, Rainier, and Welch—brought him neither profit nor engineering excellence.

Meanwhile Ford was hard at work developing a car which he put on the market in 1909 as the Model T. It was an immediate success. A first-year production of 10,607 made it the No. 1 car and the company the second largest. At a price of $950, it was in direct competition with several lower-priced cars, but its simplicity and reliability won it enthusiastic patronage.

The success of the Model T had a drastic effect on prices and brought the industry to a turning point. In 1907 and 1908, the average wholesale price of cars was just over $2,100. In 1909, when the Model T swept the field, that price had dropped 37 percent to touch $1,288. From then on the comfortable profit margins, which had enabled so many companies to prosper on a limited production, were on their way out.

On the other side of the ledger for Ford was defeat in the Selden patent suit. When the case finally came to court the A.L.A.M. had about eighty members, the A.M.C.M.A. around forty, leaving perhaps one hundred companies unaffiliated. The court's decision immediately strengthened the position of the A.L.A.M. and seriously weakened its opponents, mainly small companies with little combative power. Ford refused to give in and appealed the court's decision, so the battle was resumed in the closing months of 1909.

By now the gasoline-propelled car outrivaled all others commercially. If one failed to respond to cranking, or lay down in its tracks overcome by some chronic ailment, the owner was less apt to suffer the indignity of hearing the cry "Get a horse." Steamers were still to be seen outspeeding gasoline cars, or drawn up at wayside watering troughs to refill their tanks; electrics still glided noiselessly through city streets; but the horse was far from becoming a relic. In the classified ads of used cars for sale there occasionally appeared the phrase "Always driven by a lady." Like Charles Duryea's protestations that his vehicle was a carriage and not a machine, this gentle phrase was intended to assure prospects that the car's "wind" had not been broken by impromptu racing. With such assurances were the skittish horse-and-buggy tribe still being led to the automobile.

The industry was churning furiously. Newcomers in 1909 numbered 71; almost matching it were the number going out of business, 68. During the year there were 289 manufacturers putting some kind of car on the market.

Through the separate but cumulative effort of the 557 pioneer companies operating in the first decade (1900–1909), the industry had learned to crawl, then to stumble. And by their failure as well as by their success, they proved to the Doubting Thomases that the automobile was here to stay.

But at what a price of blasted hope and dissipation of capital! Only fifty of these companies survived for ten years or more before becoming hopelessly crippled by financial anemia. Sixteen others, although they did well, had to undergo some form of surgery, or blood transfusion, before they, too, wound up their affairs.

3
growing pains:
1910–1919

The faltering of one giant producer, the founding of another automobile empire, and the second Selden trial were the events ushering in the second decade. Any one of these three events would have been sufficient to make the year 1910 memorable.

The faltering giant was General Motors. Durant, who had an insatiable appetite for companies, had picked up twenty automobile and parts concerns within two years. He tried to acquire Ford but could not raise the asking price of $8,000,000—a bargain price as it turned out later. Most of the companies acquired in haste did not amount to much and could be had for a small payment in cash and a wad of General Motors stock, which Durant always seemed to have in copious supply. This program of expansion was accompanied by heavy outlays for expansion of facilities. The result was the greatest thing on wheels and, if the analogy can be carried further, wheels from which the air in the tires was slowly escaping.

Sales and profits had been excellent, but not good enough to carry the burden of expansion. Debts mounted and money had to be found quickly if the giant enterprise was not to go into the hands of a receiver.

Durant finally located two banking houses willing to put up the needed funds provided he stepped down from active management. He agreed to this, having no other choice, and the bankers underwrote an issue of 6 percent five-year notes to the amount of $15,000,000, secured by a mortgage on all General Motors property. The bankers kept $2,250,-000 as their commission and in addition received $4,000,-000 worth of preferred stock and $2,000,000 of common stock. The notes were then sold to the public, the purchaser getting a bonus of $20 worth of preferred stock with every $100 worth of notes.

The automobile fraternity thought the terms usurous and were not backward in saying so. The bankers defended their actions by pointing out the highly speculative nature of the underwriting. Since one of the banking houses was known for its conservatism, the explanation was not taken very seriously.

With Durant out of office and control of the corporation in the hands of a board of trustees for five years, there began a pruning and housecleaning. Unprofitable companies were sold, debts reduced, water squeezed out of the common stock, and General Motors took a new lease on life.

While Durant was toppling from his pedestal, Benjamin Briscoe, co-founder of the Maxwell-Briscoe company, was erecting one of his own. To emulate Durant, he acquired the companies making the Brush, Columbia, Courier, Maxwell, Alden Sampson, and Stoddard-Dayton cars to form the United States Motor Co. Backing Briscoe were many of the same people prominent in the Electric Vehicle Co., who thought to profit from the Selden patent.

Of the cars Briscoe gathered together, only the Brush, Maxwell, and Stoddard-Dayton were at all widely known to the public. The Brush competed with the Ford. It had a wooden axle and an oil-treated, hickory chassis mounted on four spiral springs which were snubbed by friction disks. Having a one-cylinder, ten-horsepower engine, it was hardly a "hot" competitor. The Stoddard-Dayton, at the other end of the price spectrum, was a heavy, expensive vehicle, powered by a Knight sleeve-valve engine. Briscoe's selection of companies appears to have been based on a desire to have a complete range of products rather than viable companies. Two years later, the United States Motor Co. crashed. When salvage operations were completed there was nothing left but Maxwell, which, after a lapse of fifteen years, became the nucleus of another giant corporation.

While General Motors and United States Motor were making news, the A.L.A.M. and the Ford-led A.M.C.M.A. were girding themselves for a final battle in the courts. Intimidation had swelled the ranks of the A.L.A.M. and shrunk the opposition to a mere dozen. Moreover, Durant, who had fallen out with the A.L.A.M. and was in arrears with royalties, paid up, or it was said that he did. Then, just before the case went to trial, the A.M.C.M.A. disbanded.

This trial, unlike the previous one, made clear what the fight was about. Stated as simply as possible, Selden used a modified Brayton-type engine, that is, a two-cycle engine; the defendants all used an engine of the Otto type, which was a four-cycle engine. Nevertheless, Selden claimed his patent covered any form of liquid-hydrocarbon engine of the compression type. The presiding judge, noting the difference in engines and the existence of the Otto engine before the patent was issued, held the patent to be restricted to vehicles powered by the Brayton-type engine; therefore, Ford had not infringed on the Selden patent.

Thus, in January, 1911, was terminated the long-drawn-out patent war and the attempt to create a monopoly in the automobile industry. That the A.L.A.M. objective was monopoly seems incontrovertible. The trade press reported applicants being refused licenses to manufacture and the terms and conditions of membership being made increasingly harsh. Had this not been true, some denial undoubtedly would have been made. Evidence of monopolistic intent was supplied by the Velie Motor Car Co., which claimed it had been asked an excessive fee for joining the association and had been ordered to restrict its production to 2,500 cars in 1910 and 2,000 in 1911.

While the restriction of output loomed large in the affairs of the A.L.A.M., it was not the association's sole reason for being. It had a mechanical branch which undertook the promulgation of standards, the first being for screws, nuts, and bolts, which came in 1906. The variety of these items had proliferated to create great confusion and needless cost, and no improvement could come about without industry-wide action. Later, the work of standardization was taken over by the Society of Automobile Engineers (now Society of Automotive Engineers) and its scope expanded steadily to embrace practically every item entering into the construction of a car. The value of this work in furthering the development of the automobile is impossible to estimate. The dollars-and-cents savings have been figured to run into hundreds of millions.

The Selden patent was extremely important to the Ford Motor Co. and it looms large in any history of that organization. The blows and counter-blows exchanged through advertisements brought the case to public attention long before the first court trial and made Henry Ford a hero before he gained great prominence as a manufacturer. By the time the second trial took place, the Model T had put Ford in the forefront.

What effect the existence of the patent and the subsequent prosecution had on the industry at large is hard to assess. Production of cars by both licensed and unlicensed manufacturers proceeded without interruption. The rate of new company formation rose throughout the period of litigation until 1910. In that year the number of companies leaving the industry exceeded the number entering, and the total number of companies in operation fell for the first time since the industry started. This reversal in trend cannot be attributed to the patent threat, because it continued after the settlement had banished all fear. A more plausible explanation will be offered later.

Had Ford lost the case and been refused a license, automobile history might have been strikingly different. Even if the officials of the association had succumbed to an overpowering urge to punish Ford, it is inconceivable that they would have been so stupid as to try to put him out of business. By 1910, Ford had the public and most of the press on his side, so much so that any attempt to throttle him would have brought forth loud cries of "Monopoly," unhealthy for the industry.

But, to speculate further, had Ford been put out of business for the duration of the patent's life, it is doubtful that he would have survived the financial blow and the truly low-priced car would have been much slower to make its appearance.

Bitter as had been the fight, it left little hard feeling, at least on the surface. Following the court decision, a banquet was held to which all manufacturers were invited. It had all the characteristics of a love feast. And from the trade press, which mirrored the attitude of the industry, flowed editorial sighs of relief.

The A.L.A.M. was dissolved following invalidation of the patent and the auto makers organized the National Automobile Chamber of Commerce. In the 1930's, the N.A.C.C. became the Automobile Manufacturers Association. Henry Ford never joined any of these organizations and his cars were never exhibited at the shows they sponsored. When Henry Ford II succeeded his grandfather, following World War II, the Ford company became a full-fledged member of the A.M.A.

To explain why 1909 was the high-water-mark year in number of companies requires examination of production figures. Unfortunately, data for all companies are not available, but it is known that Ford and General Motors had captured about 30 percent of the total market, with at least twenty companies sharing among them more than 10 percent. This left very slim pickings for the 250 or so remaining producers.

Ford had almost pre-empted the low-price car market and competitors could not lift output to a volume permitting comparable quality at a comparable price. Most producers were building cars to sell for $1,000 to $1,500, and the vast majority of people did not have that amount of cash money. Extending credit for the purchase of an automobile was unheard of and would be for another few years. All this made for intense rivalry, and the slaughter of companies became the order of the day.

Profits were generous, but no one wanted to reduce them. Ford's idea of an ever-larger output at an ever-decreasing price was unattractive to most members of the industry. Some auto makers tried to meet competition by including accessories as standard equipment. The Overland, for example, was offered with top, windshield, lamps, and a magneto for $1,000, the first car at this price to be so equipped. Owen, a higher-priced car, boasted a top, windshield, electric horn (instead of a bulb horn), electric and acetylene headlamps, electric and oil side lamps, and electric tail lamp, all as standard equipment.

There was talk at this time of having annual models, but it was not adopted as an industrywide practice. A producer brought out a new model when engineering advances warranted it, or when competition could no longer be met by cutting the price. New model introduction usually took place at the beginning of the year because it was logical to exhibit at the national shows to arouse the greatest possible interest just prior to the spring buying season.

About this time, James J. Hill, president of the Northern Pacific Railroad Co., declared the automobile to be an extravagance and a pastime and the money spent on it to be wasted. This widely circulated, unkind cut came at a time when the manufacturers had begun to suspect that prices were too high to attract the public.

To prove that cars were economical to operate, Maxwell-Briscoe ran a test on the streets of New York, then burst forth with this advertisement:

> The first real cost test of the automobile versus horse proves:
>
> Maxwell   —1$\frac{8}{10}$¢ per passenger mile
> Horse and buggy—2$\frac{1}{5}$¢ per passenger mile
>
> This is our answer to the charge made that the automobile is an extravagance. It proves the automobile an economic factor that would save millions of dollars if the Maxwell were everywhere substituted for the horse and buggy.

The method of conducting the test was not explained in the ad. The skeptic may wonder, therefore, how a valid cost per passenger mile could be figured for a horse which consumed a fixed amount of fuel regardless of miles driven.

Various expedients were tried to lower the cost of car purchase. The C. H. Metz Co. of Waltham, Massachusetts, offered a "knock-down" car for the buyer to assemble under what was called the "Metz Plan." The components of the car were grouped into fourteen packages, each priced at $27. Each package had to be taken in a prescribed order and paid for before the next was shipped. Package No. 12 contained the engine; No. 13 the magneto; No. 14 the carburetor, fuel tank, and hand crank. Thus the car was immobilized until the last payment of the $378 total was made. Save money and become roughly familiar with mechanical details, was Mr. Metz's advertising appeal.

With the declared purpose of eliminating the middleman and reducing the cost of a high-grade car by 25 percent, a number of New York bank officials organized the Club Car Co. of America. Membership in the club was limited to one hundred and cars were to be built only for the membership, to agreed specifications. In true banker style, they issued preferred and common stock. A $100 share was the initiation fee; five shares per member was the limit. Merchant & Evans of Philadelphia was selected to manufacture the vehicle. The company lasted just two years.

The Orson Automobile Co. of New York was similar in nature to the Club Car Co. It was organized by one hundred businessmen to have cars built to their specifications, first for themselves, then for the general public. Prominent in the group was a vice president of the National City Bank, New York. The manufacturer in this instance was the Brightwood Motor Manufacturing Co. of Springfield, Massachusetts. The wonder is that any hundred businessmen could agree on specifications. They must have done so or the company would not have survived three years.

Very wealthy people still bought European cars, but imports were no menace to anything but the pride of the domestic manufacturer. In a year (1911) when almost 200,-

000 cars were built, importation of 978 vehicles was insignificant. When the *Automobile Trade Journal* declared America to be producing cars "that can compare in every respect with the best that can be built in any other country in the world," it may have been stretching the truth a bit, but it must be remembered that Europe was producing cars for the well-to-do, whereas the American manufacturer was aiming at the mass market.

Indicative of the widespread interest in the automobile, or of a desire to create more interest, *Vogue* published an article in 1910 which told how women were flocking to the automobile and of the efforts manufacturers of high-priced cars and electrics were making to give the interiors of their cars a touch of elegance and a wealth of comfort. In still another article, it told how a number of wealthy Philadelphia ladies, who were avant-garde enough to drive their own cars, had formed a club called Moveganta Klabo, whatever that means, and were allowed to have their headquarters in the Benedict Arnold homestead in Fairmount Park in return for its restoration.

Not to be outdone, the *Review of Reviews* launched a motor department the following year. This question-and-answer column, in which the ailments of cars were discussed as well as allied subjects, appears to have been the first of its kind.

By now cars were much quieter, more reliable, and more comfortable to operate. The switch from chain drive to shaft drive, now practically completed, did much to reduce noise. Doors to enclose the front seat were in process of adoption. This warming innovation had to await the moving of the steering column to the left side, the placing of the gear shift and brake levers in the center of the compartment, and a removal of the spare tire to the rear. Once the changes were accomplished, the front seat could be entered from the sidewalk instead of the street side. Ford led off with the left-hand drive, but it was several years before it became standard practice.

The year 1911 saw the introduction of the Stutz, "The Car That Made Good in a Day," which promptly competed for the sporting world's affections with the Mercer. To own a Stutz Bearcat put a man just about as high as he could go in the hierarchy of the would-be red-blooded.

The something new on the mechanical front was the arrival of the Knight sleeve-valve engine on the Stearns, Columbia, and Stoddard-Dayton cars. Charles Y. Knight, the inventor, formed Knight & Kilbourne in 1906. Unable to interest anyone in taking out a license to manufacture, he went abroad to try his luck and there he succeeded in having his engine adopted by the Daimler company. By this circuitous route the engine came back to its native land.

In place of poppet valves, which were congenitally noisy, the Knight engine had a sleeve with ports in the wall of the cylinder. As the sleeve slid up and down in the cylinder, the intake port came opposite the intake manifold so that the charge entered the cylinder for compression. Similarly, when the charge was burned, the exhaust port in the sleeve lined up with the exhaust manifold for passage of the exhaust gases.

The Knight engine was noted for its quiet operation since it did away with the noise-making valve train. Although the Columbia and Stoddard-Dayton disappeared from the market with the collapse of the United States

Motor Co., the Knight engine did not. It was adopted in subsequent years by six manufacturers and persisted well into the 1930's on one of the Willys-Overland models.

Granted that the advertising slogan is often more an expression of hope than a statement of reality, the slogans in use in 1912 tell a great deal about the cars of that vintage, the state of the roads, and the state of the public mind. Performance was the main theme, as witness the following:

> Eats Up the Hills—Great Western
> The Car That Survives—Glide
> Pass Them All—Knox
> No Noise but the Wind—American
> No Hill too Steep; No Sand too Deep—Jackson
> Built and Tested in the Hills—Matheson

The most famous slogan of them all, dating from 1903, was Packard's "Ask the Man Who Owns One." People who knew little about cars and cared less would parrot that slogan at the mere mention of the Packard name, so persistently had it been held before the public eye.

Attempts to impart the idea of quality and lift the advertised product above those of competitors were:

> The Car of Absolute Exclusiveness—Norwalk
> The Car with a Conscience—Oakland
> The Incomparable—White
> Output Must Be Limited—Rambler
> The Choice of Men Who Know—Lozier

No matter how well a car climbed hills, or how long it survived, its engine still had to be cranked by hand. This was an obstacle of which the manufacturers were well aware, and they devoted much effort to devising a means for mechanical cranking. Amplex came out with a compressed-air starter. Acetylene, gas, rope, and spring starters were tried but none was satisfactory. All but the rope starter, which was offered by an accessory house for the Model T, were dropped when Charles F. Kettering of the Dayton Engineering Laboratories Co. developed a successful electric starter. This was introduced on the Cadillac in 1912 and the following year electric self starters were offered by many producers at an added cost of about $100.

The importance of the self-starter can hardly be overestimated. It cleared a hurdle that had prevented many men and almost all women from becoming motorists. Now, with the back-breaking, arm-twisting, bone-shattering job of cranking on its way out, the gasoline-propelled vehicle became reasonably civilized, and the electric vehicle lost its major appeal.

Three other events made 1912 memorable in the industry, although at that time their true import was not apparent. The first was a reciprocity bill passed by the State of New Jersey. The second was the inauguration of installment selling, which was to change profoundly the American public's attitude toward the incurring of personal debt. And finally, there was a court case which established the manufacturer's responsibility for the integrity of his product.

The reciprocity bill was in itself a small matter and could be passed over except that it indicated the progress made by the automobile as an established vehicle of transportation which transcended state lines. New Jersey had long complained that it served as a thoroughfare between New York and Philadelphia and had required the purchase of a license by those traveling in and through the state. This was tantamount to a tariff which burdened all out-of-state travelers.

The reciprocity bill permitted motorists to travel for fifteen days within the State of New Jersey provided the state from which the motorist came granted the same privilege. Most states were already operating under similar reciprocity arrangements and in time the fifteen-day limit was extended until licensing a car became a requirement of residence rather than of prolonged or commuting use of the roads.

Speaking of tariffs, the Underwood Bill of 1912 proposed lowering the duty on imported automobiles from 45 to 40 percent. Although the imports of that year were no more than 898 cars, the industry opposed the provision vigorously. In later years, when domestic manufacture had outstripped the foreign producers and imports were not to be feared, the industry took an equally vigorous stand against tariff on car imports because it prompted other countries to impose tariffs on our exports.

Unquestionably credit had been extended to car buyers prior to 1912, but not until the Studebaker company announced that it would accept notes from farmers and other responsible buyers of its products was there formal adoption of the practice by automobile manufacturers. The trade gave this announcement a mixed reception, but mainly deplored that a reputable company should take a step in the wrong direction. If a man could not afford to pay cash for a car, so the argument ran, he certainly was in no position to maintain it. The credit buyer would probably be a novice, and if he didn't have an accident and wreck his car he would assuredly abuse it and cause its value to depreciate rapidly.

The industry seemed not to realize what a potent device installment selling would be for promoting sales. There was no great rush to adopt it. Dealers, hearing that the easy payment plan, as it was called, would ease the transformation of prospects into buyers, gave it a try. The used-car department of the Chalmers Agency in New York City advertised easy payments in 1914; the Times Square Automobile Co., which dealt in used cars and in the liquidation of defunct makes, adopted easy payments in 1915; and so did the Maxwell Agency, on the strength of its working well in the Middle West. However, there was more public resistance to credit selling in the East. To go into debt for an article of merchandise as expensive as the automobile was unthinkable. Only those who used the automobile for income-producing activities escaped the raised eyebrow.

Actually, installment selling crept up on the industry and became well established before there was widespread discussion of its merits and demerits. This did not occur until the 1920's and will be considered later.

The manufacturer's liability for the integrity of his product stemmed from an accident. Donald MacPherson of Galway Village, New York, was driving his Buick one day when it suddenly overturned, pinning him underneath. The cause of the accident was a broken rear wheel. MacPherson promptly sued the Buick company for being negligent in equipping his car with a defective wheel.

According to a law promulgated in 1842, a manufacturer

was responsible only to the direct buyer of his product; therefore, the Buick company held that MacPherson had no case because he had bought from a dealer. Realizing the significance if MacPherson won, Detroit marshaled its best lawyers for defense, yet he did win, the jury bringing in a verdict of $5,000.

The case was an interesting one because old-time wheel-wrights testified that the quality of hickory could be told by its appearance and that only young trees yielded satis-factory wood. Some manufacturers must have believed this, for they advertised their cars to be equipped with "second-growth, hickory wheels."

Experts for the plaintiff testified that the quality of wood could be determined only by viewing the spoke ends, which the manufacturer could not do because he bought wheels assembled and painted; that young wood was no better than old; and that no adequate test for quality existed.

When the case was carried to the New York Court of Appeals in 1916, the same court that doomed the Selden patent, MacPherson won again. The court noted the ab-surdity of making a distinction between direct sale and sale through a dealer and held the automobile to be as hazard-ous an article as many others for which manufacturers were held liable for defects.

Wooden wheels had been in universal use ever since the wire-spoked wheel, offshoot of the bicycle wheel, had been abandoned. But the year after MacPherson was awarded $5,000 by a sympathetic jury, several companies reintro-duced wire wheels as standard equipment, and from then on well into the 1920's they were often offered as optional equipment, especially on cars of the sport type.

Cycle cars, too, had wire wheels. These hybrid vehicles, a sort of cross between a bicycle and a buckboard, seating two in tandem fashion and powered by what would now be described as a lawnmower engine, appeared like a swarm of insects and were as soon gone from the scene. More than two score companies were formed to manufacture them, beginning in 1913, but by 1915 those who had not abandoned them to engage in manufacture of a full-sized car were out of the picture.

The significant innovations of 1914 had to do with gear shifting. Changing speeds with the gliding gear type of transmission was an art. Many drivers never learned how to do it without clashing of the gears, and in the earliest cars it took strength as well as skill. Some drivers of cars with planetary transmissions had their troubles too, but of a different order. In one of the early manuals on the care and feeding of the Model T Ford the driver was instructed to hold the clutch pedal in a midway position, open the hand throttle a certain number of notches on the quadrant, depress the clutch pedal, run twenty feet (in low gear), then let the clutch pedal spring back into high gear. This was all very well for a level road, but to start on an upgrade required a wider opening of the throttle and a longer run, whereas on a downgrade less throttle and a shorter run would suffice. People who drove by "the book" found themselves stalling on an upgrade and making an unseemly roar on a downgrade until re-educated by a more mechanically-minded Model T owner.

Something other than a revised instruction manual was needed for the shifters of sliding gears and the maker of the S.G.V. came to their relief. In place of the gear shift lever there was a dial on the steering column. Pushing a numbered button on the dial selected the desired gear, and when the clutch pedal was depressed solenoids did the actual shifting. For reasons that have never been made public, perhaps because the system was not sufficiently reliable, the innovation failed to add luster to the S.G.V. and two years later the company was out of business.

The manufacturer of the Owen-Magnetic sought to eliminate shifting altogether and brought out a car in which the gasoline engine was used to generate electricity and the drive to the wheels was electrical. The flywheel of the engine was replaced by the field magnet part of an electrical generator. Back of a case, bolted to the engine, was a second set of field magnets in line with the flywheel set but fixed and nonrevolving. In the center of the case was a shaft with two armatures, one fitting within the flywheel, the other within the stationary magnets. This shaft, unconnected to the engine, had its rear end carrying the universal joint for the propeller shaft.

The engine was started by turning the current from a battery into the coils of the forward armature, which was kept from revolving with the rear wheels. Then the car was started by switching the resistance brushes of the flywheel generator to generate current, which in turn was taken to the rear of the case, which tried to drive as a motor. With the electricity causing the flywheel machine and armature to turn together, the car got under way. Varying the resistance had an effect similar to slipping the clutch and afforded acceleration without the hiatuses and jerks associated with conventional shifting. In high gear the flywheel generator produced just enough current to maintain a tight grip on the armature.

The Owen-Magnetic, a fairly high-priced car, was produced for six years, then faded. Gear clashing continued for fourteen years, or until General Motors introduced the synchromesh transmission, which then spread promptly throughout the industry.

In that same year of 1914, a V-8 engine appeared on the Cadillac to suggest the direction powerplant design would take. The car was immediately successful and set a new mark in high-speed, multiple-cylinder engines.

During the period 1910–1914 inclusive, 151 new companies were organized to produce passenger cars, but so great was the mortality of concerns that at the end of the period there were 101 fewer companies in business than in 1910. Production and sales expanded steadily but the increase was due primarily to Ford. With the wage of the worker ranging from $10 to $15 a week, the market for cars selling at a higher figure than $1,000 could not expand substantially. It could, and did, expand for Ford, who dropped the price of his car steadily from $780 to $490. In 1914 he accounted for 45 percent of all car sales, and to survive on what market was left, some 180 manufacturers had to work very hard.

At this point, Ford made two moves that endeared him to the general public and to labor. To the public he announced that he would rebate to buyers of his cars between $40 and $60 if he succeeded in selling 300,000 cars in one year. In 1915 he paid off—$50 to every purchaser of a Ford car. To labor he announced that he would raise the minimum wage from an average of $2.50 a day to $5. This move brought anguished cries from his competitors as well as from the heads of other industries. It was confidently declared that it would lead to disaster and that Ford would come to regret his foolish act.

The offer of a rebate to customers is easily understood. Increases in production brought lower unit cost; a lower sale price increased volume to produce a larger overall profit. Volume increases preceded lower prices, and as long as sales were maintained at a high level both manufacturer and customer benefited.

Ford never did give a clear explanation of his motive in raising wages; that is, he gave a variety of reasons, none of which indicated formulation of a well-defined policy or philosophy. There is no evidence of his espousing the idea of expanding the economy by increasing purchasing power. A quarter century was to elapse before that idea became reputable. His rivals claimed it to be a sly trick to draw to him the pick of the labor force. Perhaps the explanation is simply that with millions of dollars rolling in and his stockholders enriched beyond the dreams of avarice, Ford thought to make life more bearable for his employees by sharing the wealth.

Simultaneously with Ford's dramatic moves, the Dodge brothers, who had been fabricating parts for Ford, decided to build a car of their own and let Ford get his parts from another source. Thus was born the Dodge car, priced at $785, a hot competitor for those who were trying to win second place in the industry.

While Ford was winning press headlines, General Motors was recovering from the excesses of Durant's optimism and setting its house in order under the guidance of Charles W. Nash. Durant meanwhile was in process of engineering another coup. Just one year after losing control of General Motors, he organized the Little Motor Car Co. and the Chevrolet Motor Co. The Little company did extremely well and in 1912 produced the lowest-priced six-cylinder car on the American market. The Chevrolet company was less successful at the outset, but by 1914 hit its stride with a Royal Mail roadster and Baby Grand touring car. Both Littles and Chevrolets were made until 1915; then the Little was put to sleep and the company merged with Chevrolet. At this point the performance of the company had been spectacular enough to attract the interest of the E. I. du Pont de Nemours Co., which was seeking a good investment for the money it made in munitions.

Not every company did well. Lozier, Norwalk, and Speedwell, for example, went bankrupt. It is worth a quick look at these disasters to see what sort of money the lesser lights in the industry were dealing with while the giants were playing with millions. Lozier, producer of a large, expensive car for ten years, valued its property at $4,000,000, the receiver valued it at $2,069,000, and it sold at auction for $1,000,000. Norwalk (The Car with a Conscience) had liabilities of $40,000 and assets of $12,000. Speedwell, an eight-year-old company with a reputable product, had liabilities of $465,315 and assets of $386,640.

Before narrating events that took place in quick succession, it is necessary to remind the reader that there was a war on in Europe—the bloody conflict which came to be known as World War I. The industry paid little attention to it, its attitude being "Go away, don't bother me." The years 1915 and 1916, the years during which our country remained on the sidelines, were enormously profitable for some. Competition forced car prices lower, wages rose under the spur of manufacture of war matériel for Europe, and sales mounted by leaps and bounds, tripling between 1914 and 1916. The big companies got bigger, the weak grew weaker, and the in-betweens gained a new lease on life. Prosperity was widespread, but not spread widely enough to slow the mortality rate of those operating from hand to mouth.

The York Motor Car Co. advertised its Pullman car as "Tailored for Her Majesty the American Woman," thereby, I believe, making the first direct appeal to the woman buyer. But Her Majesty looked away and in another year the Pullman was a has-been. Packard, Winton, Kline, and Kissel all introduced a body with an aisle between the front seats to facilitate passage to the rear seat. National not only produced a twelve-cylinder model but went so far with the luxury touch as to seat the occupants in four castered armchairs. Premier, one of the true pioneers among manufacturers, brought out an aluminum engine and a Vulcan magnetic gearshift. Briscoe launched an eight-cylinder car to sell for the extraordinarily low price of $950, and Enger came out with a twelve-cylinder model at $1,095. The Haynes and the H.A.L., named for H. A. Lozier, who manufactured the Lozier until bankruptcy overtook him, also appeared with twelve cylinders. National, Briscoe, Premier, Enger, and H.A.L. did not long survive, but it can be said of these companies that they made heroic efforts.

Installment selling got another nod of recognition. The Agricultural Credit Co. having bought $5,000,000 worth of notes from Chalmers dealers, the Chalmers company adopted a credit plan whereby the customer could buy on time by "paying a small portion of the list price plus 6% on notes given on the balance."

The outlook was rosy, but floating here and there were a few fleecy clouds. A rise in the price of gasoline aroused the industry to consider counter measures. Three suggestions were made: organize cooperative refineries, experiment to see if alcohol or kerosene could be substituted for gasoline, and organize a boycott of the oil companies by the dealers. Nothing was done. What could be done but complain?

If the makers of automobiles were apprehensive of the future, they kept it to themselves and accentuated the positive. The trade press, on the other hand, had its doubts. One journal foresaw the market becoming saturated within five years, a gloomy outlook extracted from figuring on an annual production of 1,200,000 cars, a car life of five years, and no more than 5,000,000 people with the wherewithall to buy.

As the year 1917 dawned, the *Automobile Trade Journal* queried whether new car buyers could be found for 1,000,000 cars a year after 8,000,000 or 9,000,000 cars were in use. After looking into its crystal ball, the *Journal* answered its own question in these words: "We believe that the maximum demand for cars will be reached in three or four years and that manufacturers should lay their plans accordingly."

None of them did. They planned for uninterrupted growth.

Ford made plans for a new plant that would supply him with all his basic materials, make him less dependent on his suppliers, and enable him to effect economies leading to a car price of $250. To get the funds needed to execute his plan he restricted dividend payments. This action aroused the ire of the Dodge brothers, who had no desire to see the Ford company become more powerful, and had a great desire to get dividends on their 10 percent stockholding in the Ford company. They went to court about it and Ford was ordered to disgorge profits and abandon the idea of making his own steel. Now it was Ford's turn to be angry and he took the case to a higher court, which held that he must pay dividends of some $19,000,000 but overruled the order regarding steel manufacture. With this crisis surmounted, Ford began the building of the famous River Rouge plant.

Ford had no reason for any longer loving his stockholders. They had put in very little and taken a great deal out and he decided they were an unnecessary evil and barnacles on his ship of progress. By now the stockholders of the Ford Motor Co. were more interested in the status quo than in the possibility of even juicier profits through actions that appeared to them to be reckless. Henry Ford thereupon announced a desire to buy out their interests. When the stockholders demurred, he threatened to pull out of the company, form a new organization, and bring out a competitive car. This threat was effective, and with a payment to stockholders of $105,250,000 the Ford company became a strictly Ford family affair.

Durant, like Ford, was dreaming of bigger things to come. He had always regarded General Motors as his creation, which it was, and he planned to recapture control of it through stock acquisitions in the open market and by offering to swap four shares of Chevrolet company stock for one share of General Motors. Through these maneuvers Durant was able to get Pierre du Pont elected president of General Motors, and shortly thereafter the Chevrolet company gained complete control. Thus, for the time being, there existed the extraordinary situation of the Chevrolet tail wagging the General Motors dog.

Back in the saddle again, Durant began expanding General Motors operations. The individual manufacturing companies comprising the corporation were made divisions so that the corporation became an operating rather than a holding company. Not until 1918 was the tangle unsnarled that gave Chevrolet control of General Motors, but with that accomplished Chevrolet also became a division of the corporation.

The Du Pont company, which had acquired a large block of General Motors stock in 1917, thinking it to be a good investment and to insure a large market for its paints, varnishes, and artificial leathers, increased its holdings in 1918 until it held 26.4 percent of the stock outstanding. This was the stock the Supreme Court ordered the Du Pont interests to distribute to its stockholders over a period of years, beginning in 1962, because the holding was deemed a violation of antitrust laws.

Pierre du Pont's replacement of Charles Nash as president of General Motors brought a new company into being. Nash, with the backing of the banking group that lost control of General Motors, bought out Thomas B. Jeffery, who had been building the Rambler (later called Jeffery) since 1903. And with this purchase was born the Nash car.

The Woods Motor Vehicle Co., which had been building electrics since 1899, came out with a combination gasoline-electric vehicle. It represented an effort to overcome both the limited range of the electric and the nuisance of gear shifting in the gasoline car. The Woods had an extremely small engine running at high speed which was built in a unit with a generator to keep batteries charged. Once the car was started and brought to a certain steady speed with electricity, the gasoline engine took over. There were two controls, affording a choice of power. One could drive on gasoline alone or include electricity for greater acceleration.

The Pathfinder car appeared with a closed compartment under the rear to house the spare tire. This was the first time the spare tire and wheel had been protected from the elements. Heretofore, it was customary practice to put it in a fender well or hang it vertically from brackets at the rear of the car. The idea was not adopted by other manufacturers and the Pathfinder company went into bankruptcy the same year.

Chalmers did a handsome business in 1916, faltered in 1917, and was leased for a period of five years by Maxwell. Through this deal, Maxwell laid hands on $3,000,000 of new cash capital, with Chalmers getting half the profits from the operation of its company.

America's entry into the war caused the industry to suffer more from the fear of hardships than from any hardships that transpired. Production was greater in 1917 than in 1916. Nevertheless, there was a war on and the War Industries Board imposed a limit of 50 percent of the industry's previous use of steel, consumers were showing increasing reluctance to purchase cars at the prevailing high prices, and Congress slapped an excise tax of 5 percent on the sale of cars.

The industry met these threats by chorusing that the country and the State of Michigan in particular would suffer a calamity if steel was denied it. Incensed that the automobile should be classed as a luxury and taxed accordingly, the industry launched a campaign to substitute the term "passenger car" for "pleasure car." Dealers in Philadelphia instituted an advertising campaign to urge the public to "Buy Now" because prices were likely to go higher. In Springfield, Massachusetts, dealers followed suit with a campaign calling the automobile "Our Country's Greatest Asset." The industry was determined that America should have its butter.

Production did fall 45 percent in 1918, owing to a slump in the latter half of the year. And no wonder, what with heatless homes and gasless Sundays, which necessitated the filling of car tanks by Saturday night. The appearance of heaters in closed cars and the advent of radiator shutters to keep engines warm, some built-in and thermostatically-controlled, nice as they were, could not offset the chilling fact that America was engaged in war. Had prices been what they were in 1917, the mortality of companies might have been severe, but average wholesale prices had risen 40 percent and even the independents had been able to salt away a little working capital. Fortunately for the industry the war soon came to an end and in 1919 production bounced back to double the 1918 output.

There was a move to get into war work in 1918, but it

came very late and had little influence one way or the other. Many of the small companies announced cessation of manufacture for the duration of the war and never resumed operations.

Data for 1918 show a decline in number of new companies formed and in number leaving the industry. The war and the fear of a steel shortage probably caused some aspirants to change their plans. One car failing to appear on the market was the S.S.E., designed by Victor L. Emerson, credited with inventing the universal joint, the cantilever spring, and the bevel gear drive. Emerson planned to manufacture the car, but when war was declared he switched to the making of gunsights. In 1921 I was taken to see the car by a friend who discovered it reposing under a tarpaulin in a small Philadelphia factory. Even then, it was far in advance of the day in engineering design and would certainly have influenced car development had it made its debut.

The Doble steam car appears to have been another war casualty. According to press reports, the War Industries Board ruled against Abner Doble so that he was unable to get into production although he had booked $27,000,000 worth of orders. Other reports had him hopelessly blocked by patent litigation. These reports may or may not have been true. The Doble did attract a great deal of attention and favorable comment when it was shown around the country. Unlike the Stanley, which required torch heating of the fuel vaporizer nozzles to start steam generation, the Doble had a device similar to a spark plug placed beneath the boiler which heated to incandescence by electricity and ignited the fuel-air mixture. Doble moved from Detroit to California, where he produced and sold some cars in the early twenties, but the affairs of the company have defied probers and remain shrouded in mystery.

With the war over and the future looking very bright, the number of companies organized exceeded those dropping from sight, something that hadn't happened for three years. Always before the eyes of ambitious men were the examples of success and fabulous fortunes. It was fairly easy to engage in manufacture but hard to stay in business because the newcomer had to compete with well-intrenched companies. This was not so ten years earlier when even the mighty were struggling to get a firm foothold.

Up to now, dealers wishing to sell cars on the easy payment plan had made their arrangements for credit extension with local banks and finance companies unaffiliated with the manufacturers. This was not a wholly satisfactory arrangement and in 1919 General Motors organized an acceptance corporation, herald of great changes to come. While G.M. dealers were not required to deal with G.M.A.C., the availability of this credit source had the effect of encouraging the flow of this lucrative business to the parent company. Car buyers paid 6 percent per annum on the initial unpaid balance and the recourse system was practiced. In the next decade, the 6 percent plan was to come under government fire and, as will be seen when events of the 1920's are related, a bitter verbal battle ensued between dealers and manufacturers over the recourse versus nonrecourse method of financing.

Ford's giant River Rouge plant was progressing, but the high cost of buying out his six stockholders had left him low in funds at a crucial time and he was forced to borrow $75,000,000. He too had reversed his policy of reducing prices when the wartime inflation began, but successive price increases failed to offset the loss in revenue from shrinking sales.

Durant had not been exactly splurging, but preparations for a booming 1920 had strained General Motors' resources. Other companies, too, planned for a bigger output with all that it meant in new plant facilities and orders to parts makers.

In the five-year period 1915–1919, 142 companies had passed from the scene, 112 new ones had been organized, and there were 133 companies (156 fewer than in 1909) left to battle for a share of the market so certain to expand in the coming decade.

4
bust and boom:
1920–1929

The decade beginning 1920 was the period of the great shake-out, and when it was over and past the manufacture of cars was more firmly concentrated in still fewer hands.

The trouble began in 1920 when the entire industry walked to the edge of a precipice and all but a very few fell over. The biggest and boldest seemed least aware of the yawning chasm, approached most confidently, and fell the farthest, but they were also most able to pull themselves back to safety by virtue of their corporate muscle.

You would never notice that anything out of the ordinary had happened if you consulted production figures. Output was greater in 1920 than in 1919, only 22 percent less in 1921, and then the climb was steadily upward through

1929. As a matter of fact, the first quarter of 1920 was a record breaker, justifying the rosiest expectations. And then something happened—the bottom began falling out of the car market.

The chasm grew deeper and deeper and the manufacturers fell into it. They couldn't gauge the bottom, they thought it only a shallow dip, and when they did hit bottom the only explanation they had was "Somebody pushed me." Looking around in characteristic fashion for scapegoats, they hit on the Federal Reserve Board and the public. They blamed the Federal Reserve Board for restricting credit and thereby bringing on the depression; they blamed the public for conducting a buyers' strike. What they did not see, or refused to admit, was that prices had been raised too high for the public to absorb the projected production. Between 1917 and 1920, prices had risen 57 percent. The term buyers' strike was a misnomer, but comforting.

By September, when manufacture was grinding to a stop, Henry Ford announced a slash in prices "to help the restoration of business to normal conditions." Since the war had ended, said Ford, "war prices should be reduced. . . . Although rich in natural resources, the country's progress is being held at a standstill through the greed of profiteers. Now is the time to call a halt to war methods, war prices, and war greed."

Members of the industry did not think of themselves as profiteers. They had been doing only what comes naturally and Ford's statement angered them. The opinion was unanimous that Ford's cut in prices could not be carried out successfully and this forecast came near to being correct. Nevertheless, within one month twenty-eight manufacturers had followed suit and made their first price reduction.

To contribute to the chaotic situation around Detroit, the factories began laying off men in droves. With production slowed, the need for workers dwindled, and the paying of wages became a drain on depleted treasuries.

In an editorial published at the close of the year, the *Automobile Trade Journal* said. "Cut out the hard times talk and instigate a policy of optimism which is bound to reflect itself in trade dealings. Conditions are not as gloomy as they appear." But the realities could not be talked away and, indeed, no one quite understood what the realities were.

The Big Three—General Motors, Ford, and Willys-Overland—were in the worst straits and each took measures to meet its own peculiar circumstances. General Motors issued some common stock to raise money, but Durant himself was in hot water. He had been accumulating stock and was in debt to his brokers to the tune of $30,000,000, and there was need to unload. Rather than see his stock dumped on the market and the price collapse, Du Pont made a deal whereby it took over 2,500,000 shares for $23,970,000 in cash and $3,480,000 in securities. And once again Durant left General Motors.

The extent of the G.M. debacle became apparent in the balance sheet of 1921, which contained these items:

Write-down of inventories—$16,603,073.

Refunds to dealers and distributors on price reductions—$2,441,376.

Cancellation of commitments, rebates on 1920 sales and miscellaneous losses—$11,421,102.

Special reserve established to cover anticipated losses and unforeseen contingencies pertaining to 1921 and prior years, but not at present definitely discernible—$14,000,000.

The total amount exceeded $44,000,000 and the total liquidation loss announced in the spring of 1923 was $84,-869,893. It was at this time that production of the Sheridan and Scripps-Booth cars was discontinued.

Ford succeeded in paying off $25,000,000 of the $75,000,-000 loan obtained earlier, but even $50,000,000 was too much to permit complacency. At the close of the year he ceased manufacture and turned to assembling the components on hand, which made some thirty thousand cars. These he shipped out to his dealers for cash and, by one expedient and another, raised sufficient money to pay off the loan and rid himself of the fear of banker control.

Dealers were angered by Ford's summary action. They had the alternative of refusing to accept cars and presumably losing their franchises, or raising the necessary funds, hoping to recoup when business turned better. Most of them chose to play along with Ford rather than sacrifice what had been a valuable franchise and probably would be again.

Henry Ford made one serious mistake at this time of stress. He allowed William S. Knudsen to leave the organization. Knudsen had been a key man in the development of Ford's production technique and shortly after quitting the company he was giving the benefit of his knowledge and experience to the Chevrolet Division of G.M., Ford's hottest competitor.

Willys was already loaded with bank loans when the crisis developed and his only hope was to keep renewing loans so the bankers would not take over. In the final showdown a bank agreed to make a loan provided Walter Chrysler was taken in to straighten out Willys's affairs. Chrysler did move in, but Willys was able to "escape" the loan. Willys's troubles were compounded by the formation of a separate corporation and the building of a $10,000,000 plant in New Jersey for the manufacture of a Chrysler-sponsored Willys car. The car was never built and the plant stood idle until bought some years later by Durant for $4,000,000 to expand the productive facilities of his Durant Motors.

While Chrysler was tinkering with the Willys-Overland company to get it to run on all cylinders, he was also brought into Maxwell to do a similar job. Walter Chrysler is now on stage, if only in the wings, but beginning to show the capacities which would bring him to the top in later years.

Two holding companies were organized in the first part of 1920, when business was flush and the outlook bright. One was the United States Automotive Corp. with satellites in the form of the Lexington Motor Co. (cars), Ansted Engineering Co., Connersville Foundry, and Teetor-Hartley Motor Corp. The other was Hare's Motors, embracing the Mercer and the Locomobile, both high-priced cars, and the Riker truck. The holding company had a contract for factory operation and sales, but the manufacturing companies retained their identity. Hare's Motors, according to press releases, anticipated an annual business of $200,-000,000 within five years. "Expansion will be limited only by the time factor." An unforeseen factor—the depression —shortened the time factor. Within two years, the company was dissolved.

Typical of the loose business methods all too common in the era of expansion, which sent many a company to the wall, was an incident occurring in a distributorship which I joined following a change in management. The new management ordered two highly qualified men to take a parts inventory. This brought to light a stocking of shelves and bins with old, used parts, replacing new parts which had been sold for personal profit by stockroom employees of the previous regime. All told, the inventory write-down approximated $72,000. When this was brought to the attention of the new head his response was "Write it back up, boys. If we show a loss like that we'll never get any more money from the bankers."

The year 1921 was ushered in with factories closed or operating part time and an overtime production of oracular pronouncements. "Business is fundamentally sound," was the exorcising cry. Manufacturers joined hands to break the buyers' strike with a campaign to convince the public that rock-bottom prices had been reached. They hadn't, but maybe if the public could have been persuaded a floor would have been put under prices. As it was, the public was not convinced and prices continued sinking throughout the year.

Durant, whose response to disaster was to bounce, announced the formation of Durant Motors in January. He still had many admirers and supporters, but they were not to be found among bankers. To raise funds he created his own stock-selling organization. I had occasion to accompany a district sales manager on his rounds of bars, restaurants, small shops, and shoeshine parlors and observe the readiness of these small-time employers and smaller-time employees to part with their hard-earned money to "get in on the ground floor of the General Motors of the future." A sale of 500,000 shares at $12 a share (with the salesman getting $1 per share) was a remarkable feat for 1921 and proof of the public's unshaken faith in William Durant, or in the industry's power to produce gold.

At that particular time public faith was based on a great deal of ignorance. The only cars in the G.M. line then making money were the Buick and the Cadillac. The Chevrolet Division lost $5,000,000 in the year. Yet, as matters turned out, the public would have done far better to buy General Motors stock than Durant's. That's where the pot of gold at the foot of the rainbow lay.

While Durant was beginning at the bottom for the third time, two other men whose names were famous throughout the industry were seeing their dreams shattered. They were Henry M. Leland and Louis Chevrolet. Leland, who had been most responsible for endowing the Cadillac with quality through precision manufacture, had brought out his own high-priced Lincoln car in the unfortunate year of 1920 and now, stripped of working capital, he was forced to put the Lincoln Motor Car Co. on the auction block. Henry Ford picked it up more out of a personal friendship for Leland than from the desire to add a high-priced car to his line. In addition he paid off company notes endorsed by Leland and his son.

Louis Chevrolet, who had designed the first model of the car bearing his name and had formed the American Motors Corp. in 1916 to manufacture the American car at Plainfield, New Jersey (sloganed "America's Smile Car"), saw his organization go into the hands of a receiver.

Having pulled the Maxwell company together and brought the Maxwell name back into good standing, Walter Chrysler was strengthening his position and biding his time until he could launch a car under his own name. A move in this direction was to organize the Maxwell Motor Co. to take over the assets of Maxwell-Chalmers.

Eddie Rickenbacker, famed World War I ace, served no apprenticeship before having a car on the market bearing his name. Backed by Walter Flanders and B. F. Everitt, two members of the E-M-F triumvirate and subsequent producers of the Flanders and Everitt cars, respectively, Rickenbacker capitalized on his war fame with the hat-in-ring symbol for his car emblem and, as it were, grew out of the depression.

Although failures increased slightly in 1921, they were not what made the year stand out prominently. It was a revival of interest in steam cars. Eight companies were formed to manufacture them, all reaching the point of producing at least one pilot model. The revival brought forth a variety of engines and steam generators, but no manufacturer succeeded in finding a way to generate steam fast and adequately. The flurry of interest and activity was all over within five years. Two of the companies had charges of fraud brought against them.

The sudden burst of interest in the steam car was prompted by the high price of gasoline, coupled with dire predictions that supplies of crude oil would soon be insufficient to yield the needed gasoline. Some method, therefore, would have to be found to utilize a less-refined product. The steam car seemed to offer one solution because it was less finicky about its fuel diet. Some also thought the steamer could be built for less money. The dire predictions soon proved to be unfounded. Cracking processes were developed which produced more gasoline from a barrel of crude oil, new oil fields were discovered, and interest in the steam car lapsed.

Late in 1921 the price of cars had sunk nearly to its prewar figure and the public began re-entering showrooms. *Automotive Industries,* which reflected industry opinion, had this to say at the year's end:

> Part of our business depression has been real; it has been caused by economic factors resulting from the war and could scarcely have been avoided. Part, however, has been psychological, the result of fear. This last has been unnecessary and has caused unnecessary financial loss and human suffering. It should never have been and can be dispelled readily by a more optimistic view of conditions, by a firm belief in the essential soundness of industry, and by determination to go forward on this basis.

Ringing words, those, but no true explanation of what had happened. Nowhere a hint of the industry's contribution to the trouble; no suggestion that the steady pushing up of prices had brought on the buyers' strike. Presumably the real cause had yet to be recognized. But it is fair to ask what would have happened had the public not gone on strike. Would not prices have held firm and, perhaps, been pushed even higher to perpetuate the inflationary situation and precipitate a more widespread and deeper depression at a later date?

The total adverse effect of a depression or recession is not inflicted immediately. The victim first suffers a headache, but cannot put his finger on the cause. His condition worsens so he tries wonder drugs (campaigns). Rarely are these effective so he gets a blood transfusion (new working capital) and goes on a dict (reduces inventories). If he survives, always problematical, there is apt to be a long period of convalescence accompanied by good resolves and a strict regimen.

It is another characteristic of a depression that misery likes company. The weak join with others who are weak in search of strength. While the psychological benefit from holding hands may be great, the entwined companies usually sink together.

In spite of a production of over 2,000,000 cars, which established a new record, 1922 was a year of recovery and a mounting death rate. Ford made half the cars and a dozen manufacturers made most of the remaining million so that only crumbs were left for the small companies. To get a true flavor of that year, one has only to read headlines. Here are a few:

Creditors of Earl Motors, Inc. Confer with Bankers

Owen-Magnetic Property Offered for Sale by Receiver

Pan American Sale Ordered

Saxon in Difficulty; Begs Creditors for Extension of Time

Creditors Plan Rehabilitation of Maibohm

Rumored Lafayette and Pierce to Merge

Creditor's Merchandise Claims Against Templar $1,000,000

In March, the Frontenac Motor Car Co. was organized with financier Allan Ryan as chairman of the board and Louis Chevrolet as vice president and designer. In August, Mr. Ryan went bankrupt and a year later the Frontenac company followed suit.

The Associated Motor Industries was incorporated to embrace the manufacturers of the Dixie Flyer, the old-line Jackson and National, and six other companies variously engaged in the manufacture of engines, gears, trucks, and bodies. Creditors of National gave their permission for the company to join the group and the A.M.I. became the National Motors Corp. but, as we said, combining weak companies, whatever it promises in economies, does not automatically create strength, and a year later National was washed up.

C. Harold Wills, who had been one of the shining lights at Ford, realized his dream of building a high-quality car of modest proportions with the launching of the Wills–St. Claire. The car featured extensive use of molybdenum alloy steels and an eight-cylinder engine with overhead valves driven by an overhead camshaft, something new in the world of engines. Hardly had Wills got under way when he ran into financial difficulties. Bankers granted a revolving credit of $6,900,000 to tide over the organization for a year. In 1923 the C. H. Wills Co. went into receivership and was reorganized as the Wills–St. Claire Motor Co., which survived until 1927.

Wills's experience provides a classic example of an industry axiom. Given a high-quality car of moderate size and above-average price, and a large car of average quality and average price, the public will choose the latter. Packard tried putting quality into a small package with its "single six" of 1920 and got nowhere with it. Size and price must be related, and the wise manufacturer learned it early.

In spite of the about-turn in production in 1922, price cutting kept many a manufacturer from putting on any fat. Trailing companies found themselves once again with hope, but better profits were needed to get on solid ground and better profits were hard to come by.

Durant was making the Star (to compete with the Ford and the Chevrolet), the Flint, and the Durant. His financial operations, like those of John North Willys, were too complex to be reported here with clarity. Both men fought up and down hill in a struggle to reach the top until they were mortally wounded by the next depression.

The liveliest news and a pleasant departure from the more common tale of woe was a rumor that General Motors was about to produce a "copper-cooled" car, a colorful but descriptive name for a car with an air-cooled engine. Franklin was still using air-cooled engines and was floating a stock issue to finance a low-priced, four-cylinder model; the air-cooled Fox car had just appeared in Philadelphia, but for the manufacturer who had everything to venture an air-cooled car was news indeed. However, its real significance had nothing to do with air cooling.

Charles Kettering, who joined General Motors after developing the electric self-starter and was its research head, began working on an air-cooled engine in 1918 and by 1920 reported its development sufficiently advanced for pre-production tests preparatory to introduction in 1921 as a replacement for the water-cooled engine in the Chevrolet 490. But the program became fouled up and the car was not shown publicly until 1923. It was unveiled at a hotel at the time of the New York Automobile Show and made quite a hit although nothing was shown but a chassis.

The basic difference between the copper-cooled engine and other air-cooled engines lay in the use of copper instead of cast iron for the finning to radiate heat from the cylinder, and one of the problems had been to unite metals with dissimilar coefficients of expansion. Convinced of the superiority of the engine, General Motors had plans to bring out a six-cylinder model to power the Oldsmobile, but this was postponed.

According to Alfred P. Sloan, Jr., who was president of General Motors at the time, 759 copper-cooled Chevrolets were built. Of these, 239 were scrapped by the production department, 100 were sold at retail, and the remainder were scattered among the factory and dealer organizations. By the middle of the year all were recalled because they were defective in performance.

With a big sales year in prospect and production of Chevrolets and Oldsmobiles practically at a standstill, the only recourse was to call off the program and revert to the proven water-cooled engines. In *My Years with General Motors*, Mr. Sloan says that had the company programs been held up in the face of an expanding market by the uncertain development of the engine, "I do not believe there would be a General Motors today; we would have missed the boat."

General Motors did not again play with air cooling until it brought out the Corvair thirty-six years later, but by that time Dr. Ferdinand Porsche had developed a remarkably successful air-cooled engine to power the Volkswagen and the engineering spadework had been done beyond peradventure.

As far as I know the full story of the copper-cooled fiasco had never been told to the public until related by Mr. Sloan. No mention of it appears in the "foresight saga" entitled *The Turning Wheel,* written by Arthur Pound for the twenty-fifth anniversary of General Motors. We can be grateful to Mr. Sloan for the full disclosure because the facts are relevant to the entire industry as well as to G.M.'s later success.

What happened to G.M. happened to countless companies. Their products were defective or failed to catch the public fancy. But unlike General Motors they had no life preservers—no proven engine or car to fall back upon; no companion line of cars to soften the disaster. One blow and they were out of business. The moral is, of course, don't put all your eggs in one basket, as Durant recognized when he put General Motors together. But most car makers had all they could do to produce the one egg.

The value of the copper-cooled experience to the organization, according to Sloan, lay "in what it taught us about the value of organized cooperation and coordination in engineering and other matters. It showed the need to make an effective distinction between divisional and corporate functions in engineering, and also between advanced product engineering and long-range research."

"All is not gold that glitters" and "Beauty is only skin deep" seem to be the maxims exampled by the automobile show of 1923. Outshining the copper fins of the Chevrolet was a gold-plated McFarlan chassis. Six months after serving as a conversation piece, the McFarlan was sold to a woman in an Oklahoma city whose family had acquired wealth in oil wells.

It wasn't a gold-plated year for Mitchell, Haynes, Winton, Apperson, and Dorris. Mitchell resported a $2,000,000 loss on the previous year's operations. The cost of developing a new model plus an inability to sell cars at a satisfactory profit resulted in selling below the cost of production. Result: receivership, and the end of the Mitchell, which had been in business for twenty years.

Haynes, Winton, and Apperson decided to merge to form the Consolidated Motors Corp. and it was rumored that Dorris might join. The objective, news reports said, was to be like General Motors. To companies weak in the knees, to be like General Motors was to reach the Promised Land. Haynes and Winton stockholders agreed to the merger and a New York bank proposed to back it, but the creditors of Haynes and Apperson raised objections and the plan fell through. In 1924, Haynes, Winton, and Dorris decided to call it quits and with their demise three pioneer companies passed into automobile history. Haynes dated from 1904, Winton from 1897, and Dorris from 1905. Apperson, dating from 1902, struggled on.

Walter Chrysler, who had been consolidating his position step by step, dumped the Chalmers, deciding the reputation of this once proud make of car was beyond resuscitation. At the year's end he became president of Maxwell and a few days later papers of incorporation for the Chrysler Motor Co. were filed. Alfred P. Sloan, Jr., became president of General Motors, succeeding Pierre du Pont. The ascendancy of these two men to high command posts ushered in a new era in automobile manufacture. This, of course, was not apparent at the time, and it is only with hindsight that the statement can be made.

Let's take a look at the domestic car which made its bow to the public in January, 1924. Front and rear bumpers were now standard equipment, following the example set by Westcott in 1919. A score of manufacturers had adopted four-wheel brakes and a few were offering straight-eight (eight-in-line) engines. Both these advances had been introduced by Duesenberg in 1920. Lamps and radiator shells, which had hitherto been painted the color of the car, were now glittering with nickel plate and some producers were offering foot-controlled headlamp dimmers and power-operated windshield wipers as standard equipment. Gone were the days of driving with one hand and swinging the wiper with the other.

Balloon tires had made their appearance and were both exclaimed over and frowned upon by engineers. The switch from high-pressure tires to balloons could not be made without redesigning the steering system and that took time to accomplish. Balloon tires (doughnuts as they were sometimes called) are a thing of the past, but they did serve to make the transition from the hard-riding, high-pressure tire to the soft-riding, low-pressure tire.

Several manufacturers began experimenting with fabric bodies under license from abroad. The French Weymann body promised to be lighter in weight than the combination wood and metal body and some exponents heralded it as the body of the future. Apperson was the first company to offer a car so equipped, in 1925, and that was the end of Apperson.

The most important events of 1924 were not mechanical in nature. They were the advent of the truly low priced closed car and of Duco, which revolutionized the painting of cars.

The Hudson company, which had been steadily reducing the price of its six-cylinder Essex coach, posted a figure of $895, which was $5 less than the price of the touring car. At the same time, the Hudson open- and closed-body models were offered at an identical price. This was revolutionary and as far reaching in effect as the introduction of the self-starter. It made of the automobile an all-season vehicle for every class of buyer. No longer would heaters dissipate their warmth through the cracks in the side curtains, or compel the driver to assume the wet task of installing side curtains when overtaken by a storm. Hudson having set the course, other manufacturers were forced by competition to follow, and from then on the increase in sales of closed cars was matched by the decline in sales of open models. Only sport models with rumble seats withstood the change and in time they, too, became extinct.

Prior to the development of Duco by the Du Pont company, the painting of a car was the bottleneck in the production process. The application of fillers, primers, lead coats, varnish coats, rubdowns, and intervals for drying took anywhere from ten to fifty days, depending upon the quality of the job. It was a slow, costly process even though labor rates were low, and there had to be large storage facilities. With the arrival of Duco, painting a car could be accomplished in a couple of days, a period more consonant with the time required for assembly.

With closed cars growing in popularity, there arose a demand for a better antifreeze than alcohol. Owners were complaining that alcohol boiled away without warning, often with dire effects to the engine. A trade correspondent suggested using a mixture of honey and water, but before there could be any run on honey a permanent antifreeze in the form of ethylene glycol came on the market.

The launching of a Chrysler car, while it startled the automobile world, pleased the public, and was highly important to the future of Chrysler Motors, lacked the significance of the Hudson price slash. The Chrysler car did represent a decided engineering advance. It had a high-compression engine, new to passenger cars, four-wheel brakes, balloon tires, and very snappy lines. It gave the impression that Chrysler might become a pacesetter in the industry. The car was not cheap, but the buyer got his money's worth. If the prospective buyer did not have the money to buy, which was around $1,500, there was an improved Maxwell selling for half that price. A year later, with the Chrysler selling well, the Maxwell was discontinued and with it was extinguished a name known to the motoring public for twenty years.

Henry Ford now advocated a decentralization of the industry. He envisioned small factories dotting the countryside for the making of components and accessories. By such an arrangement he thought the worker could have one foot in industry and one on the land and thereby lead a more secure and balanced life. When the industry went into one of its frequent tailspins, the worker would have his plot of ground, hoe his vegetables, and keep at least his dinner pail full until business picked up again.

The idea may not have been practical, but it showed that Ford was aware of the dislocations created by the industry's growth. Factories were once spread widely over the eastern half of the nation, but had gravitated to Detroit to sprawl all over it. Detroiters now depended entirely on the industry for their welfare—an industry which gyrated between giving full employment and no employment, feast and famine. Ford made a few moves to implement his idea. He established small plants within trucking distance of Detroit, but nothing came of it in the long run. In time a form of decentralization did come about with the installation of assembly plants at strategic locations. But this wasn't exactly what Ford had in mind.

All in all, 1924 was a very good year for the majority of auto makers. Output slackened, but not enough to scare anyone. There were, of course, some failures, most of them an aftermath of the depression. In the five-year span 1920–1924, there were 126 companies leaving the industry and only half as many newcomers. In addition to the cars already mentioned as disappearing from the market should be noted the Mercer, which was discontinued after some 25,000 cars had been built; the Crane-Simplex, a superbly engineered car; the Premier, which had been on the market for twenty years; and the Stanley, the last and best-known of the steamers.

In retrospect the manufacture of automobiles appears as a hazardous undertaking—failures so far exceeding successes. But this was not apparent to the public, perhaps because the successes were so eye-catching and the possibilities of miracles (profits) still so strong. Charles M. Schwab, president of United States Steel, must have thought there was hope for the small companies because he bought into Stutz. And there were thousands like him.

The sale of cars on the installment plan had been increasing steadily, following the inception of the practice around the middle of the teens, then accelerated so that by 1925 about one half of all cars were sold on credit. No one seemed to know where it was leading, or how it would end. It grew like Topsy and now it had become a source of bitter conflict.

Generally speaking, auto makers and dealers thought well of installment buying because it sold cars that otherwise would not have been bought. Bankers and economists, on the other hand, were apprehensive lest it get out of hand and wreck the economy. Clothiers, furniture dealers, and other merchants catering to consumers complained that people were buying cars instead of the solid necessities of life.

The free-for-all discussion bursting out in 1925 and continuing on into the next year might have been postponed a few years more had not warfare broken out between manufacturers and dealers. There were, therefore, two lines along which the discussion ran. There was concern over the impact of installment selling on the national economy, and the narrower concern for its effect on individual welfare.

Customarily cars were sold with a one-third down payment and completion of payment in twelve months. That was regarded as sound because the buyer's equity would be large enough to make it worthwhile for him to complete his payments. If he failed to make his payments, the dealer could repossess the car and resell it without incurring financial loss. Had these terms been adhered to strictly there would have been less to talk about, but they were eroding under the stress of competition. In many instances, down payments had been reduced to 25 percent and pay ment terms lengthened to eighteen months.

H. Parker Willis, consulting economist to the Board of the Federal Reserve Bank, made a public statement urging substantial down payments, a strict limitation of terms, and closer supervision to see that the line between sound and unsound financing was not crossed. Oscar F. Meredith, assistant cashier of The Bank of America, New York, issued a similar plea and urged cooperation among all parties con cerned.

Dealers charged manufacturers with applying pressure on them to make sales and the public with pressing for easier terms. The dealers in turn applied pressure on the finance companies to lower their rates. When the finance companies lowered their rates without tightening their terms, the weak ones went out of business.

Dealers also objected to the recourse system of financing and demanded the opportunity to use a nonrecourse system. Recourse meant that if a credit sale backfired the dealer bore the responsibility. He had to take back the car, sell it for what he could get, and hope to come out even. With the nonrecourse system, it was the finance company that took the responsibility and suffered any losses. If we are going to use the recourse system, said the dealers, factory discounts should be larger so that we can set up reserves against repossession and resale.

Manufacturers favored the recourse system, holding that without responsibility for the quality of credit extended, the dealers would sell to poor risks and impair the soundness of the credit selling.

The dealer's situation was made more difficult by the used-car problem. A large proportion of his sales involved a trade-in, which meant selling one or perhaps two used cars following a new car sale before he knew where he stood as regards profit or loss. Far too often he ended up with a loss on the multiple transaction.

The manufacturers declared installment selling to be basically sound and to prove it, pointed to the almost negligible losses from repossessions. But something had to be done to make the situation less chaotic, and that something was a move to establish connections with a large finance company to assure some regulation. The manufacturers also saw to it that insurance was tied in with the installment sale, where previously the dealer had arranged his own insurance with a company of his choice. At this, agents and brokers of insurance companies were up in arms and had their say because they saw themselves losing most of that business.

Those who took it upon themselves to speak for the public limited their comments to criticizing the manner in which rates were presented to the public. The true cost of financing was concealed, they said. If the advertised rate was 6 percent per annum paid on the initial balance, the public assumed it was simple interest such as paid by savings banks, whereas in fact it was much more than 6 percent. It was many years before this point would be settled.

There were no last words spoken in this installment credit controversy, but to wind up the subject temporarily, two quotations will suffice.

O. H. Cheney, president of the American Exchange–Pacific National Bank, New York, declared that rate warfare had put the automobile industry in the position of selling credit. And as for the loss ratio, it meant little in good times. "There was a time," he said, "when automobiles were sold on merit. Later, automobiles were sold on advertising 'talking points,' now they are being sold on numerology."

A more penetrating comment was made by William F. Foster of the Pollak Foundation. He said general opinion held installment selling to be all right if not overdone, but that it would be nearer the truth to say that installment selling is helpful to business because it is overdone. He noted that it did influence consumption but that the purchase price came from future income. Installment selling, he declared, "cannot permanently produce prosperity."

As we can see clearly with the passage of time, installment selling did expand the market enormously by channeling purchasing power in that direction. Without the forced saving imposed by an installment contract, thousands upon thousands of people would never have been able to accumulate the purchase price; their income would have been spent for more immediately gratifiable wants. Without credit, many more thousands would never have been able to buy any but the lowest-priced car. However, once sales had been lifted to a higher plateau and future income locked up, credit could give no more stimulation to sales and further expansion of the market depended upon national growth and a general rise in purchasing power. That installment selling "cannot permanently produce prosperity" was amply demonstrated four years later when the great depression came.

Purchasing power was rarely discussed in those days. Its relation to sales was barely understood because time selling had obscured the realities. There was talk of sales reaching a saturation point, but it meant different things to different people. To the manufacturer it seemed to mean the point where everybody owned a car, and that point was still far off.

But the limit to the market for new cars was a lot closer than production figures indicated. Every new car sold eventually swelled the number of used cars on the market, and the mounting production of 1921 through 1923 worsened the used-car situation to plague both manufacturer and dealer. It plagued the manufacturer because as long as a car would run it stood in the way of a new car sale. It plagued the dealer because he had to keep his trade-ins moving into consumers' hands and at a price that would keep him from going bankrupt as a dealer in "old iron." The expedient of shipping used cars to South America, where there was no competition from local manufacture, was tried, but it could not significantly ameliorate the situation.

Some manufacturers set quotas for their dealers and these dealers knew they were expected to sell their quotas or run the risk of losing their franchises. To a dealer who was having a hard time selling his quota, an easing of financing terms looked attractive. If the quota was not sold, did it signify overproduction and forcing by the factory, or a poor dealer? That was a moot point on which dealer and manufacturer could not see eye to eye.

Although the dealer was far from satisfied with his position vis-à-vis the manufacturer, he was selling new cars just about as fast as they could be shipped to him. The first quarter of 1925 was such a booming one that even the weak sisters got a reprieve; hence, when the news came out that Dodge Brothers was for sale, it came as a shock to an industry which could understand the selling of a weak company, but not the disposal of a strong one. Dodge had risen slowly and steadily to the Number 1 position among the independents. Its past year's sales grossed $191,000,000 with a profit of nearly $20,000,000.

But the company was, in fact, for sale. The Dodge brothers had died in 1920 and their widows thought it best to dispose of the property. The House of Morgan, acting for General Motors, bid $124,650,000 cash, or $50,000,000 in cash and $90,000,000 in non-interest-bearing notes to be paid off serially in nine years. Dillon, Read & Co., a New York banking house, offered $146,000,000 in cash and secured the property. Thereupon, the bankers resold the company to the public for $160,000,000, represented by $75,000,000 in 6 percent bonds and $85,000,000 in 7 percent preferred stock. With each share of preferred was given one share of Class A nonvoting common stock. For itself, Dillon, Read kept 500,000 shares of Class B common stock, which had the voting power, and 650,000 shares of

Class A stock. Thus the bankers made a profit of $14,000,-000 (less expenses) and retained complete control of the company.

This was a whopping profit to make on a turnabout transaction where the risk was practically nil. It is interesting to compare this deal with the refinancing of General Motors in 1910. In that instance, where the risk was great, the bankers underwrote a $15,000,000 note issue and for their pains received $2,250,000 in cash discount, preferred stock with a cash value of $3,851,054, and control of the board of directors. Whatever the reader's conclusions, one can understand why the manufacturer turned to bankers only as a last resort.

The year 1925 marked the thirtieth anniversary of the industry, but only three of the makes of cars on the market had been before the public since 1900. These were Stearns, Packard, and Locomobile. There had always been an F. B. Stearns Co. in Cleveland, Packard began life as the Ohio Automobile Co. in Warren, Ohio, and the Locomobile Co. of America had undergone one reorganization and a transfer to Durant control. Had Haynes and Winton remained in business one more year they, too, could have taken their places in the Hall of Fame—as survivors in the deadly combat of automobile manufacture. It can be seen that it was deadly for since 1900 about eight hundred companies had disappeared from the scene.

At this quarter mark of the century there came about a change, or rather the beginning of a change, in industry policy. Alfred P. Sloan spoke of it in a talk to G.M.'s General Sales Committee.

"In my judgment," he said, "General Motors as a whole

is relatively weak in sales endeavor. As a matter of fact, the entire automobile industry has been built up and around people of mechanical and technical characteristics rather than commercial, and I think we are just beginning to realize the great importance of the commercial side of the business."

Amplifying this statement in *My Years with General Motors,* Sloan writes: "When it came to the product, the policy meant continuous eternal change." He also said General Motors would put emphasis on selling "the bigger and better car."

People with a mechanical and technical bent had dominated the formative years of the industry and many of them lacked the commerical sense necessary for survival. In the 1920's many companies were headed by ex-star salesmen who had little understanding of production and to whom a balance sheet was a bore. After them came men who climbed to the top position via accountancy or finance, or who exhibited a native skill for management like Mr. Sloan. Each era produced the leaders thought best equipped to serve it.

Without the mechanically-minded men for whom perfecting the automobile was a life pursuit, there would have been far less to exploit commercially. What Mr. Sloan said called the turn and his remarks are highly significant because they heralded the coming of a practice eventually to become industrywide—the introduction of the annual model to induce obsolescence rather than to launch engineering improvements. And the "bigger and better car" led to the practice of trading up—inducing the public to buy a larger, more expensive car.

These policies were diametrically opposed to that of Ford, which was to build an ever-cheaper car through standardization of model, and they were effective policies with which to battle him. Whatever the policies—Ford's or General Motors'—they put the smaller, independent manufacturers between the upper and lower millstones. Price competition meant shaving profits; annual model change increased production costs. Price cutting hurt the dealers, too; it lowered the value of used cars that had been taken in trade. Annual models forced the dealers to unload unsold cars at cut prices at the end of the model year.

To get a dynamic image of the industry at this juncture it is best to regard it as a race rather than as a business enterprise. Ford was out front, selling two cars to Chevrolet's one. Close behind were bunched about ten auto makers going at top speed. With all contenders driving as if to set speed records, the contest was grueling and someone was bound to get hurt. The inadequacy of the track seemed far from mind; all were driving to hold their position and, if possible, to better it.

With Ford and Chevrolet certain to hold first and second positions, the hottest competition centered around cars selling for about $850. Pontiac, the General Motors competitor in this group, put on a remarkable performance for a new car. When a tally was taken at the end of 1926, it was obvious that, while relative positions had changed little, some of the drivers had failed to go ahead as expected.

General Motors improved its position vis-à-vis its competitors by completing the purchase of the Fisher Body Co., in which it had already acquired a 60 percent stock interest in 1919. Fisher then became the body division of

G.M., but the Fisher name was retained and became widely known through the advertising of "Body by Fisher."

The wear and tear began taking its toll in 1927. Ford was the major victim. Dodge, too, suffered and the producer of the Paige car turned its business over to the Graham brothers. People who lived through that period may recall that the Model T had remained virtually unchanged since its inception. It now came in a limited range of colors instead of black only, but no advances had been made in comfort or performance. By contrast with other cars, notably Chevrolet and Mr. Willys's Whippet, the Model T was sadly out of date. What the public wanted now was more comfort and snappier performance, and installment selling had put cars with these qualities within its reach.

Paradoxically, the popularity of the Ford had begun to militate against its sale. There were just too many of them on the road to give distinction to ownership. You often heard people say they were tired of being one of the masses; that they itched to lift themselves out of the Ford class—a remark which indicated the passing of cost as the primary consideration in the minds of many people.

Dodge was in much the same situation as Ford, with a good, sturdy car produced year after year with minimum change and no yearly model. Both Dodge and Ford, though doing a big business, had slipped numerically as well as relatively. Further price reductions could not reverse the trend.

Chevrolet sales exceeded those of Ford for the first time in history in the month of April, 1927. By mid-year Ford had shut down his factory and announced the bringing out of a new car to satisfy a changed market. This was big news to the motoring public and an ominous warning to com-petitors and to many small accessory and parts makers. There had grown up around the Model T a large industry devoted to supplying gadgets to improve appearance and components to improve performance. An indulgent Model T owner could spend hundreds of dollars dolling up his car and many did. Two examples will suffice to show the range of articles available.

There was the Craig-Hunt cylinder head to be had for about $100 which would convert the Model T's L-head engine into a sixteen-overhead valve job in the interest of greater speed. There was also a device to please the economy-minded. It was known as a Speedler and sold for $5. It consisted of a watch-case dial with three small ports at the end of a perforated tube which could be screwed into the intake manifold. Opening and closing of the ports was controlled by a Bowden wire leading to a small lever on the steering column. As the car gained speed, opening the ports allowed air to enter the manifold so that speed was increased without further opening of the throttle. In effect, the Speedler altered the mixture in a way not possible with the simple float carburetor. On descending a hill, the throttle was shut, the Speedler opened, and the engine acted as a brake because it lacked an explosive charge, and it also cooled down substantially, ready for the next upgrade. At a forty mph speed, gasoline mileage would increase as much as ten miles to the gallon, which was a considerable gain. During World War II, a similar device was used on the P-47 Thunderbolt fighter plane to inject a charge of water into the engine manifold when a sudden and short-time burst of speed was needed.

The public was avid to know what the new Ford would look like. Could Henry Ford design and produce a car capable of putting him back in the lead position? Would such a car have to be priced higher than the Model T? Whatever his competitors thought, the public gave Ford the benefit of the doubt. Many prospective buyers must have held off in a wait-and-see attitude because, when production figures are examined, they show no filling of the void left by Ford, and a drop of about three quarters of a million in production for the year.

The wear and tear showed up in another way. Manufacturers had gone into the 1927 season with the expectation of even better sales than in 1926 and they had lowered prices still further to meet competition. When the bigger market did not materialize, but instead the market shrank, those who lost both volume and profits were placed in a precarious position. They were, of course, the independents.

Primarily there were two factors standing in the way of expansion. There was trouble in the farm belt and in the South and Middle West. Farmers were not prospering enough to buy the cars Detroit was making for them. Again, used-car sales now controlled new car sales. Until the accumulating used cars could be digested there was too much unused transportation lying around to plague and weaken the dealers. There was much discussion of accelerated junking of used cars, but when dealers sold used vehicles to junkers they were not necessarily scrapped. Far too often they were repurchased by prospects who offered them as trade-ins on new cars. In desperation it was suggested that the market value of old cars by make and by year be published to acquaint the public with true values. All well and good, but a dealer did not have to abide by the published price and if put under sufficient financial pressure he tossed the quoted price out the window. The buyer was in the saddle.

So serious was the used-car situation that when suggestions were made in the press to have compulsory car insurance for the protection of the public, the American Automobile Association urged its clubs to fight the move lest it hurt used-car sales.

Low profits were general in industry. Competition in 1927 was not alone between companies within a single industry but between industries. And the cry heard around the country was "profitless prosperity." With sales trending downward and prices following suit, with productive capacity in excess of normal demand, and with the lesson of 1920–1921 still in mind, manufacturers began buying from suppliers on a hand-to-mouth basis. This was sane and orderly, but upsetting to the suppliers, who could not well plan production ahead.

Observing life to be precarious for a large manufacturer having no car to sell in the under-$1,000 market, Studebaker launched the Erskine to sell for $835. Great things were expected of it, but it failed to win public favor. With seven or eight cars selling for less money, a newcomer at $835 had to offer something exceptional and the Erskine did not. Peerless, whose niche had been in the higher-priced quality group, thought it best to tap a lower-priced market and brought out a smaller model six to sell for $1,300. This car, too, failed to set the world on fire.

At the annual automobile show of 1928 there were fewer

manufacturers exhibiting their wares. There were fewer chassis on display and more body models. The public was manifesting, or being led to manifest, less interest in the vitals of a car and more interest in its outward appearance and the comfort it offered. This was a compliment to the general excellence of engineering and an indication that the automobile had come a long way. Here too was a hint that style was to play a more important role in the future.

Now back to the track.

The year 1928 opened with Chevrolet in the lead. Ford had just come out of the pit, where he had been forced to stay for a half of last year's race. He was trailing the field and dreadfully slow in getting up speed. The contestants offering cars around $850 were still bunched and crowding each other. Cars in the upper price brackets had also raised their speeds.

Ford's Model A was an immediate success, a vast improvement over the Model T in every respect and selling at only a slightly higher price, which was still under the Chevrolet figure. But Ford was having great difficulty in resuming mass production, and it was the fall of the year before he got the Model A rolling off assembly lines at the old Model T rate. This was fine for Chevrolet and for Willys, who had been cutting Whippet prices and offering what seemed to be more of a package than his competitors.

Second only to the Model A and Ford's manufacturing difficulties as attention getters was a "silly" move made by Chrysler. He bought the Dodge company. Dodge had been slipping and, as all manufacturers knew by this time, once a company starts a downhill course it takes superhuman effort to arrest the slide and push it back up. Dillon, Read

& Co., having no desire to see its once-great triumph turn
into a fiasco, was eager to sell—how eager is indicated by
the terms of the sale, which were more to Chrysler's liking
than Dillon's.

Chrysler paid no cash for the company. He agreed to assume the bonded indebtedness, give one share of Chrysler
common for one share of Dodge preferred, one share of
common for five shares of Dodge Class A common, and one
share for ten shares of Class B, the voting common stock
held by Dillon, Read. The only fixed obligation Chrysler
assumed was payment of interest on the $56,000,000 of out-
standing bonds, which amounted to something over
$3,000,000 annually.

Shortly after the Dodge acquisition, Chrysler launched
two new cars—the Plymouth and the De Soto. Thus, he
had four baskets for his eggs, nicely spaced as to price. The
purpose of his "silly" act now became clear. The Dodge
purchase gave him something he sadly lacked—a factory
equipped to turn out all the components of a car, which
freed him from dependence on suppliers. Chrysler was now
a multi-make producer like G.M.

All production records were broken in 1928. Chevrolet
was leading the procession. Ford was gathering speed after
that very slow start from the pit, and it looked as if he
might ultimately overtake Chevrolet. A faster pace had
been set in the under-$1,000 group and even high-priced
cars were moving faster. The wand of prosperity was wav-
ing over the public, encouraging it to indulge in more luxurious cars. With the notable exception of Durant, most
companies realized fair profits, though not all did better
than in 1927. Among the independents, Hupmobile distin-

guished itself with a car that caught the public fancy. Company earnings were 212 percent higher than those of 1927. Hupp expanded its production facilities by acquiring the Chandler-Cleveland Motors Co., formed two years earlier by a merger of Chandler and Cleveland. Moving in a contrary direction was Peerless with an operating loss of just over $1,000,000.

Studebaker, desiring to have a car in its line to suit every purse, acquired a controlling interest in Pierce Arrow. Pierce was a high-priced car, one of the three P's—Packard-Pierce-Peerless—which stood for years as symbols of quality, any one of which a man would buy if he had no concern with cost. Pierce looked like a good bet to capitalize on the buying spree then in progress, and in 1929 it justified expectations by going from the red to the black financially.

If the industry was patting itself on the back for the record it had turned in, it had cause to, but there was always someone to ask the embarrassing question "How were the sales made?" and to cry alarm at the handling of installment credit. Once again, Oscar F. Meredith, now vice president of The Bank of America, New York, raised his voice to warn that finance companies were being imperiled by price cutting on installment paper.

"If there is an overgrown child in the family," said Mr. Meredith, "it is neither advisable nor proper to rid ourselves of the child, but we should see that it does not indulge in so much indigestible food that its health is dangerously if not permanently impaired."

Before moving back to the track to watch the last race of the decade, a pause is in order to take a look at company offerings. Chrysler had introduced rubber engine mounts to absorb vibration. Stutz and Rickenbacker adopted shock-proof windshields. One type had wires running through the glass horizontally; the other was a glass-celluloid sand-wich. Hypoid gears appeared on the Packard and this inno-vation opened the way to lower the body in relation to the chassis and the ground. To increase all-around comfort, hot-water heaters made their appearance and so did crank-type window lifts.

When the 1929 race began, Ford was far out in front again with Chevrolet trailing. Ford's pace was furious and so well sustained for most of the year that the industry racked up a production record of nearly 4,500,000 cars, a record that was not exceeded, or even reached again for twenty long years.

Looked at from the standpoint of production figures alone, the year appears to have been a healthy one, but there was more to it than production record-breaking. After a stunning first-quarter performance, sales began to taper off, but not to an extent regarded as abnormal for the season. But the decline persisted, especially in the far South and West. Automobile publications blamed the situation on the bad weather, but when the sales decline continued with clearing weather, that explanation had to be aban-doned. Production figures show General Motors taking cognizance of the situation and tapering off production in an effort to maintain some sort of balance between output and sales; other companies kept going at top speed out of exuberance or fear, it is hard to say which. By August, there was concern lest the demand for call money in the stock market increase finance rates and so curb sales.

Ford cut prices and prayers went up from the industry that no one would follow suit. None did. Some companies were making money; others losing it; no one wanted to see an upset of the price structure. Marmon brought out a lower-priced model under the name Roosevelt and E. L. Cord came into the market with his namesake. The Cord was the first American front-drive car ever offered to the public, and its body lines were both advanced and captivating. Had all its admirers purchased, the Cord would have been a sensation, but price precluded that. It sold for just over $3,000, which was high for those days. Two high-priced cars disappeared from the market—the Locomobile and the Stearns, which had been before the public for thirty and thirty-one years, respectively.

The break in the stock market which came on October 26 signaled a retreat. The crash caused no panic; recessions had been faced before. Sales were falling off steadily and in the face of a shrinking market there was nothing to do but try to hold some balance between production and sales and that could only be done by curtailing output.

Milan V. Ayres, economic analyst for the National Association of Finance Companies, declared that finance paper should be eligible for rediscount by the Federal Reserve Banks. The head of General Motors Acceptance Co. said there was no fundamental reason for anything more serious than a very short pause in business and in so declaring he probably voiced the opinion of 99 percent of people, economists included.

Both birth and death rates of companies were low in 1929. Competition was too hot to encourage risk capital; profits were adequate to keep most well-established companies afloat. During the decade 1920–1929, there had been 67 new companies formed and 161 on which the curtain fell. Since 1900, 882 companies had failed or retired from business and there were now only 26 left to fight for their lives.

It was still possible to become an automobile manufacturer by buying components from parts companies and assembling them, but it was impossible to cut much of a figure this way or to survive in competition. Fifty-five percent of the companies in business in 1920 were assembling to the extent of buying their engines; by 1929 the number had dropped to 35 percent and they were the small producers. With competition at fever heat, the manufacturer could ill afford to share any profits with suppliers. Companies were growing more vertical as well as horizontal. The rich were getting richer; the poor were getting poorer.

5 the great shake-out: 1930–1941

Talk of the troublesome phenomenon known as the business cycle was as prevalent in 1930 as is talk of gross national product (GNP) today. The cycle of boom and bust was thought to be inherent in the economic system and the common concern was whether the country was in a recession—a short and shallow dip—or a depression—a prolonged and deep disturbance.

Hoping for the best and wishing to believe the stock market crash to be a thing apart and not a reflection of a basic disorder, the industry groomed itself for a prosperity hailed as being "just around the corner." The volume producers tended to shade the prices of their products; those who were suffering the most financially tended to raise prices to protect their already slimming profit margins. Cadillac opened the year with a sixteen-cylinder model, the phaeton priced at $6,650, and followed with a twelve-cylinder job later in the season. A sixteen-cylinder model was also introduced by Marmon. Gardiner exhibited a front-wheel-drive car with body by Baker Raulang, one-time makers of electric vehicles.

The introduction of high-priced, multicylinder models turned out to be badly timed. Even the wealthy tended to be cautious. The producers of custom-built bodies were especially hard hit. For years it had been the practice of men of distinction and dowagers to have bodies built to their order by such firms as Fleetwood, Darrin, Waterhouse, and Wolfington to be mounted on Packard, Pierce, Cadillac, and Locomobile chassis. After the depression those who wished to have distinctive bodies bought importations from Europe, where custom body building was never abandoned.

Bad as the slump was, the dealers around the country expressed more concern regarding factory policies than over business conditions. What they demanded, though they were in no position to enforce their demands, were four basic changes.

First, they wanted the manufacturers to keep production just under the demand of the market. This was understandable because the dealer was being squeezed between the need to find nonexistent markets for new cars and the need to get rid of used-car stocks. Though this demand was reasonable, it was like asking for the moon.

They wanted a resumption of closed-territory contracts. It was one thing to compete with dealers of rival products and quite another to compete with dealers handling the same line. The manufacturer preferred open-territory contracts because they kept the dealers on their toes.

The dealers also wanted year-end, leftover models sold to them at clean-up prices. Why, they asked, should they be expected to suffer losses because the manufacturer overproduced?

Finally, they wanted the factories to adopt junking plans.

In the automotive world, the dealer-factory relationship was regarded as the dominant problem. If this seems strange in view of the state of the nation, one must remember that it was widely believed the recession would be self-cured if it was waited out, whereas the dealer situation required action.

C. E. Eldridge, president of Reo, decried the policy of making frequent model changes for the purpose of making car owners dissatisfied with what they had. It is not necessary, he said, for the improvement of cars. Eldridge spoke truly: it never was necessary. However, it was a sales stimulant and it served to transform a durable good into a consumable, thus permitting greater production.

Ford did open up junking lines to handle three hundred cars a day, but junking alone could not sell cars, though it may have been a help to dealers. Compared to the previous year production fell more than 1,500,000 cars, or about 37 percent. The depression of 1921 occasioned only a 22 percent drop in output. Nevertheless, in the last month of the year, the automotive press reported that the industry felt the depression to be nearing an end and that 1931 would be a year of progress. A less optimistic note came from Colonel Leonard P. Ayres, vice president of the Cleveland

Trust Co. He expressed the opinion that the depression was severer than expected and that recovery would be slow.

Studebaker withdrew its Erskine car from the market; Marmon did the same with its Roosevelt. General Motors discontinued production of the Marquette, companion car to the Buick, and the Viking, companion car to the Oldsmobile, both of which had been introduced the year before. All four discontinued cars had one thing in common—they failed to live up to their sponsors' expectations.

Ford and General Motors made most of the cars and garnered most of the profits in 1930. The independent manufacturers saw their sales slashed more than one-half and their profits down to where they could barely survive. It is perhaps no wonder that there began to be talk of a buyers' strike, as when sales receded in 1921. In 1921, prices were inflated and the public would not, or could not, reach for them. When prices were cut, purchasing resumed. The situation in 1930 was wholly different. There was no peak from which prices could descend; values were solid, but purchasing power was lacking. With millions of people unemployed and their number growing larger, even those who had money and a job were uncertain of the future and could very easily continue to run their old cars until the skies brightened. One might have expected an increase in the number of cars sold on credit, but the ratio of credit to cash sales remain virtually unchanged.

Exports, too, declined just when they could have been most helpful. For years the manufacturer had counted upon the foreign market to sop up surplus production, and it had been thought exports should run around 12 percent of total production for the health of the industry. By 1929, exports had risen to about 17 percent of domestic manufacture, but the following year, with the depression worldwide, exports shrank even more than the home market.

What the automobile manufacturer was facing was a situation which had not confronted him for more than a decade. For the time being, the automobile had reverted to being a durable good and could no longer be regarded as a consumable item. While this situation lasted, there was not enough business to be had to produce profit margins for all manufacturers. Put another way, manufacturing facilities were grossly overbuilt for the market then existing.

To any readers to whom the depression of the 1930's is history as remote as the Civil War, it should be emphasized that the economic trouble extended to all industry. The automobile industry took greater punishment than most others because a new car was not an essential in a home where the breadwinner was out of work.

The automobile producer has always been an incurable optimist; at least that is the pose he has found best to present to the public. When 1931 rolled around he was busy binding up his wounds and planning for better times. A new crop of eight-cylinder cars was offered to the public. More cars boasted silent transmissions and free-wheeling. Some cars were larger and more powerful than their predecessors because, said the manufacturers, the public wants bigger and more powerful cars. The real reason in many instances was to avoid cutting prices. If you offered a larger package, you didn't have to apologize for the higher price. At the same time, there was a move in the direction of eliminating unprofitable lines and reducing the number of slow-selling body models.

Walter Chrysler forecast a 5,000,000-car year, which overshot the mark by 2,000,000. Albert Erskine raised the Studebaker schedule from 64,000 to 100,000, with plans to bring out the Rockne as a replacement for the Erskine in the low-priced field. The death of Knute Rockne, who had been appointed to promote the car, delayed its introduction. Only two companies had the temerity to enter the industry. Norman DeVaux, having acquired Durant of California, launched the DeVaux to sell for $625. Mercer Motors Corp. of Elkhart, Indiana, announced that it would revive the Mercer, proceeded to show illustrations of the revitalized sport car, and then faded. It wasn't a propitious time to enter the arena. The independents lost several members. Kissel merged with New Era Motors with plans to continue building the Kissel and to manufacture a front-drive car known as the Ruxton. A receivership ended that move. Moon and Gardiner consolidated their sales and engineering staffs to effect economies and then made a graceful exit. The Moon company was a true pioneer. It began to manufacture in St. Louis in 1905, and in addition to the Moon it made the Diana and the Windsor. Gardiner had been in business eleven years.

Among the obituaries of the year, the death of the Jordan company deserves special mention. Edward Jordan began assembling cars in 1916. He did very well until squeezed out of business by competition and the depression. It was his advertising, rather than his car, that most distinguished his career in the automobile world. He produced a Playboy model and advertised to the "young in heart." He it was who introduced moonlight and romance ("Somewhere West of Laramie") into automobile copy (the word "carefree" had yet to be blared), and if he did not sire today's advertising themes, he at least mothered them.

Around the middle of the year, Herbert Hoover declared a moratorium on war debts in an effort to alleviate the depression, which was now worldwide. The industry greeted this act as a master stroke. It is hard to understand the enthusiasm unless prompted solely by affection for the President. Then followed press statements that the automobile was leading the way to recovery—a hope unfulfilled. Production and sales were still declining.

Gerard Swope of General Electric came forward with a plan for the stabilization of industry and employment. This was followed by a host of similar plans. There was also a warning that unemployment insurance might be on the way and that industry had better start working out plans to its liking, or the government might impose regulations, any kind of which would work a hardship.

To add to the manufacturers' unceasing headache, the dealers continued to complain of mistreatment. They objected strenuously to contracts which forced them to accept shipment of, as, and when tendered by the manufacturer. They also abhorred contracts cancelable on ten to fifteen days' notice by either manufacturer or distributor. The manufacturer countered that he had to have control because so much was at stake. The dealer was thinking similarly about his own survival.

A visit to the track to view the contestants at the year's close would show Chevrolet out in front again, Ford trailing, and Chrysler in third place. General Motors and Chrysler made money; Ford lost money. Aside from these Big Three there wasn't much of a race left. The 1931 performance did show the Ford Model A to have seen its heyday and, recognizing this fact, Ford announced a V-8 model to be on the way.

In January, 1932, there were nine thousand fewer dealers than in January, 1931. Since neither Ford nor General Motors lost dealers, the figures tell a vivid story of what was happening to the sales outlets of other producers. Even though some dealer consolidation came about through the handling of several lines rather than a single one, such moves accounted for a small amount of the shrinkage. The demise of dealers was calamitous and it was the independent manufacturer who was taking the beating.

Normally, sales in the first quarter of any year are heavy because of new models. Not so in the first quarter of 1932. Production, which had been poor at the beginning of 1931, was now ruinously low. Auburn, Graham, and Nash made a little money; General Motors made over $9.5 million. Since Ford was practically out of production with the grooming of the V-8, he could not have made money, and everyone else lost. Some of the losses were very large. Chrysler dropped $2,000,000; Hudson about $1,125,000; Packard $1,500,000, and Willys $1,000,000. Four companies were able to pay dividends by dipping into their reserves. These were Auburn, Nash, Chrysler, and General Motors.

As the mid-year approached, came the bitter realization that the industry could not lead the nation out of the depression. More car for the same money plus a flattering of the public had lost its magic power to make sales. To add to the gloom it was reported that dealers had at least $50,000,-000 in accounts receivable, mostly ninety days past due and uncollectible. Downward adjustments became imperative and among the steps taken were a reduction in factory staffs and a lowering of wage rates. It was said around Detroit that sales managers had become engineers, while engineers had become production managers.

Whether delivered prices should be substituted for F.O.B. prices was a question now raised within the industry. The dealers were not enthusiastic; the publication of delivered prices would make it difficult, if not impossible, for them to pad the selling prices. The manufacturers concluded that the practice would have to be universal if those who followed it were not to be handicapped by those who did not, and they turned thumbs down. A quarter century later the government settled the matter through legislation requiring the manufacturer's suggested selling price in itemized form to be affixed to the window of any new car on sale.

Handicap or not, the Auburn company went ahead to cut prices and then advertise the delivered price to the consumer. Then, contributing to the feeling of instability, General Motors Acceptance Corp. raised its finance rates to offset the decline in volume of cars sold on time, and the government imposed a 3 percent excise tax.

Prices had very little meaning. Automobiles had become distress merchandise and the dealers set up the cry that they could no longer make any money and, as if to prove it, they continued to go out of business. Many producers were in no better shape. DeVaux-Hall Motors, having experienced one year of life, went under and was purchased by Continental Motors. Continental had been the biggest supplier of engines to the industry, but had lost business steadily as more and more companies took over the production of their own engines. Presumably the purchase of DeVaux-Hall was to give Continental an outlet for its product; the car name was changed to Continental, but in another year production was terminated.

Ford's delay in getting his V-8 on the market may have been due in part to his desire to cast the engine block and crankcase in a single piece. Thousands of engines had to be scrapped before he was able to perfect the process. It is doubtful if a commercially-minded organization with hungry stockholders could have persisted in carrying through such an expensive development at such a critical time. When the V-8 did appear it was priced at the Model A figure of $490 and the Chevrolet price was promptly dropped to meet it.

In the middle of the year, Henry Ford began to speak his mind in newspaper advertisements. In an ad entitled "Henry Ford on Self-Help," which occupied a third of a page in the *New York Times,* he plunged into his old theme of having one foot in industry and one on the land because the alliance between a man and a plot of ground was superior to any form of unemployment insurance. He followed this with another entitled "Henry Ford on Farm and Factory," in which he propounded the idea of chemistry being the link between farm and factory to produce security for all.

Ford's ideas were too simple for solving an international financial crisis. He did, at least, recognize the economy to be sadly out of balance and he groped for a means to correct it. John North Willys had his own idea of what was wrong and a hint of what to do about it. Farm products and incomes, he said, had been reduced about 50 percent, while cars selling for $750 or less had decreased in price only a little over 4 percent in the previous three years. The lowest-priced car on the market sold for $410. The same model sold for $385 in 1928 and $350 in 1927. In short, transportation sold for less when incomes were greater. Willys's highlighting of the disparity between prices and incomes was thought by the trade to herald a lower-priced Overland.

The economic life of the nation was coming to a standstill when 1933 rolled around. The used-car problem was still critical and no nearer a solution than it had been ten years earlier. There was talk of establishing central depots, backed by the manufacturers, which would handle all used cars and free the dealers to sell new cars without trading. Nothing came of it. The manufacturers wanted no part in distribution. They had no intention of courting suicide.

With business getting progressively worse, year-end reports of output and profits made a very sad picture. Production in 1932 was one-fourth of what it had been in 1929, the year of the stock-market crash. Charles Nash, who had the reputation of being able to make money in all kinds of weather, did show a profit of just over $1,000,000. General Motors made $165,000 after generous write-offs. Chrysler lost millions, but he had been readying a low-priced Plymouth six to compete directly with Ford and Chevrolet. It was in the low-priced field that sales were to be made and Walter Chrysler wasn't to be left behind.

Sales of just over a million cars in a country accustomed to absorbing many millions and now so dependent upon the automobile for every kind of transportation may seem extraordinary, but perhaps the really extraordinary fact is that so many were sold. On the average, the per capita income had been slashed just about in half. Hundreds of thousands of people who did have jobs were not sure they would have them tomorrow. Few were inclined to tempt fortune by purchasing a new car. Prosperity had been just around the corner for a long, long time and there was widespread suspicion that the distance to the corner might be lengthening, as indeed it was.

Willys-Overland finally went into receivership in 1933 after more than a quarter century of ups and downs. John North Willys never ceased trying for the number one spot and at times he performed extraordinarily well. Following this debacle came the appointment of receivers for the Studebaker Corp., which shook the industry more profoundly than the Willys failure. Studebaker had been a stable organization, not meteoric like Willys-Overland. Many reasons were given for the collapse. One was President Erskine's attempt to gain control of the White Motor Co., truck manufacturers; another was the failure to make a success of either the Erskine or the Rockne cars, which would have anchored the company firmly in the low-priced field. With a line of cars all selling for over $1,000, Studebaker was left with a poor hand to play the depression. Equally serious was its decision to pay two dividends which had not been earned, thereby depleting much-needed working capital.

Casualties of the year were Peerless, Marmon, and Du Pont. The Peerless company had been making clothes wringers when the automobile was still in its cradle. Its first car appeared in 1900 and over the years its product gained a fine reputation. Unable to climb down successfully from its perch as a maker of high-priced, high-quality cars, manufacture came to a stop. Nordyke & Marmon was one of the true pioneers. A manufacturer of flour-milling machinery, it launched its first car in 1904 and ever since had built a quality product, but a rather expensive one. The Model 34, brought out in 1916, featured aluminum fenders, body, and engine, which gave it a weight of 3,540 pounds although it had a 130-inch wheelbase and seated seven passengers. The Du Pont, on the market for sixteen years, was classed as a distinguished-looking sports car.

Although output rose 40 percent in 1933, to reach a million and a half cars, this was far from satisfactory for an industry which had facilities for building as many as four and a half million. Moreover, the average wholesale price had sunk to $496, the lowest it had ever been, or ever would be again. Low production coupled with low prices were the ingredients for disaster.

When the banks were closed by government order and subsequently reopened if their doors still had hinges, people sighed with relief and began to feel more optimistic. This change in attitude was reflected in purchases of cars, which mounted steadily—insufficiently to make all manufacturers fat and happy but enough to fend off more receiverships.

The dealers, too, profited from the slight upturn in business, but they still found it hard to lay their hands on the cash required to pay for the cars shipped to them by the manufacturer. An easing of the situation was gained by having the finance companies "floor plan" cars to the extent of 90 percent, with the dealers putting up the remaining 10 percent in cash. In this way, the dealers had cars to display in their showrooms and the manufacturers got the cash.

For the first time in many years consideration was given to the feasibility of manufacturing a small car. The question was, would the public purchase a car with a smaller, more economical engine requiring more frequent changing of gears? No one had the answer. Some studies made at the time indicated the cost to a going concern for designing and launching such a car would run in the neighborhood of $15,000,000, and that was more than anyone cared to gamble when the skies were so cloudy.

Meanwhile the manufacturers were being stormed with suggestions to cut the work week and spread such work as there was over a larger number of workers. The automobile manufacturer received more than his share of these suggestions because the industry was still regarded as the bellwether that would lead the country out of the deadly morass of the depression. The attitude of the industry toward the idea of spreading work is rather well summed up in a statement emanating from the Cleveland Trust Co. It said:

> The present campaign to spread work and to increase wage payments can have little effect in financing the output of capital goods . . . to restore prosperity we must revive production of durable goods, which involves the floating of corporate bonds, and that in turn requires the restoration of full faith in the future of money and credit.

The automobile industry was eager to revive the production of its durable goods. The only question was, who was going to buy them?

The Motor and Equipment Manufacturers Association compiled its views on legislation and submitted them to President Roosevelt. In the light of subsequent events and what we understand of the depression today, they make interesting reading:

1. Balance all budgets (national, state, and local).

2. Impose a federal turnover sales tax of not more than 1% in the event that more revenue is needed.

3. Eliminate capital gains and losses from personal income taxes and treat both alike.

4. End direct government competition with private business.

5. Adopt uniform state motor vehicle codes and ban any diversion of motor vehicle taxes for use other than roads.

By the middle of the year both production and sales had made a substantial revival, and with the clouds of uncertainty rolling away industry spokesmen began a bitter attack on the Roosevelt program. Notably absent from the chorus was Walter Chrysler, who slashed prices and brought out the "Airflow" design. This pioneering attempt at streamlining attracted much attention and comment, but not public approval. It was a bit too advanced.

Among the many acts of the New Deal to which manufacturers took exception was the National Recovery Act (NRA). In effect it legalized price fixing, which didn't interest the manufacturers. On the other hand, the parts makers and dealers welcomed it. To the parts makers it promised an end to ruinous competition; to the dealer it meant putting a ceiling on used-car allowances. To make it work, the public had to be re-educated. Long accustomed to the idea and fact that the higher the new car price, the higher the used-car trade-in value, the public could not understand how a used car could now have a fixed value.

In spite of the impediments the auto makers claimed the New Deal was throwing in the way of recovery, the year 1933 ended with sales up about a half million from the year before. This was a heartening increase of about 41 percent. On the strength of this recovery, 1934 opened with prices on new models up from 8 to 10 percent, and in some instances the dealer's discount was cut. And still sales climbed.

Henry Ford approved NRA at the outset but considered it full of faults, and being used too much to make money instead of aiding human values. Later, he said he saw nothing wrong in the thirty-hour week, that the world's work could still be done. However, when the government backed labor in its right to organize, he turned violently against the New Deal and all its works and his treatment of labor became savage. It was then that he inveighed against the theorists "who had never met a payroll"—a phrase that was to echo and re-echo down the years.

Alfred Sloan didn't like the labor provisions in Section 7-A of NRA and spoke out quite frankly and at some length in the G.M. annual report. He urged industry to stand and, if necessary, to fight for a square deal. He wanted employee representation through company unions rather than an independent union to carry on collective bargaining. He contended that the more industry was let alone "the more rapidly we will achieve our objective—the well-being of the American worker."

The American worker employed by the automobile industry did not share Sloan's preference for the company union, knowing full well that it would give him no leverage and that he would be licked before he started when it came to making demands on the industry.

Walter Chrysler stood off labor until a strike crippled operations, then capitulated. It is, perhaps, because Chrysler was a mechanic at heart that he was the least violent of the crowned heads. Other companies had their strikes, but the real showdown battles were fought by Ford and General Motors.

It is interesting to note that Ford and General Motors, the companies gaining the most from the recovery, should have been the most virulent in their attacks on the government. They and Chrysler were in fact the only companies other than Nash to make a profit in 1934. In the first five months of that year the Big Three got 91 percent of the business. The independents were just about holding their own and their sales outlets were shrinking. Why was there no outcry from them? Were they letting the giants speak for them? Or did they regard the Big Three as a greater menace than the government?

The cars for whom the bells tolled in 1934 were the Franklin and the Cunningham. The H. H. Franklin Manufacturing Co. of Syracuse, New York, began manufacture of an air-cooled car in 1901 and spent its thirty-five years of business life swimming against the water-cooled tide. And it did well. Few companies could point to more loyal, enthusiastic owners. Never a large producer, James Cunningham & Sons of Rochester, New York, made a high-grade, expensive car for twenty-five years; then, down but not out, it went on to other manufacture.

Along about October, William B. Stout declared, "We can't keep on selling $1,000 cars to buyers with $800 incomes." Stout was not then a car producer. He had been co-designer of the Scripps-Booth, which General Motors bought and scrapped, and he had shown he knew how to meet a payroll by building the Stout all-metal, trimotored airplane, which he sold to Ford to his own profit and to the profit of his backers. His declaration made sense as subsequent events were to show, but his pronouncement fell on deaf ears. In 1935, he designed and built a beetle-shaped car, well-named the Scarab, so roomy inside that a foursome could sit around a table. This car, be it noted, was not for people with $800 incomes.

Besides being something of a genius, Bill Stout was a good showman. The story is told that when he was soliciting funds for the building of his plane he sent prospects a letter containing a folded paper airplane. He reasoned that executives would be intrigued to see if the paper planes would fly and would toss them around their offices. This, according to the story, is just what they did and in the process became softened up to a "touch" when he called upon them. Leastways, he got the money, and the "suckers" got a generous return on their investment.

It was his custom when driving the Scarab through small towns of an evening to have his chauffeur switch on all lights and gather his guests around the table to make at least the pretense of playing cards. Thus the Scarab, which never went into production, acquired fame.

Another oddity of the period was Buckminster Fuller's Dymaxion car. Fuller is known for his geodesic structures rather than for his car, but the car did have novel features to recommend it. It was a three-wheeled vehicle, shaped much like a tailless porpoise, the single wheel in the rear doing the steering. Aside from its unusual shape and construction, it featured a unique system of suspension to reduce drastically the unsprung weight in the interests of a better ride. Between 1932 and 1935, Fuller built three experimental models, all of which were sold. A fourth model was projected but never built and Fuller moved on into other fields.

Although production and sale of cars mounted in 1935, the independents failed to share proportionately in the improvement. The long-drawn-out period of scant business had exhausted their working capital to the point where they were incapable of bringing out advanced models to wean buyers from the Big Three, nor were they able to rebuild their devastated dealer organizations. Packard alone took a brave and expensive step to produce a car better suited to the consumers' pocketbook and came out with an eight-cylinder car to sell for $1,060. As a rule, the producers of high-priced, high-grade cars were unsuccessful when they tried to produce for the medium-price market, but Packard was the exception, and its new model lifted the company out of the deficit class of operators. Hudson, too, made a profit for the year, and the Studebaker receivership was lifted. Hupp, which deserved to share in the recovery, became snarled in a battle for control of the company which seriously impaired its performance.

The National Recovery Act, which the manufacturers detested, was thrown out by the Supreme Court, but the Wagner Act, which the manufacturers liked even less because it fortified labor's right to bargain collectively, was passed. And the automobile factory worker, having undergone a long period of low wages, intermittent work, and worse, unemployment, became restless and manifested dissatisfaction by calling strikes. Even so, 1935 output was up a million from 1934, and again it was the Big Three who got the lion's share.

John North Willys died, thus ending the career of one who was truly a pioneer. In his lifetime, the Willys-Overland company produced upward of 2,500,000 cars and in 1923 it ranked third in output among the manufacturers. Willys was an exponent of the low-priced car, ever running at the heels of Ford, and ever hopeful of getting top position on the totem pole.

With output climbing another 400,000 in 1936 to top 3,500,000, there were some crumbs falling to the small companies. Hudson cleared $3,000,000. Both Studebaker and Nash showed gains, but Willys-Overland, which had slipped since Mr. Willys's death the previous year, underwent a reorganization, and Reo ceased the manufacture of cars in favor of trucks.

Two events highlighted 1936. One was the filing of bankruptcy papers by that colorful personality, William Crapo Durant. He listed liabilities of $914,000 and assets of $250. The other event was the merger of the Nash company and Kelvinator, maker of household refrigerators.

The Durant company had been losing money since 1925 and by 1930 the phantom empire had broken up and was no longer a factor in the industry. Durant had been unable to get his various subsidiary companies moving ahead, and the executives who followed him in the management saddle were incapable of rescuing them.

Durant exemplifies the success coming to a man whose genius and the times are in harmony, and equally well the failure that follows when the times and the situation change and another kind of genius is needed. He had vision and the drive needed to give birth to giants, but it was these very qualities which kept him from imparting stability to his creations. That stability had to be given by others, notably Alfred Sloan, who had great managerial genius. I recall listening to Durant as he cast a spell over a group of his salesmen and thinking what a great missionary the Church lost when he went into the manufacture of cars.

The merger of Nash and Kelvinator was important to the future of Nash if only because it brought to the presidency George W. Mason, who was most responsible for the later introduction of the compact car.

The recovery of business continued into the fall of 1937 and the automobile press was proud to announce that over one-sixth, or more than 16 percent, of the national income was now being spent on motor vehicles and their operation. With an increase in output of about 300,000 cars, the industry came within hailing distance of a 4,000,000-car year, but the independents failed to get any of the increase.

The Wagner Act, which the auto makers had cold-shouldered in the hope and expectation that it would be declared unconstitutional, was held constitutional by the

Supreme Court and workers began to strike. To make matters even more uncomfortable for the industry, the Federal Trade Commission took a careful look at the practice of advertising a 6 percent time payment plan, found it misleading, and ordered it stopped. The true rate of interest ran 12 percent or higher.

There was a general rise in commodity prices, and when the new models were exhibited at the fall shows they bore a higher price tag. However, there was a recession in sales in the early fall of 1937 and the stock market took a nose dive. This time the auto makers were not to be caught napping; they curtailed manufacture of cars with unseemly haste and dismissed workers from their jobs. Despite the high volume for the year, the Big Three had lower profits and the independents slipped back into the sea of red ink. Nash discontinued production of its Lafayette, Hupp was in a dormant state until fall, and Stutz was declared bankrupt. Manufacture of Auburns, Cords, and Duesenbergs ceased, but under the able management of its president, Roy Faulkner, the Auburn company made a successful switch from the building of cars to the manufacture of diversified metal products.

The halt in recovery lasted until the end of 1938 and resulted in production being slashed almost in half, or down about two million cars. But prices did not drop; they rose about 8 percent. Always in the past—in the recession of the early twenties and in the black days of the great depression, not yet out of mind—prices had fallen. For all practical purposes competition was dead, or so near to death as to be ineffective. Henceforth, prices would climb steadily upward.

The recession of 1938 dealt the death blow to the Pierce-Arrow Motor Car Co., and so passed into limbo one of the oldest automobile manufacturers, older than any of the Big Three. For thirty-eight years, the name Pierce had stood for quality. Of the three P's—Packard, Pierce, and Peerless —only Packard remained in business.

Ford, who had suffered from lack of a vehicle to sell in the medium-priced field, introduced the Mercury. Thus, he now had the Ford, Mercury, and Lincoln with which to battle General Motors and Chrysler, already well established in all price ranges. Hupp got a transfusion in the form of new capital and resumed production. Its new models looked like the Cord since the bodies were struck from Cord dies, and it appeared as if Hupp were ready to make a strong comeback. Hudson dropped the Terraplane and Studebaker brought out its Champion model, which did so well the company was able to announce a profit. The only other independent able to do this was Packard.

The ups and downs of the industry, its unstable state of feast or famine, caused the practice of installment selling to be given another hard look by its critics. Was the easing of credit terms responsible for overselling, thus creating a boom and the subsequent corrective slump, with its dire effects on all industry? A conference to discuss the subject of installment selling was called at the White House. Representatives of the industry attending said they realized the need for more conservative financing methods, but not to the point where sales would be impaired. This was a non sequitur.

In June of 1938, Arthur Fertig, a retail consultant specializing in installment selling, surveyed the situation in an article in *Automotive Industries* with a frankness that was painful to the producers.

> At the present stage of our national economy [he said], the consumer's dollar is inadequate to create a market for anywhere near 4,000,000 passenger cars annually without sharp repercussion. This repercussion is being felt as a used car problem of serious proportions, in repossessions and overtrading which is exhausting the capital of dealers, and in a near-pauperization of the marginal consumer. An approximate 20 percent is too high a proportion of the national income to be spent for individual transportation, given the purchasing power of today.

It was Mr. Fertig's contention that the low rate of car repossessions, so often pointed to as indicative of the soundness of credit financing, told nothing about the state of the nation. The consumer was indebted to banks, credit unions, personal loan companies, and credit sources other than finance companies, and the total indebtedness was far greater than realized. Since the automobile accounted for the largest dollar volume, and it was dollar volume that counted, the single item of the automobile brought the downfall of too many people.

And then came the unkindest cut of all. Fertig called the industry middle-aged and said it was trying to keep a youthful figure at the sacrifice of the national health. One producer attempted unsuccessfully to refute Fertig and the head of the association of finance companies claimed it was 10 percent, not 20 percent, of the national income that went for automobiles. To this Fertig replied that if 10 percent produced the dire conditions, then 10 percent was too much.

Since companies other than the Big Three were selling few cars, it was obvious to whom the admonition was directed. But the manufacturers had something more serious to combat than criticism. Dealers all over the country were in revolt. Responding to complaints and recognizing the seriousness of the situation, the Federal Trade Commission held hearings. In Wisconsin, the dealers subordinated their own feuds long enough to get protective legislation passed and similar attempts were made unsuccessfully in other parts of the country. General Motors had the added headache of being charged by the FTC with coercing its dealers to finance through the General Motors Acceptance Corp.

The Big Three did liberalize and clarify dealer contracts, but a survey made several months after such action was taken found the dealers with a highly skeptical wait-and-see attitude. The new contracts served to dissuade the dealers from seeking further legislation and a slight upturn in business removed some of the discontent.

The upturn in 1939 was not pronounced. The industry was able to make half a million more cars than in the low year of 1938, but there was need for an output of more than two and a half million to produce the profits to which the Big Three had become accustomed and for the independents to break even. Meanwhile the Federal Trade Commission had concluded a study of manufacturer-dealer relationship and issued a report in which it claimed that there did exist inequities in dealer agreements and that they should be remedied.

A small car at last materialized. Powell Crosley, Jr., boldly stepping in where others feared to tread, introduced the Crosley car. The vehicle weighed less than a thousand pounds and sold for $325. It was unveiled at R. H. Macy & Co.'s department store in New York and at Bamberger's in Newark, New Jersey. It was widely believed to be the first time that a department store had merchandised an automobile, but this was not so. The enterprising New York merchant John Wanamaker sold the Searchmont car and later the Ford, in neither case with much success.

In August of 1939, Paul Hoffman, one of the three receivers who had lifted Studebaker out of its receivership and was now president of the company, gave an address before the National Institute, Northwestern University, which struck some fresh notes. With reference to the Federal Trade Commission he said:

> In its long history [it] has been Public Friend Number One of free competitive enterprise. Has business recognized this fact and given its vigorous support to the Commission? Unfortunately, the answer is "no." Minority groups have attacked the Commission unfairly, and there has been resentment of its so-called interference with business which has not been justified. The Commission makes no attempt to control or manage business, but merely to police it to its own advantage.

He did take his stand with other industry leaders against NRA, saying:

> We must fight against minority groups who are willing to sell out free enterprise by seeking governmental help in the form of price or production controls or licensing laws.

Hoffman's attitude toward labor and unionization was far removed from that expressed by Ford and Sloan, as his remarks showed:

> We must cease defending all employers and condemning all labor leaders and begin to use some discrimination. . . . We have been too prone to rush to the defense of those reactionaries who were openly opposing or attempting to sabotage the clear right of the worker to join or not to join a union as he chose and to bargain collectively.

Unfortunately, Hoffman's words went unheeded by those who could have exerted leadership and labor's fight to unionize was unduly prolonged and punctuated by strikes and violence on both sides.

There was a continuation of the recovery in 1940 with manufacturers striving to get back to a 4,000,000-car year. They almost achieved their goal, falling short of it by a mere 300,000. Willys launched the Americar, a well-designed, smaller car at a moderate price, but the year also saw manufacture of the last Hupmobile. The Hupp Corp., a worthy member of the independent group, never did recover from the disruptive and exhausting struggle with the notorious Archie Andrews, who sought to gain control of the company after the depression had weakened it.

Hardly had the industry climbed back from the recession when war clouds began rolling westward from Europe. At the request of the government, the auto makers began manufacture of war matériel. Packard and Ford began working on aircraft engines, Chrysler started to make tanks, and General Motors engaged in manufacture of machine guns and trucks.

In 1941, production came within a few thousand of the four-million-car mark. Warned by the government that output would have to be cut 20 percent on August 1, the car producers pushed out an enormous number of cars in the early months of the year. Nothing startling took place in design and engineering of new models. Nash went to the unitized body, and General Motors took the LaSalle off the market.

The independents, Hudson and Willys, joined the Big Three in war production. Delmar (Barney) Roos of Willys Overland, produced the initial design for the vehicle which came to be known as the Jeep and as ubiquitous as the scrawled epithet "Kilroy was here." Manufacture of the Jeep was undertaken by Ford as well as Willys.

With a government clamp-down on production, the output of cars tapered off to a little over 200,000 in 1942 and practically ceased in 1943 and 1944, the total for those two years being a mere 700. But the industry was now turning out guns instead of buttered-up cars. The biggest companies became prime contractors and the small ones took on whatever they were capable of manufacturing. There was no lid on the production of war goods and profits were assured, that is, for everybody but the dealer. For the duration of the war, he survived as best he could by working off the accumulation of used cars and keeping them running.

America had become the arsenal of democracy and the automobile industry was leading the parade.

6
middle-age spread:
1945–1966

Rumors were rife as World War II drew to a close. Three of them in particular highlight the times.

It was said that full production would resume immediately on the cessation of hostilities so that pent-up demand for replacement vehicles could be satisfied.

Aircraft manufacturers were reported planning to enter the automobile business to offset the slump in demand for aircraft. And some prophets declared the automobile would benefit greatly from the application of aircraft design practice.

Lower-priced cars were heralded. Henry J. Kaiser, the industrialist, captured headlines by declaring America's need to be a good $500 automobile. He hinted he would supply it.

None of these things happened.

There were widely published forecasts that the postwar era would bring radically engineered new cars. These forecasts came not from the industry but from the Gee-Whiz School of feature writers. They saw the cleanup of old cars creating a unique opportunity to start afresh without depreciating cars in owners' hands, in used-car lots, and in showrooms, and they turned loose their imaginations to give the public something to dream about. The manufacturers, on the other hand, had good and substantial reasons for not turning these dreams into realities, as we shall see.

The government lifted the ban on car production in the middle of 1945, but set quotas for the remainder of the year and the first three months of 1946. But there was no such thing as "instant" mass production.

Plants had to be reconverted, contracts had to be made with suppliers, who themselves had to revamp facilities, and labor had to be reassigned and retrained. The situation was aggravated by a terrific shortage of materials, by price ceilings imposed by the Office of Price Administration in the interest of curbing inflation, and by an epidemic of strikes. The best the industry could do was to build 60,000 cars in the half year. The next year it raised output to just over 2,000,000, of which the six independents built 15 percent. The industry called 1946 "a year of calamity."

Bad as were the immediate postwar years for the industry as a whole, they marked the end of calamity for the Ford company. During the late thirties the company had faltered at almost every step under the guidance of the aging Henry. He dissipated his waning energies in fighting unionization, warring with the government, and embarking on ill-conceived ventures. Worse yet, the company had become a police state replete with gestapo headed by Ford's trusted advisor and evil genius, Harry Bennett. The company had long since yielded second place to Chrysler, and by 1945 affairs were in such a chaotic state that an aroused family pressured Henry into turning over the reins to his grandson, Henry II. With that, the skies brightened, but not until 1950 was the company able to dislodge Chrysler to regain its old position, second to General Motors.

Aircraft manufacturers had second thoughts about car manufacture; they elected to turn out consumer goods of lesser cost which were in great demand.

No lower-priced cars made their debut when the ban was lifted from production. Henry Kaiser organized the Kaiser-Frazer Corp. and launched the Kaiser car to sell at a price three times the $500 figure. The Frazer, a "sister ship," followed promptly. In 1946, Kaiser had designed and built a front-drive car, but production was postponed, as it turned out, indefinitely. For a newcomer, Kaiser did astonishingly well. Having lost $19,000,000 in 1946, he made $19,000,-000 in 1947. And in both years his products outsold those of the other five independents. The Kaiser started a new trend in styling by integrating the fenders with the body so that the seats ran the full width of the car.

The first cars to be made by the old-line companies were modified prewar models. There was little time or opportunity to design and test radically new models while the companies were engaged in war work. The cars bore a higher price tag because all costs had risen. How inflated prices had become in relation to prewar prices was made clear when Henry Ford II told OPA that the car costing $681 to build in 1942 cost $962 to build in 1945. Given such costs, the delivered price of a so-called low-priced model ran over $1,000 and the once most popular field of cars selling for around $750 was deserted.

The industry was well aware of this void and there was much discussion of building a lighter-weight, cheaper car, since what it was building, it was said, could not be sold at an appreciably lower figure. Still, the producers hesitated. Would the public buy the lower-priced cars in heavy volume if they were offered? The public, mused the auto makers, never had shown a preference for the small, inexpensive model when it was available. And this is true, but it is not the whole truth about the small car.

The so-called small car had never been offered at a price differential which the consumer thought offset what he had to forgo in performance, comfort, equipment, and appointments. He was too much aware of what he would be doing without, just to gain a small saving in first cost and operating expense. Nor did the consumer get much encouragement to buy. When the cheaper model was just the lowest priced in a line, with no distinction of its own, the dealer too often treated it as a gimmick to get the prospect into the showroom to sell him a more expensive model.

Nevertheless, plans for the building of a lighter-weight, cheaper car were announced by Ford and Chevrolet, with the idea of having readily salable cars in the event of a recession. The press reported General Motors getting ready to build a special factory. Then, as 1946 drew to a close, both Ford and General Motors abandoned the small car project because of the tight material supply and other troubles.

Spokesmen for the industry are forever proclaiming, "We struggle unceasingly to give the public what it demands." It is a noble thought, but it is a myth, repeated so persistently as to assume the stature of a fact. It is a phrase used to explain or justify upward price movements, annual models, increase in engine horsepower, absence of small cars; in fact, any sales policy or engineering design a company believes will be most profitable.

Juxtapose this echoed statement with Mr. Sloan's remark that the automobile owner must be made dissatisfied with what he owns so that he will come into the market for a new car, and the myth stands revealed for what it is. A satisfied owner is undemanding. Even when dissatisfied he is undemanding; he makes a selection from what is available. The vast majority of car owners are not educated buyers; they are indoctrinated buyers, which is greatly to the advantage of the manufacturer.

Even when manufacturers analyze sales, what are uncovered are preferences, not demands. No questionnaire gets down to engineering fundamentals, nor should it. What the automobile is to become or to be is strictly within the province of the manufacturer. The car buyer is unqualified to make demands. He buys what strikes his fancy, the producer struggles to catch this fancy, and if he succeeds he creates a demand which has to be met by his competitors.

The public, for example, did not demand the lowering of bodies which created humps in the floor of the passenger compartments and brought smaller-diameter wheels with a consequent reduction in tire life. There was no alternative to taking it and liking it. When the manufacturer very clearly turned this liability into an asset by installing a console, the public fell for it in a big way and, seemingly, without regret for the loss of a passenger seat.

What new wrinkle will make the public dissatisfied to the point of trading in the old bus is the riddle of the industry which great minds try to solve once a year. The reasons for buying any particular car are legion and often irrational. Take the lady who was avid for a really small car and wildly approving of the compacts. When she bought, she chose the biggest compact offered. Or take the man who studied the specifications of all the makes offered in the size and price range he desired, then bought the heaviest because, as he said, "It weighs four hundred pounds more than any of the others so I get more for my money." That he might be buying metal at the expense of performance never entered his head.

At the close of hostilities, the industry did not have to worry about the vagaries of public taste. The demand was for anything that would roll. And the struggle was to build them fast enough. By 1947, output exceeded 3,500,000 and while the independents shared in the rise, it was the Big Three again who got the disproportionate share. In 1948 there was a climb to a near 4,000,000 perch and in 1949 the 5,000,000 mark was exceeded for the first time in the history of the industry. The independents, who got 15 percent of the business in 1946, were now getting only 13 percent.

The rise in production in 1946 and the advance in car prices, which left the market for a truly small car unexploited (except by the Crosley Corp.) was regarded by many free enterprisers as creating a highly opportune time to join the family of car producers. Thus, between the years 1947 and 1950 approximately twenty-five new organizations were formed. Most of these turned out to be paper organizations or got no further than the drawing-board stage with their product. However, there were some who made a good try. Small cars appeared under the names Bobbi-Kar, Playboy, and Davis, and conventional-sized cars under the names Tucker and Darrin. This rash of newcomers represented the last attack on the citadel of automobile manufacture and by 1950 it was all over. The only new car to live beyond that period was the Checker and it was built by a company which had been producing taxicabs since the 1930's.

The Bobbi-Kar, hailing from San Diego, had the engine placed in the rear, weighed about a thousand pounds, had a wheelbase of eighty inches and was to sell for $500–$600. The company moved from San Diego to Huntsville, Alabama, where it was taken over by an outfit named Keller, and funds for production were sought in vain.

The Playboy was also a rear-engine car. It featured an all-steel, all-welded, integral body and frame, four-wheel independent suspension, automatic drive, a wheelbase of ninety inches, and a price in the neighborhood of $950. As many as fifteen pilot models were built in 1948 and with each new design the company found it necessary to advance the prospective price until it reached $1,300–$1,500. Attempts to raise capital through sale of franchises to dealers and stock to the public failed to bring in the needed funds, and after building some ninety-seven experimental and demonstration cars, the Playboy company went to the wall in 1949, having spent nearly $2,000,000.

The Davis car was a three-wheeler with the single wheel in front. It was designed with a wheelbase of 108 inches, a weight of 1,328 pounds and was to be powered by a Hercules engine.

These three cars were both distinctive and unconventional in design and evidenced considerable thought along the line of designing to cut cost. Perhaps they were too unconventional and would have failed to win public favor even had the companies been able to get production rolling. The public had not been lining up to buy Powell Crosley's more conventional small car in numbers one usually associates with profitable production. He hit his peak in 1948 with an output close to 28,000, and was able to pay a dividend. He had pioneered an engine made of all-steel stampings, copper-hydrogen-brazed, with cast crankshaft supported by five main bearings, and with overhead camshaft and valves. This engine failed to live up to expectations and was replaced by a conventional cast-iron engine. The 1949 model, for which an output of 50,000 was scheduled, featured such advances as bonded brake linings, valve rotors, and disk brakes. Nevertheless, production fell to 8,800 and continued downward until the company was sold in 1952.

The Tucker Corp. was the most flamboyant of the newcomers. Preston Tucker promised a revolutionary car and attracted a great deal of attention. Hardly a month went by without a press report of some great step toward expansion, but there were also reports of trouble in raising working capital. Tucker hit upon the scheme of selling franchises to prospective dealers and in this way obtained over $7,000,000, and he also sold stock to the public. By the end of 1947, he reported an expenditure of $11,000,000 to get ready for production. Then came an investigation by the SEC, the placing of the corporation in the hands of trustees, and a mail fraud trial in federal court from which Tucker was exonerated. On studying the situation, the trustees calculated that it would require an expenditure of $71,000,000 to get into production on a three-hundred-car-per-day basis, and the corporation was liquidated.

The Darrin, which was conventional in design and powered by a Continental engine, was priced at $1,950, which put it in direct competition with the strongest companies in the business. No more was heard of the Darrin.

While these failures may be interpreted in many ways, they do make obvious the extreme difficulty faced by a new company trying to enter the charmed circle of producers. The time has long passed when a company could start business in an old building, purchase components from suppliers, and put together a car that the public would buy in preference to an established brand. Failures serve to emphasize the massive nature of automobile manufacture, the need for huge amounts of capital, not only to get established but to keep going.

The only company formed after World War II to meet with success was the Kaiser-Frazer Corp., and the word "success" must be qualified. In three years of operation it became the number one producer among the independents and when it bought the great Willow Run plant in 1948, it looked as if Henry J. Kaiser was a man to reckon with. The next year moves were made to acquire iron and steel facilities which were necessary if a company was to profit on large production. At the same time output dropped 60 percent, and to move cars prices were cut. There was a loss of $30,000,000 on the year's operations and a scurrying around to find new capital.

In 1950, with the Kaiser and Frazer cars meeting tough competition, the company brought out a smaller car named the Henry J and losses were cut to $13,000,000. Kaiser then obtained money from the Reconstruction Finance Corp., the Frazer line was dropped, and efforts were made to push the Henry J. But there were never more than 58,000 sold in a single year and that was not enough to make the company prosper.

Even the long-established independents were having a rough time holding their own against the Big Three. When production jumped 1,500,000 to total just over 6,000,000 in 1950, the independents' share in the volume fell from 13 percent to 11 percent. For these producers, price cutting was not the answer. In any price battle the Big Three stood to be easy winners. The independents' best chance lay in offering something new, attractive, and different, and preferably in the lower price range. Thus we find Willys bringing out a station wagon (which was a great success) and a glorified and more comfortable version of the civilian Jeep, called the Jeepster; Hudson going to the monobuilt body, later called unitized construction, which was first used on the Zephyr model of the Lincoln, and a smaller car known as the Hudson Jet; Nash testing the market reaction to a small car built abroad, which came to be known as the Nash Metropolitan, and launching a brand-new model under the old name of Rambler.

The Nash Rambler was the forerunner of the compact. It had a 100-inch wheelbase which made it unconventionally short, an 82-h.p. engine, and a weight of 2,400 pounds. Its convertible body had a frame over the windows which provided for side windows and served as a slide for a power-operated top. The introductory price was high—$1,808, justified only because the car was a convertible and lavishly equipped, which put it in a class by itself.

The regaining of the number-two spot by Ford, which came in 1950, was a tribute to the management of Henry II. As soon as he took over from his grandfather he cleaned house and gathered about him able men to help him rebuild the company and give it the sound managerial control it sadly lacked and must have if it was to recover and go forward.

The onset of hostilities in Korea hit all producers across the board. In November, 1950, Regulation W required the shortening of time payments from twenty-one to fifteen months, much to the disgust of the auto makers, who saw in the tightening of credit terms a curb on sales. To top this off came the setting of production quotas and a freeze of wages and prices. Once again the industry took on contracts to produce war matériel and for a time production was split between supplying the government and the public.

Output shrank by 1,300,000 cars in 1951 with the independents getting a 1.5 percent increase of the total volume, but this did not necessarily mean that they were better off. Hudson, for example, lost $1,250,000 in contrast to a profit of $12,000,000 in 1950.

With government quotas still being in effect, production fell another million in 1952. To ease the situation for the independents, who were less able to offset losses by taking on war work, the National Production Authority assigned a larger share of the car production quota to Nash, Kaiser-Frazer, and Willys-Overland. Even so, Kaiser lost money. In the first six months of 1952 the loss was $8,500,000, and the stockholders, seeing this drain while profits were being made in war work, formed a committee to force the company out of the automobile business, but its efforts were unsuccessful. In an effort to expand volume, Kaiser induced Sears, Roebuck & Co. to try selling the Henry J under the Allstate nameplate in several of the Southern states. Had this test proved successful, the big mail-order house might have been back in the business of merchandising cars after a lapse of forty-three years. And it would also have represented an alliance of sorts between Sears, Kaiser, and Willys, since Willys was building the engines for the Henry J. The following year, 1953, Kaiser-Frazer acquired Willys-Overland, the latter becoming Willys Motors, Inc., and a subsidiary of Kaiser Motors Corp.

Kaiser's losses and Willys's profits prompted the deal. The year 1952 was the best Willys had had in twenty-two years. Production was 168,216 vehicles, of which about one-third were Jeeps for the Army. With a merger, Willys' earnings would have the Kaiser losses as a tax write-off—and there were other benefits. The Kaiser operation was a sprawling affair and with the merger consummated there began a shrinking and consolidation.

The pressure of the Big Three and the effects of two wars were very apparent in the performance of the remaining independents. When the government took the brakes off production in 1953, output soared over the 6,000,000 mark and the seven independents built 300,000 fewer cars, or 35 percent less, than eight independents did in the previous 6,000,000-car year of 1950. Cars were being pushed onto the market to the detriment of the independents and of all the dealers. The National Automobile Dealers Association reported profits before taxes for new car dealers fell from 4.3 percent of sales in 1952 to 0.8 percent in 1953, while three car makers (names unstated) made profits of 16.46, 6.51, and 5.9 percent on sales.

Paul Hoffman, who had returned to Studebaker as board chairman, told a group of salesmen in Toronto that production should be limited to the number of cars a dealer could sell at a profit with intelligent selling; that manufacturers should ship no cars without an order from the dealer, nor should they pressure dealers to move cars at little or no profit just to maintain the manufacturer's production position. Officials of the Hudson company endorsed Hoffman's statement, but otherwise there was only one comment from the industry. A Chrysler vice-president made a nonanswer to the effect that the saturation point had been predicted many times since 1908 and would be still forecast when the industry was producing 8,500,000 cars annually.

The Frazer was discontinued in 1951, the Crosley company ceased production in 1952, control having been bought by General Tire, and the Henry J was dropped in 1953. Far more significant were the two mergers effected in 1954. Nash and Hudson were joined to form the American Motors Corp., and Packard, which had added to its line by resuming the building of luxury models and was losing money, teamed up with Studebaker to form the Studebaker-Packard Corp.

Merger is no sure road to salvation for weakened companies, as has been said. It has been demonstrated time and again in automotive history. Devolving upon the management is the need to make great and wise physical changes and to weld the personnel of the units to form a smooth working team. All this takes time and the outcome may hang in the balance for several years. The year following union saw American Motor's output increase 70 percent and Studebaker-Packard's 60 percent without making profits. Some of this gain could be attributed to the general improvement in market conditions which lifted total industry production by nearly 2,800,000 to establish the all-time record of 7,900,000 cars. Time was to show, however, a great difference in the competence of the management.

George W. Mason, president of American Motors, died a few months after the union was effected. Under the skillful management of his successor, George Romney, the company survived the indigestion of merger and began to cut its losses. Studebaker-Packard, on the other hand, floundered almost from the start under its management.

Another independent having a rugged time was Kaiser Motors. None of its cars was selling well, and it announced a cessation of car manufacture to concentrate on utility and commercial vehicles. This meant pushing the Jeep here and in worldwide markets.

From the industry's standpoint, the year 1956 was one of harassment by the government. It opened with Senate hearings on dealer-factory relationships, inspired by complaints from individual dealers and by a campaign waged by the National Automobile Dealers Association. What disturbed dealers most was the tenuous hold they had on their business, which could be canceled by the manufacturer, variously on thirty to ninety days' notice, leaving them, they said, with nothing for their families. Out of this hearing came some relaxing of contracts. G.M., for example, extended its dealer contract from one to five years, terminable by both parties on thirty days' notice.

Then came an antitrust suit charging General Motors with a monopoly of the bus business. This sent shivers down the collective spine of the Big Three lest it lead to similar action as regards car manufacture. G.M. did have 85 percent of the bus business. The government did not win this suit until 1965. This was followed by a House Commerce Committee hearing on highway safety. At the close of the hearing, committee members reported being impressed by what the manufacturers had told them of their efforts to engineer safety into vehicles. The car makers had been unenthusiastically contributing financial support to several organizations to carry on safety studies.

Meanwhile the Cornell Aeronautical Laboratory and the Liberty Mutual Insurance Co., working jointly to design a safe car, displayed the fruit of their researches. Among other innovations, the car had a lever replacing the steering wheel and passenger seats facing backward, features which the manufacturers felt were too revolutionary to be accepted by the public. They saw, too, several serious production problems.

By the middle of the year, car sales had slipped badly and cutback followed cutback. Harlow Curtice, president of General Motors, blamed the restrictive credit policy of the Federal Reserve Board, and the heralding of revolutionary designs in the offing, which he thought caused the public to postpone purchases. It seems more likely that the record-breaking sales of the previous year had removed many people from the market. Whatever the cause of the decline, all companies were hard hit. The first six months of Chrysler earnings, for example, were $18,600,000 as compared to $70,000,000 for the same period of the previous year. There was talk of Studebaker-Packard merging with the Curtiss-Wright Corp., but what came out of it was a management agreement by which Curtiss-Wright fed the auto maker vitamins in the form of defense work.

In 1957, American Motors ceased manufacture of the Nash and Hudson. The Rambler, which had acquired a healthy reputation, was pushed to the fore with emphasis on the compact. There was also talk of merging with some other company. To this rumor Romney replied that while he had an open mind to any practical arrangement, he would continue to struggle to overcome operating losses.

At the same time that the Hudson and Nash were bowing out, Ford's Edsel was bowing in with what turned out to be a two-year lease on life. No flop has ever received so much publicity, perhaps because no car had ever been given such a tumultuous pre-launching buildup. General Motors had its "copper-cooled" fiasco, its Marquette and Viking, which also lasted just two years; Chrysler had its "Airflow" design, which was too advanced in style for public acceptance; but in none of these instances was the public made so aware of the misstep. The Edsel did have some mechanical defects, its styling made no hit, and it was priced at an unpopular figure. It had the added misfortune to run smack into the recession of 1958 when the industry's production fell back close to the four-million mark.

The Edsel was not a new design from the ground up. Except for the grille and trim it was constructed essentially from existing components, hence the widely circulated statement that the venture cost the company $250,000,000 seems wildly exaggerated. Even though the car failed to capture the market, sales to dealers alone brought in substantial revenue at a time when sale of all cars to consumers was running low.

When Ford undertook to design the Edsel, cars were gaining in size and advancing in price and the introduction of a car in the medium-price range seemed logical. But the market was changing. American Motors had been pushing the compact Rambler, and in the year when the Edsel came on the market the importation of small foreign cars doubled and thereafter continued to mount by leaps and bounds. What the public seemed to want was a compact.

Production rose by 400,000 cars in 1957, but this was not enough to account for the better profits of the Big Three. From General Motors came a statement that the gain seemed to be due in part to customer preference for high-priced options because dollar sales rose faster than deliveries. Studebaker-Packard, still struggling, arranged to market the German Mercedes-Benz.

The average wholesale price of cars had risen 120 percent since resumption of manufacture after World War II. And the rise was striking enough to attract attention in Washington. In March of 1958, the Senate Anti-Trust and Monopoly Subcommittee held hearings. George Romney of American Motors, speaking his mind freely, declared competition could be fostered by splitting up General Motors, Ford, and the UAW (United Automobile Workers), thus dissociating himself from both the establishment and labor. Otherwise little came out of the hearings to make news. Various groups in Washington continued to study the price situation. High prices were suspected of causing the recession then facing the nation and suggestions were made which did not sit well with the manufacturers. One idea was to continue 1958 models unchanged through another year and to pass on to the public the resultant saving of $250 per unit as a price reduction. Another idea was to refund a part of the excise tax provided the car makers would pass it on to the buyer.

There were several reasons why these suggestions were unwelcome. The thought of outsiders tinkering with prices gives the manufacturer nightmares, because prices relate directly to profits. The higher-priced cars were selling best when the overall sales volume was down and these were the cars yielding the highest profit margins. By the year's end, production was almost two million cars lower than the previous year, which placed output just where it was in 1952, when the Korean War forced a downward adjustment. The excise tax idea was unappreciated, according to industry spokesmen, because it would mean more supervision, more paper work.

Price reductions as large as $250 per car could have had a very unsettling chain-reaction effect. Drop the price of the Blitz car $250 and overnight all Blitzes stocked by dealers and in owners' hands would depreciate sharply in value. The dealer would suffer serious loss unless the manufacturer was willing to bail him out; the consumer, who had bought on time, would be paying on the old value and might resent it enough to call it quits; the values backing the millions in loans made by finance companies and banks would become fictitious.

Now that about 80 percent of all sales are financed, installment selling serves as an effective barrier to the lowering of prices of established makes. If less-expensive cars are to be offered to the public without upsetting what passes for a price structure, they must be introduced as new makes. And that is exactly what is being done.

Various expedients were used to adjust to the recession. Chrysler got its managerial personnel to donate a week or two of unpaid working time in lieu of a salary cut. Studebaker-Packard, now forced to stand on its own feet by termination of the agreement with Curtiss-Wright, dropped the Packard, last of the three P's, and introduced the Lark.

With the exception of American Motors, the auto makers regarded the compact with dislike. They regarded the small European car with both dislike and disdain. They declared the public's interest in smaller cars to be a passing aberration. Once the novelty had worn off and the status bestowed by ownership had lessened, they said, Americans would buy bigger, more luxurious cars. However, lest their judgment be wrong and the market run away from them in this undesired direction, the Big Three brought out compacts. The 1959 crop was General Motors' Corvair, Ford's Falcon, and Chrysler's Valiant. Still smaller cars could be imported from foreign subsidiaries to meet whatever demand developed.

Were the manufacturers correct in their appraisal of the market? Subsequent events seemed to prove they were. As larger, more lavishly styled and equipped compacts were put on the market they outsold their plainer kin. And whatever plans were formulated for introducing truly small cars to compete with such foreign invaders as the Volkswagen and Renault were shelved. The plainer kin, be it said, were barely in evidence. Buying the "dolled-up" models was made easy because they were the ones on the showroom floor ready for delivery. If the prospect wished to purchase an unadorned, true compact, it often had to be ordered from the factory with a delivery date far enough in the future to be discouraging.

There was an element of novelty in the first compacts which helped their sale. There was also a small revolt against what some people called the "Detroit Juggernaut." It seems undeniable, too, that there was a strong appeal to status in the imports. But among those who embraced the European car were many who were searching for a better product. Novelty, of course, has a way of wearing off, and the search for status makes for fickle buyers. Nevertheless, it should be noted that the swing away from the compact to the larger, more luxurious, but not necessarily better, car conformed to the will of the Big Three. The giants cajoled and led the public back to the type of car they wished to produce. And the public, being able to lay its hands on the wherewithal to indulge itself, was easily led.

The policy of upgrading, as enunciated by Alfred Sloan in 1925 and first used by General Motors to lead the public out of the Model T camp and into the camp of Chevrolet, became fully implemented and industrywide during the 1950's, Ford and Chrysler following suit, if not cheerfully, then by necessity.

Rephrased, the policy ran like this: Since the annual market for new cars is limited and can no longer be expanded profitably by lowering prices, the only way dollar growth can be sustained is to sell a larger package to bring in more profit per car.

All in all, the policy of trading-up assures the industry of getting its full proportionate share of the rising consumer income. And as long as our society remains affluent and price competition, as the industry once experienced it, does not raise its ugly head, the policy is a profit-making one par excellence.

The offering of a "larger and better" (more expensive) car was coupled with options on engines, other components such as automatic transmissions, power brakes, and power steering, still greater emphasis on styling and a corresponding de-emphasizing of price. There was no need to fear price cutting by the independents, now reduced to American Motors, Studebaker-Packard, Kaiser-Jeep, and Checker, who lived wholly by sufferance.

Emphasizing styling raised the status of the stylist in the manufacturing hierarchy, to the discomfiture of the engineers. They complained of being placed in a subordinate position with their function reduced to overcoming the engineering problems created by the stylist. And there was a measure of truth in it. For example, lowering the hood to gain a more pleasing silhouette restricted the flow of air to the engine and space for components, and it was up to the engineer to find a way around these difficulties.

Styling includes the element of comfort as well as appearance. Serious efforts were made to design the seat to fit the occupants. Measurements were taken of the human body to find the best common denominator, manikins were then constructed from these measurements, and the seats built to conform to the manikin. In earlier days the comfort of seating was a matter of chance. I recall an instance where the car company president's wife was the arbiter. She was driven to the factory, seated in the car, and if she found it comfortable the design was approved; conversely, if the seat failed to fit her particular (and peculiar) dimensions, alterations were made.

Style, luxury, and comfort provide the theme for advertising copy. The appeal is to our dreams, to the Walter Mitty in us, since there is little or nothing else to talk about to make us dissatisfied with what we own, as witness:

> Distinguishes Your Way of Life
> For Young People of All Ages

Recognizing the swelling number of young people coming into the market for cars, the auto makers have been quick to exploit their immaturity and to encourage irresponsible driving. Here are typical examples from advertisements:

> You can start billing yourself as The Human Cannonball.

> If this [make of car] doesn't do for your driving what red capes do for bulls . . .

This is a far cry from the "pitch" which once sought to convince the skeptic of the reliability and stamina of the product.

Between 1955 and 1964, the period between two seven-million-car years, the Big Three broadened their lines to have cars for a wide range of pocketbooks and taste. In earlier times, offering a wide range of models at various prices to please the greatest possible number of prospects was often debilitating to profits because it raised costs. Lines were expanded under pressure from dealers who wanted to have vehicles to match all competition and then were contracted when the point of no adequate return was reached, such that repetitive action resembled that of an accordion. Today models are designed so as to have many interchangeable components. The same body shell, for example, will be used for several makes and given distinctive appearance by altering the front grille, fenders, and hood, and varying chrome treatment. Again through similarity in basic design and highly developed scheduling it has become possible to assemble a wide variety of models in an almost infinite variety of colors and interior treatment on a single assembly line. If you have wondered why cars of different make produced by one manufacturer have a fleeting resemblance, there is your answer.

This flexibility in manufacture, which has grown greater over the past twenty years, has been hard on the independent, whose means to survival seemed to lie in offering a type of car not provided by the giants. Studebaker tried the unusual with its fiberglass-bodied Avanti, ran into difficulties in production of the bodies, and lost out commercially. In 1963 the company moved its manufacturing to Canada and then ceased all production in 1966. American Motors, having made the greatest percentage gain of any producer, not excluding the Big Three, found itself at the crossroads with a shrinking market for the compact car and boldly set out to compete head-on with its larger models. Unsuccessful in this attempt, it cut the price of its Rambler American and mobilized sales effort behind it. The Kaiser-Jeep Corp. brought out a four-wheel-drive wagon following in 1967 with a Jeepster Commando, a four-wheel-drive roadster powered by a V-6 engine, designed to compete for the thriving sports-car market. And Checker continued to nibble away on the fringe of the market with a sturdy vehicle, stable in design, which you can enter without removing your hat.

Boom times always stimulate production of a car of distinctive design and quality with price a secondary factor. The Excalibur SSK, introduced in 1965, and the new Duesenberg, introduced in 1966, fall in this category. The Excalibur is a modern version of the famous Mercedes SSK, which won the hearts of sport fans in the 1920's and is a classic car in every sense of the word. The Duesenberg, which sought to capitalize on a name famous from 1921 to 1937, was to be (it was stillborn) the most lavish car on the road and set a high mark for speed, luxury, and price—a mere $20,000.

The Cord front drive, another revival of the year 1966, went bankrupt after producing short of one hundred cars. Though differing from its predecessor in having an air-cooled engine and being four-fifths its size, it was a replica of the old Cord in styling and it reintroduced the separation of hood and fenders, as does the Excalibur. Indicative of the esteem in which the original Cord was held was the Hupmobile company's use of the Cord dies to form the body of its 1938 model in a desperate attempt to recapture its position in the market.

It is significant that the manufacturers of these three recent arrivals all utilized engines obtained from established car manufacturers. The Excalibur has a Chevrolet-Corvette engine, the Duesenberg had a Chrysler power-plant, and the Cord a Corvair engine. By this action the newcomers avoided an enormous and well-nigh prohibitive expense. It is also noteworthy that all three vehicles were inspired by cars greatly admired in an earlier age.

When the Cord appeared in 1929 there had been no front-drive (as distinct from the four-wheel-drive) car for a quarter century and then only as an experimental car developed by Walter Christie, the famous racing driver. In 1929 a front-drive Ruxton was announced by the New Era Motors Co. and a year later came a front-drive Gardner. Neither car reached the production stage and both companies failed shortly thereafter. The eclipse of the front-drive lasted thirty-six years, or until General Motors reintroduced it on the Oldsmobile Toronado and on the Cadillac Eldorado.

The appearance of high-priced, ultra-luxury vehicles has always in the past signaled the end of a period of booming business. The termination of the World War I boom was marked by the introduction of the Lincoln; President Hoover's "New Era" flamed out with an announcement of twelve- and sixteen-cylinder Cadillacs and a sixteen-cylinder Marmon. Production did slip back in 1966 so history repeated itself. Output in the early part of 1967 was also disappointing, but there were many factors contributing to it. There were nationwide heavy snows, money became tight, and the safety of the Detroit product was brought into question. More important, perhaps, was past production. With the exception of the years immediately following World War II, when the replacement market could hardly be filled fast enough, the industry has never been able to break past production records without an ensuing slump. The year 1966 was no exception. The model year ended with a huge carry-over which dealers had to work off at reduced prices (with financial assistance from the manufacturers) in competition, as it were, with the 1967 models. The relapse, coming after three years of heavy production, was not so astonishing after all.

The 1966 production of 8,604,712 passenger cars was still large by any standard. Though down some 700,000 from the previous year, output was the second largest in the history of the industry. And this record, following boom years, explains in a measure why there came a real slump in 1967, when production fell almost 2 million from the peak of 1965. However, the industry came out of the corner fighting hard, and in 1968 production bounced back to 8,848,620. Among them, the Big Three giants manufactured 97 percent of all the cars made in the United States, with the lion's share, 48.1 percent, issuing from General Motors' factories.

On the bleached bones of nearly nine hundred companies, which once kept competition honed to a razor edge, the survivors now sit securely, planning and pushing the conquest of new markets.

7 the opaque crystal ball

No complex mechanism other than the human body is sub-
jected to more abuse by more people than the automobile,
yet it functions extraordinarily well. It took the brains
and labor of thousands of people and a half century to
bring the car to its present state of refinement. But that in
no wise diminishes the magnitude of the feat.

By providing luxurious, private transportation which
can be bought on credit, the industry has made it possible
for the vast majority of our population to be not only king
(or queen) for a day, but for every time he (or she) sits
behind the wheel until the next annual model appears. No
wonder automobile manufacture is America's most patron-
ized and pampered industry.

Tracing the rise and fall of companies leads rightly to a

consideration of why so few are left to bestow this largess of kingship upon the public. Why did so many companies start forth gallantly only to fall by the way? Is it in the nature of the business to gravitate into so few hands? In a sense, yes. But this does not explain why some companies succeeded while others failed.

One might conclude that success hinges on producing a superior product, but history denies it. Scores of excellent cars were designed and put on the market, but the companies building them are not with us today. Paramount to corporate life was working capital. Funds had to be available to keep plants modernized, to conduct engineering, to cultivate markets, to maintain parts and sales distribution outlets. There had to be, in short, a proper balance between all phases of the business and the money to do what was needed to overcome any weakness. This, increasingly with time, required a close control of costs. A slighting of any phase could be crippling in very short order. And so, in the last analysis, success comes down to the competence of management. The leaders of the industry were outstanding men and no small part of their competence was their ability to pick excellent lieutenants. In the shadow of Ford, Durant, Sloan, and Chrysler stood a company of brilliant men.

The industry solved the problems of mass production at a fairly tender age; it never has put the distribution of its product on a rational basis. The used-car problem is no nearer solution today than it was forty years ago and it will remain unsolved as long as the industry refuses to adjust production to transportation needs, or until the manufacturers discover how to build a car that will "fall to pieces all at once and nothing first" like the Deacon's wonderful one-hoss shay, thus reaching the zenith of obsolescence engineering—that is to say, probably never.

Looking at the situation casually, one might conclude the Big Three "had it made." Our society has gradually become geared to the use of cars by the millions, which insures a replacement market huge by any standard. Moreover, the growth in population is steadily expanding the market and the government is committed to use every means at its disposal to maintain the public purchasing power upon which the industry depends.

Having consolidated their position in the domestic market, the auto makers have moved aggressively to capture foreign markets, through purchase of going concerns, the establishment of subsidiaries, and expansion of overseas plants. This move has caused some concern among our friends. Writing in *Maclean*'s (Canada, 1965), Alan Edmonds expressed it this way:

> The economic well-being and prosperity of Canada and the U.S. depends to a significant, perhaps even alarming, extent upon 1966—and every other year, for that matter—being a good one for the auto industry.
>
> The auto makers know this, and are privately haunted by it. Their industry, more than any other, is dominated by the need to grow, to expand, to sell, sell, sell and provide motive power to keep the eternal circle of our consumer economy moving.

Charles E. Wilson, a former president of General Motors, expressed a similar idea with startling brevity in his widely publicized remark to the effect that what is good for

General Motors is good for the nation—a statement for which he was ridiculed in the press. If history tells us anything, it is just the reverse. The industry is the beneficiary of prosperity, not the creator of it. Nevertheless, it does have enormous power to influence the economy for good or ill because of its tremendous size and scope, and the more so because that power is concentrated in so few hands. It is a paradox that an industry so devoted to the principles of the competitive system and so free of monopolistic practice should become virtually a public utility in the field of transportation. If, as Mr. Edmonds wrote, the auto makers are haunted, this precarious climax to the war of attrition, rather than any fancied responsibility for keeping the economy going, could be the specter.

If auto manufacture were to be declared a public utility by the government, it would not be relished. The industry has always been quick to fend off regulation and it is too jealous of its commanding position to accept it graciously now.

Where the industry goes from here is any man's guess. In outward appearance it seems impregnable to strong competition and its product to have reached an engineering plateau, but in a dynamic economy such as ours change is a certainty, and there are forces now at work which even the most astute manufacturer cannot quell. The most potent forces working for change are the articulated demands to do something about air pollution and highway casualties.

The State of California was the first to take action to compel the use of smog-controlling devices on automobiles, prompted by the serious smog situation in Los Angeles. Many objections were raised by the manufacturers, some of them specious. Spokesmen for the industry, for example, argued that it would be unfair to rural and small-town Californians to be put to added expense just to help out Los Angeles. Nevertheless, a law was passed calling for smog-control devices to be installed on all new cars sold in the state, but allowing the industry time to work out the complex chemical problems needing solution before an effective device could be developed. Since then all new cars sold in the United States must be similarly equipped.

Starting with the control of crankcase blowby, the attack on the air pollution problem has branched to include the reduction of emission of unburned fuel in the exhaust through engine modifications and by burning the hydrocarbons that reach the exhaust manifold, and, finally, by checking the evaporation of fuel in the system. There is even discussion of altering the formulation of the fuel itself to achieve a less noxious exhaust. Both auto makers and petroleum companies are now carrying on extensive research in the basic problems of pollution caused by the internal-combustion engine.

The industry showed strong distaste for tackling the problem of safety, but it could no longer be swept under the rug after Senator Ribicoff opened hearings in Washington and Ralph Nader's *Unsafe at Any Speed* focused public attention on the problem.

The industry met the first onslaught with negative pronouncements and persuasive advertisements. It declared the vast majority of accidents to be caused by the drivers of cars. This cannot be denied. In the universe of motordom there are drivers with inadequate vision, slow reaction time, lack of experience or inability to profit from it, emotional instability, and poor judgment. If these people were banned from the highways the accident rate would surely tumble, but the public has yet to clamor for elimination of the greatest hazard of all—the inebriated driver. To ban the unfit would be tantamount to amputation of legs, so dependent are we on the car. Moreover, it would curb the sale of cars, which the industry would find disturbing.

The safety now demanded, said the auto makers, would raise the cost of cars to the public, adding that safety cannot be sold. This concern for the public's pocketbook rang hollow in view of the industry's policy of the more expensive package. And one can be equally suspicious of the cry that safety cannot be sold. It was unduly modest. Advertisements stressed the adoption of two-speed windshield wipers, external rear-view mirrors, and padded instrument panels. While these were soothing, they were all minor items in the large issue.

There are two parts to the safety issue and neither public statements nor advertisements has distinguished between them sufficiently to clarify the controversy in the public mind.

First, there is the design of the present-day car. Critics declare it to be unsafe and have cited highway casualties as proof. They press for a redesigning of the car's structure so that in event of a collision, or other accident, the occupants would have a far better chance of survival. This might be termed the "fool safe" issue.

Secondly, are the faults in the design of components which can cause an accident. This might be termed the "fail safe" part of the issue.

Legislative bodies and persons most concerned with slaughter on the highways opened up their guns on the first part. In so doing, they gave the industry a profound shock. Here was a demand to cease delaying tactics and solve a problem requiring a great deal more knowledge of the nature of accidents, a re-examination of the product so laboriously developed over the years, and engineering development to meet the requirements revealed by research.

Replies to criticism revealed the industry to feel confronted by a crisis. John S. Bugas, vice president of Ford, asked the Senate Commerce Committee to let the industry conduct its own safety program free of government interference. Later, he told the House Commerce Committee he endorsed mandatory federal safety regulations. Obviously, this would put all members of the industry on the same footing.

Henry Ford II declared the auto industry to be the most important industry in the economic picture of the United States and warned that if Congress fooled around with model changes, or did something irrational, it would upset the economy of the country very rapidly. This statement was reminiscent of the earlier one made by Charles Wilson, only phrased negatively—what is bad for the Ford company is bad for the U.S.A. It raised two questions which the industry might better have left sleeping, to wit, the power of the industry vis-à-vis the government, and the qualifications of the industry to control the economy of the country.

Joseph C. Harsch, writing in the *Christian Science Monitor,* made an oblique answer to this gentle threat, as follows:

The motorcar masters of Detroit are correct when they say that today theirs is "the most important industry in the economic picture of the United States." And one may hope they will police and regulate themselves without government coercion, for self-discipline is always preferable, at least in theory, to outside discipline.

It will, however, be a new departure if they do. To date no industry in its moment of being the biggest and most important has yet managed to teach itself humility. The grace has had to come from either disciplines imposed by an outraged public, or from successful competition.

And the sins of the American automobile industry are not limited to a lack of due concern for safety features in their product. They have also tended to behave as though the highest purpose of the American community was to consume automobiles.

In the *SAE Journal* (May, 1966), organ of the Society of Automotive Engineers, James M. Roche, president of General Motors, gave a thoughtful and broad presentation of the problems confronting automotive engineers, most importantly air pollution and safety, then closed with this sentence:

> We cannot afford to indulge in what might seem like lofty ideals at the cost of immobility, a lower standard of living for the public, and the risk of falling behind in world-wide competition.

Mr. Roche failed to explain how a safe, nonpolluting car could bring about any of the three mentioned woes. One might expect the opposite—a positive benefit to the public. Moreover, exports from American factories are no more than 2.5 percent of the total output. Foreign markets are being served largely by overseas plants and affiliates.

The industry did take prompt action with regard to the second part of the safety issue by making public, via Washington, the faults in design which came to light on cars in consumers' hands, and what had been done about them. The wisdom of doing so was obvious, though it was done under pressure. The practice of notifying dealers of defects and requesting them to make corrections when cars were brought in for service had long been in operation, though perhaps not so meticulously. If there is anything new in this "campaigning," as it is called, it is in notifying owners to bring their cars in for attention.

There are, however, other faults caused by careless manufacture or assembly. These are annoying rather than dangerous to the owner. The auto makers know that a certain proportion of cars shipped from the factory will be unfit for delivery and they rely on the dealer to put them in proper shape. There are various ways of handling the expense. Usually, a sum is allotted by the manufacturer, which, according to the dealers, is rarely adequate to cover their costs if they do a forthright job.

While this scheme is more practical, and certainly more profitable to the manufacturer, than more thorough inspection, it is haphazard in view of the uneven quality, integrity, and capability of dealers, and it has been the source of much consumer dissatisfaction. In earlier times, the disgruntled consumer could swing his patronage to another manufacturer in the hope of having better luck and treatment. That avenue is now practically closed to him, hence one reason for the heightened interest in the foreign car, as has been pointed out.

Events moved swiftly in the safety issue. Following hearings in Washington, the government set standards to be met in the 1968 models. Some of them were opposed by the manufacturers on the grounds that time was inadequate for their incorporation, and accordingly the requirements were relaxed.

When reference is made to the "safe car," it is valid to ask, "What do you mean by safe?" By what criteria is judgment made? Until safety can be measured, tested, and defined, the objectives to be achieved through design and construction remain controversial to the extreme.

Several institutions and individuals have built "safe" cars for demonstrating purposes, but none of them has fired much interest. Then, in 1965, the Legislature of the State of New York, prompted by a program developed by State Representative Edward J. Speno, passed a bill authorizing and financing a study to:

Determine the feasibility of designing a prototype safety car for limited production, and

Develop safety definitions and tests for eventual legislative use in setting minimum performance standards that would be fair and reasonable.

To free the study from a traditional approach to design, manufacture, styling, testing, and sales practice, it was decided to employ systems engineering techniques used in the aerospace industry. Accordingly the prime study contract was awarded to the Republic Aviation Division of the Fairchild Hiller Corp.

The final report of the study, which was issued late in

1966, concluded that it is feasible to design a vehicle that will reduce injuries from moderate through fatal by at least 50 percent in the event of head-on collision at 50 mph, side impact at 40 mph, rear impact at 50 mph, and rolling impact at 70 mph.

Needless to say, the study has met with some criticism by automotive engineers, but how valid they are cannot be determined until prototypes have been built and tested. This hinges on further legislative appropriations or federal financial assistance.

The New York State study very wisely eschewed the setting of a design to which manufacturers would have to adhere rigidly. Should tests of prototype cars support the findings of the study, it would then be up to the legislature to decide whether or not to establish the safety goals in law, leaving it up to the manufacturers to attain them by whatever design and methods of construction they wished. All this, of course, is very much in the future. Safer automobiles are not going to be brought into existence by any overnight miracles. Even when the causes of accidents are pinpointed, research and development to overcome them tend to be evolutionary rather than revolutionary.

The most significant engineering development visible on the horizon is in the field of power generation. The gas turbine has been under development and test for more than a decade, and should it prove to be practical, superior to the internal combustion engine, and promise to be more profitable, it could be the next truly radical change in the product.

Reportedly the gas turbine does not pollute the air. This is an advantage that could grow in importance as the number of vehicles on the road increases and the demand for pollution abatement mounts. The turbine has few moving parts, which augurs well for maintenance. It is said to be very free of vibration at this stage in its development. Drawbacks are its requirement for diesel fuel or lead-free gasoline, and an excessive noise from components, but neither of these is insurmountable. Still to be resolved are the problems of excessive fuel consumption and durability of parts.

For a time there was much discussion of using atomic energy for car propulsion. The idea that a tiny amount of atomic fuel could run a car almost indefinitely had an enormous appeal to the general public. However, experience has shown the problem of shielding to be impossible of solution by any practical means, and for the time being, at least, the idea of being pushed around by the atom has been shelved.

A revival of competition through the rise of new companies formed to build "just a real good car," as Durant once advertised, seems most unlikely. To enter the lists with an orthodox vehicle and engage in competitive styling would be to court suicide. Anything the newcomer could spring on the public could be imitated by the entrenched companies and made their own with devastating speed. It seems incontrovertible, therefore, that if a newcomer is to have any chance of success it will have to offer a product radical enough to set it apart and capable of being sold on its own incomparable merit. Needless to say, this would take huge amounts of capital.

The unorthodox product might be an electric or steam vehicle which incorporated designs for safety.

Interest in the electric vehicle has been heightened by the air-pollution problem. If the internal-combustion engine cannot be taught to digest its exhaust to the point of reducing pollution to safe levels, the electric could arouse even greater attention.

The car makers already have experimental electrics on the street and are not to be caught napping. Other parties manifesting interest in the electric vehicle are the manufacturers of storage batteries, to whom the prospect of greatly increased battery sales is attractive, the public utilities which are eager to sell current for battery recharging, and a few nonautomotive companies looking for promising fields into which to expand.

The electric vehicle lost out in competition with the internal-combustion-engine-powered car because its range between charges was at best forty miles. Even though that range had been doubled or tripled, there was still the drawback of relatively slow speed. Limited range is still the chief obstacle to be overcome to win public acceptance and this awaits the development of a much superior storage battery. Existing batteries lack energy storage capacity and are prohibitively heavy and costly. Still, investigators probing the possibilities are optimistic that a wholly practical battery can be developed. General Motors, for example, reports experimenting with a variety of batteries and batteries in conjunction with heat engines. Among batteries under test are zinc-air and lithium-chlorine types. The latter, like the sodium-sulphur battery, is hampered by its high operating temperature.

Convinced there is a limited market for an electric vehicle for urban use, a few companies have tried out experimental cars, but how many people would be satisfied with a limited-range, limited-speed car, even as a second car for local shopping and short-run commutation, remains to be seen. Some investigators consider electric propulsion best suited for taxicabs and stop-and-go delivery service vehicles.

To make the electric practical and attractive in spite of its limited range and the uncertainty of prompt improvement, it has been suggested to have charging stations scattered throughout a city, much like parking meters, at which the car owner could simply plug in for a recharge when not using his car. A coin-in-slot device would provide means for payment, or, in a more sophisticated system, the current used would be recorded and the user billed for it monthly. Charging stations could serve taxicabs, which normally operate over a limited range, run at relatively moderate speed, and spend a certain proportion of the day at designated stands. Were electric taxicabs used in a city like New York, for example, both air pollution and noise would be greatly reduced.

From the industry itself has come the idea of embedding conductors in the pavement of highway lanes from which current could be drawn by passing vehicles. This would entail expense for installation, presumably borne by public agencies, and for that reason alone unlikely to become a reality in the near future. Moreover, a dual source of power would be required until all roads were equipped. This is reminiscent of early attempts to combine gasoline power and electricity, notably in the Owen-Magnetic car.

Many researchers, probing the field of electric power generation, believe far more success will attend development of the fuel cell than can ever be had from improvement in storage batteries. Great advances have been made in the hydrogen-oxygen type of fuel cell, which would run on the products of electrolyzed water. Ultimate cost, weight, and efficiency have yet to be determined. Many problems remain to be solved before valid comparisons can be made with the internal-combustion engine. We do know that it would eliminate noise and smell. At this stage in its development, it promises to be no more expensive to operate than a gasoline engine.

Steam propulsion would have to overcome great obstacles to win acceptance because so few people have any knowledge of its characteristics. Nevertheless, it has many advantages lacking in other power sources. Tests show burning fuel for steam generation to be less polluting than firing it in an internal combustion engine. Surely this is a bright feather in the steam cap.

A steam-propelled vehicle needs no clutch or gearset; thus there is no need for a transmission, manual or automatic, which adds to weight, complexity, and cost. The power is always constant and can be applied through a very simple engine operating at low rotating speeds.

The steam car of forty years ago, the last to be built, was the equal of the gasoline-powered vehicle of today in acceleration and smoothness of power application, and superior to it in its simplicity, number of moving parts, and quietness.

In a technical treatise comparing gasoline and steam power, J. D. Neiss of the Lewis Institute, Chicago, wrote in 1917 as follows:

No commercial gasoline vehicle has ever been built in which the builder did not attempt to secure the characteristics of constant power, which is possessed by the steam plant in ideal form.

The gasoline engine will never be the equal in performance of the steam engine until it is provided with a gearbox having an infinite number of speeds; until the gears in this box change themselves without attention on the part of the driver and in fact without his knowledge and in such a way as always to give the ratio best suited to the work at hand, until the change of gears are made without noise and without interruption of the tractive effort; until the engine secures overload capacity and starting torque. . . . Faults may be found with the steam car, but absolutely not with the characteristics of the steam engine, which propulsion approaches the ideal for automobile work.

There is a prophetic quality in this analysis. By multiplying the number of cylinders in the gasoline engine and adding an automatic transmission, the industry has at long last achieved the performance objectives outlined by Mr. Neiss.

The last steam car to be built, the 1924 Stanley, was a vast improvement over the 1917 model, which acquainted me with the performance and pleasures of steam propulsion, but room for improvement was even greater. Since 1924, enormous advances have been made in metallurgy, in heat generation, and in automatic controls. If this new knowledge were applied to overcoming the drawbacks of the earlier steam car, there seems to be no good reason why the results might not be a lighter-weight, high-performance, simpler, and less costly car—all qualities beneficial to the consumer.

The industry has shown no enthusiasm for the steam car; nevertheless, its members are experimenting with steam propulsion and at least a half dozen research organizations are similarly engaged. General Motors has exhibited two experimental steam cars. More important, the National Air Pollution Control Administration, Department of Health, Education and Welfare, has placed contracts with two research concerns to determine if steam propulsion is a feasible replacement for the internal combustion engine. If steam power is found capable of reducing air pollution to tolerable limits, legislators would have facts useful in setting standards that the industry would have to meet with whatever power source it elects.

The air pollution problem balloons as car use increases, and coupled with the problem of safety, it has created what is perhaps the most crucial period in the history of the industry. As if these two problems were not enough to conjure with, the industry also faces persistent invasion of imported cars and rising costs of manufacture.

In 1959 compact models were introduced to stem the flow of imports, but imports continued to enter. In subsequent years the compacts were enlarged until they were no longer compact. Now the enemy is to be repulsed by a new crop of cars—the Ford Maverick, the American Motors Hornet, and other small cars yet to make their debuts.

Small, unadorned cars may serve to check importation. That remains to be seen. They do enable the manufacturer to hold down price in the face of rising costs and so put him in a more favorable position to compete with the foreign invader. Other indications of a cost problem are an adjustment of warranties to make them less generous, and an erosion of the long-established policy of creating obsolescence through radical change in styling, as evidenced by the 1970 models.

In many ways the automobile industry is paradoxical. It has reached a state of maturity, yet it concentrates on undisciplined growth, which is uncharacteristic of a mature organism. Inherent to growth is change, yet of the industry it could be said the more things change the more they stay the same. Change has become the industry's bugaboo, for its members have become too large, have too much at stake, to strike out voluntarily on revolutionary paths. Freeing itself from the restrictions of competition has brought the industry no flexibility; it has become the prisoner of its own need to keep operating at peak. The nation now depends upon the industry for its essential mobility; the industry depends upon the patronage of the nation for its survival.

Let us take our leave of it now, locked in this mutual embrace.

introduction
to the lists

On the following pages are listed alphabetically all makes of passenger cars produced commercially in the United States from 1895 to 1966, together with the names of the producing companies and other vital data.

To compile a list that would be significant and something other than an indiscriminate assemblage of names, it was necessary to arrive at a valid definition of a company. After much deliberation, it was decided that to qualify as a bona fide company an organization must have manufactured a car and sold to the general public. The reason for making so arbitrary a decision will be explained.

When the automobile was first developed, hundreds of individuals built cars and gave them names by which their experiments live on in records. Blacksmiths and mechanics, men with a mechanical turn of mind, and the equivalent of today's "do it yourself" enthusiast tried their hand to see if they could build a vehicle that would run. They were no more manufacturers than the men who, in later years, fashioned radio sets to their own satisfaction. While these enterprising men have their proper place in automobile history, they do not constitute part of the industry in my opinion and are excluded from the compilation.

A degree of flexibility has been used in applying this definition, since I realize that identical standards could not be applied to the producer of 1901 and, say, 1921. Call it historical perspective. The effect has been to apply the definition loosely in the formative years of the industry and tighten it as the years advanced, risking that some undeserving car makers of the earliest years would be listed, while some deserving few would be slighted in the later years.

Excluded from the list are racing cars, taxicabs, and cycle cars, all of them passenger cars in a sense. Also excluded are the few companies building and exhibiting a car for the sole purpose of stock selling (as proved in the courts), the hundreds of companies filing for incorporation but failing to advance beyond the paper stage, and the hundreds more progressing to the point of designing their product, but expiring before getting into production. In the aggregate these excluded ones constitute a good-sized army.

Some companies have no history; others have more than the facts of their brief life warrant. Borderline cases all, they appear in a supplementary list "B," following the basic "A" compilation. Among them are a few whose product was introduced at automobile shows, but never appeared on the market.

The opening statement that "all makes of passenger cars produced commercially in these United States . . ." are listed is a gross exaggeration. No such claim can be made for any published list, of which there are a number. Too many data have been irretrievably lost to permit full compilation.

When the industry was young, there were small manufacturers who sold their cars over a very limited territory and were wholly unknown outside of it. Their existence went unrecorded. The Martell Motor Car Co., No. 516 in the list, is a good example. I passed the factory daily on my way to grade school, saw the product in use in the community, but never once in years of research have I found the Martell car mentioned. The successor concern, the Lenox Motor Car Co., which sought a wider market, was given press mention and its Lenox car described in detail.

Press reports in the early days were often inaccurate and always open to question. Much of the labor of compilation, therefore, went into winnowing fact from fiction in the interest of accuracy. When the compilation was begun in 1923, there were many old-timers who were reached to clear up discrepancies, but the men who nurtured the industry are now rarely to be found among the living and that source of information is no longer available.

In recent years, manufacturers have tended to blur the distinction between make and model as if to benefit from a striking model name while retaining the cultivated reputation of make. Where this is the case, I have been guided by advertising and by common usage of names. Thus you will not find listed such recent introductions as Pontiac's Firebird, Plymouth's Fury and Barracuda, Dodge's Dart, Chevrolet's Camaro, Oldsmobile's Toronado, Mercury's Cougar, and American Motors' Rambler American. All these are more strictly models than makes.

A word of acknowledgment is due *Motor*. It was a listing of 639 manufacturers appearing in the March, 1909, issue of that magazine that inspired the undertaking of this compilation. *Motor*'s list was reworked to eliminate truck manufacturers and to revise data when fact warranted. Thereafter, when time was available, the list was brought up to date.

While the code provided with the list is self-explanatory, comment on its use may be helpful.

The dates appearing immediately after the make of car are years of production, not model years. The dates following company names also represent years of production and not necessarily the span of corporate life, since there is usually a considerable time lag between organization and production and a similar interval between cessation of production and company dissolution. When the year of cessation could not be ascertained with certainty, the apparent year is set in italics.

While a receivership indicates bankruptcy, both terms are used. Receivers often continued manufacture and sometimes were able to restore corporate health. The term "bankruptcy" is used when insolvency was definite and production ceased. Receiverships are noted with the code

(R) for the light they throw on the frequency of corporate financial illness. When car manufacture ceased, but the company remained in business, the code (C) is used, with the new product indicated, when known.

SYMBOLS AND ABBREVIATIONS
USED IN THE LISTS

A—Acquired

B—Bankrupt

C—Car (when used in company title)

C—Production discontinued. Company continued in other
    manufacture

Car.—Carriage

D—Retired from business

E—Electric vehicle (when used after make)

E—Entered from other business (when used before com-
    pany dates)

F—Former make or company

G—Gasoline

HW—High-wheel vehicle

M—Motor

M.C.—Motor Car

M.V.—Motor Vehicle

Ms—Motors

N—Name changed to

R—Receivership

Rg—Reorganized

S—Steam vehicle

T—Transferred through sale, consolidation, or otherwise

( )—What is enclosed appeared in original company name,
    was later dropped, and portion between parentheti-
    cal material and "Co." substituted.

V—Vehicle

cars and companies—
basic list A

A

1. ABBOTT (1916–1918). Abbott Corp., Detroit, 1916–1918B. (F) ABBOTT–DETROIT (see 2).
2. ABBOTT–DETROIT (1909–1916). Abbott–Detroit M. C. Co., Detroit, 1909–1913. (R) 1913. (T) Abbott M. Co., 1913. (T) Consolidated C. Co., 1914. (Rg) Abbott Corp. (see 1).
3. A.B.C. (1906–1910). A.B.C. M. V. Co., St. Louis, 1906–1910B.
   Abendroth & Root Mfg. Co. (see 324).
4. ACE (1920–1922). Apex M. Co., Ypsilanti, Mich., 1920–1922.
5. ACME (1903–1909). Acme M. C. Co., Reading, Pa., 1903–1911. (R) 1906. (N) S.G.V. 1909. (Rg) S.G.V. Motor C. Co., 1911 (see 741). (F) REBER (see 684).
6. ADAMS (1906–1907). Adams Auto. Co., Hiawatha, Kan., 1906–1907D.
7. ADAMS–FARWELL (1904–1913). Adams Co., Dubuque, Ia., E1904–1913C.
8. ADRIAN (1902–1903). Adrian M. Wks., Adrian, Mich., 1902–1903D.

Advance M. V. Co. (see 439).

9. A.E.C. (1912–1914). Anger Engineering Co., Milwaukee, 1912–1914.

10. AEROCAR (1905–1907). Aerocar Co., Detroit, 1905–1907B.

11. AHLAND (1916–*1917*). Ahland M. C. Co., Detroit, 1916–*1917*.

12. AJAX (1901–1903). Ajax M. V. Co., New York, 1901–1903B.

13. AJAX (1925–1926). Ajax Ms. Co., Kenosha, Wis., 1925–1926. Nash subsidiary. (T) NASH, 1926.

14. ALBANY (1907–1908). Albany Auto. Co., Albany, Ind., 1907–1908B.

15. ALCO (1910–1913). American Locomotive Co., Providence, R.I., 1906–1913C. (F) BERLIET (see 82).

16. ALLEN (1913–1922). Allen M. C. Co., Fostoria, O., 1913–1922B. (R) 1920.

Allen & Clark Co. (see 148).

17. ALLEN–KINGSTON (1907–1909). Allen–Kingston M. C. Co., Kingston, N.Y., 1907. (T) Kingston M. C. Co., 1908. (T) Bristol Engineering Co., Bristol, Conn., 1908. (T) New Departure Mfg. Co., 1909 (see 706).

18. ALLSTATE (1952–1953). Sears, Roebuck & Co., Chicago. Marketing HENRY J experimentally.

19. ALPENA (1910–1914). Alpena M. C. Co., Alpena, Mich., 1910–1914B.

20. ALTER (1914–1917). Alter M. C. Co., Chicago, Plymouth, Mich., 1914–1917B.

Amalgamated Ms. Corp. (see 24).

21. AMBASSADOR (1921–1924). Yellow Cab Mfg. Co., Chicago, E1921–1926. (N) HERTZ (see 391).

21A. AMBASSADOR (1965–to date). American Ms. Corp. NASH model, 1927–1957; RAMBLER model, 1957–1965.

22. AMERICA (1910–*1911*) Motor Car Co. of New York, American & British Mfg. Co. (see 652).

American Auto. Mfg. Co. (see 434).

American Auto. & Power Co. (see 651).

American Bicycle Co. (see 413, 823, 870).

American Chocolate Machinery Co. (see 861).

American Locomotive Co. (see 15, 82).

23. AMERICAN (1902–1903). American M. C. Co., Cleveland, 1902–1903B.

American M. Co. (see 515).

American Ms. Corp., Kenosha, Wis., 1954–to date. (See AMBASSADOR-21A, AMX-33A, HORNET-403A, HUDSON-408, JAVELIN-425A, NASH-580, RAMBLER-670, REBEL-683A).

24. AMERICAN (1916–1923). American Ms. Corp., Plainfield, N.J., 1916–1923. (R) 1921. (T) Amalgamated Ms. Corp., 1923B.

25. AMERICAN (1905–1914). American M. C. Co., Indianapolis, 1905–1911. (Rg) American Ms. Co., 1911–1913B. (T) J. I. Handley Co., 1913–1914B.

26. AMERICAN ELECTRIC (1899–1901). American Elec. V. Co., Chicago, 1899–1901D.

27. AMERICAN MERCEDES (1900–1907). Daimler Mfg. Co., Long Island City, N.Y., E1900–1907D. Burned out.

28. AMERICAN MORS (1906–1909). St. Louis Car Co., St. Louis E1906–1911C. (N) STANDARD SIX (see 779). (F) KOBUSCH (see 462).

29. AMERICAN SIMPLEX (1905–1911). Simplex M. Co.,

Mishawaka, Ind., 1905–1912. (N) AMPLEX (see 32).

American Voiturette Co. (see 123).

30. AMERICAR (1940–1941). Willys–Overland Co. (see 887).

31. AMES (1910–1915). Ames M. C. Co., Owensboro, Ky., E1910–1915.

32. AMPLEX (1912–1913). Simplex M. Co., Mishawaka, Ind., 1905–1912. (T) Amplex M. C. Co. 1912. (R) 1913. (F) AMERICAN SIMPLEX (see 29).

33. AMS–STERLING (1916–1917). Consolidated Ordnance Co., Amston, Conn., 1916–1917. (F) STERLING (see 792).

33A. AMX (1968–to date). American Ms. Corp.

34. ANDERSON (1907–1910)(E). Anderson Car. Co., Detroit, E1907–1923 (see 235).

35. ANDERSON (1908–*1910*). Anderson Car. Mfg. Co., Anderson, Ind., 1908–*1910*.

36. ANDERSON (1915–1925). Anderson M. Co., Rock Hill, S.C., 1915–1925B. (F) ROCK HILL (see 704).

Anger Engineering Co. (see 9).

Angus Auto. Co. (see 327).

37. ANHUT (1909–1910). Anhut M. C. Co., Detroit, 1909. (T) Barnes M. Co. 1910B.

Apex M. Corp. (see 4).

38. APPERSON (1902–1925). Apperson (Bros.) Auto. Co., Kokomo, Ind., 1902–1925B.

39. ARBENZ (1911–1918). Arbenz C. Co., Chillicothe, O., 1911–1918. (F) SCIOTOT (see 730).

40. ARDSLEY (1905–1906). Ardsley M. C. Co., Yonkers, N.Y., 1905–1906D.

41. ARGO (1915–1916). Argo M. Co., Jackson, Mich., E1915–1916. (T) Hackett M. C. Co. (see 362).
42. ARGO (1912–1917)(E). Argo E. V. Co., Saginaw, Mich., 1912–1917.
43. ARGONNE (1919–1920). Jersey City Machine Co., Newark, N.J., 1919–1920B.
44. ARIEL (1905–1906). Ariel M. C. Co., Boston, Mass., Bridgeport, Conn., 1905–1906. (T) MARYLAND (see 520).
    Associated Ms. Corp. (see 242, 423, 581).
    Atlanta M. C. Co. (see 880).
45. ATLAS (1907–1913). Atlas M. C. Co., Springfield, Mass., 1907–1913B. (T) Lyons–Atlas 1913 (see 503). (F) Knox M. Truck Co.
46. AUBURN (1903–1937). Auburn Auto. Co., Auburn, Ind., 1903–1937C (see 178, 254).
47. AULTMAN (1901(S). Aultman Co., Canton, O., 1901.
48. AURORA (1907–1908). Aurora M. Wks., North Aurora, Ill., 1907–1908B.
49. AUSTIN (1903–1917). Austin Auto. Co., Grand Rapids, Mich., 1903–1917.
50. AUSTIN BANTAM (1930–1936). American Austin C. Co., Butler, Pa. 1930–1936. (T) Bantam (see 64).
51. AUTO–BUG (1909–1910). Auto–Bug Co., Norwalk, O., 1909–1910. (T) Norwalk 1910 (see 590).
52. AUTOCAR (1899–1912). Autocar Co., Swissville, Ardmore, Pa., E1894–1912C—trucks. Merged with Pittsburgh M. V. Co., 1899.
    Auto. Co. of America (see 338).
53. AUTOMOBILE FORE–CARRIAGE (1900–1901). Auto. Fore–Carriage Co., New York, 1900–1901D.

Auto. Parts & Equipment Co. (see 824).

54. AUTOMOTOR (1901–1905). Automotor Co., Springfield, Mass., E1901–1905D. (F) METEOR (see 539).

Auto Vehicle Co. (see 826).

55. AVANTI (1962–1963). Studebaker Corp., South Bend, Ind. (see 802).

55A. AVANTI (1966–to date). Avanti M. Corp., South Bend, Ind., 1966–to date.

B

56. BABCOCK (1906–1912)(E). Babcock E. V. Co., Buffalo, N.Y., 1906–1912. (F) BUFFALO (see 107).

57. BABCOCK (1909–1913). H. H. Babcock Co., Watertown, N.Y., 1909–1913C.

58. BADGER (1909–1911). Badger M. C. Co., Columbus, O., 1909–1911D.

59. BAILEY (1907–1916)(E). S. R. Bailey & Co., Amesbury, Mass., E1907–1916.

60. BAILEY–PERKINS (1907–*1911*). Bailey–Perkins Auto. Co., Springfield, Mass., 1907–*1911*.

61. BAKER (1899–1917)(E). Baker M. V. Co., Cleveland, 1899–1915. Merged with Rauch & Lang (see 674).

62. BALDNER (1902–1903). Baldner M. V. Co., Xenia, O., 1902–1903D.

63. BALDWIN (1900–1901)(S). Baldwin Auto. Mfg. Co., Connellsville, Pa., 1900–1901B.

64. BANTAM (1936–1940). American Bantam C. Co., Butler, Pa., 1936–1940. (F) AUSTIN BANTAM (see 50).

65. BARLEY (1923–1924). Roamer M. C. Co., Kalamazoo, Mich., 1923–1924C—trucks. (F) ROAMER (see 702).

Barley Mfg. Co. (see 702).

66. BARNHART (1905). Warren Auto Co., Warren, Pa., 1905.

Barnes M. Co. (see 37).

Bartholomew Co., The (see 348).

67. BATES (1903–1905). Bates Auto. Co., Lansing, Mich., 1903–1905B.

68. BAUER (1914–1915). Bauer Machine Wks., Kansas City, Mo., 1913–1915C. (F) GLEASON (see 347).

69. BAY STATE (1906–1907). Bay State Auto. Co., Boston, Mass., 1906–1907B.

70. BAY STATE (1922–1926). R. H. Long Co., Framingham, Mass., 1922–1924. (R) 1923. (T) Bay State M. Co. 1924–1926B.

B.C.K. M. C. Co. (see 457).

Beardsley & Hubbs Mfg. Co. (see 214).

71. BEGGS (1918–1923). Beggs M. Co., Kansas City, Mo., 1918–1923B.

72. BELDEN (1907–1911). Belden M. C. Co., Pittsburgh, 1907–1911.

73. BELL (1915–1922). Bell M. C. Co., York, Pa., 1915–1922.

Bellefontaine Auto. Co. (see 828).

74. BELMONT (1910). Belmont Auto. Mfg. Co., New Haven, Conn., 1910B.

75. BENDIX (1907–1909). Bendix Co., Chicago, Logansport, Ind., 1907–1909. (F) TRIUMPH (see 833).

76. BENHAM (1914). Benham Mfg. Co., Detroit, 1914B. (A) S & M M. Co., 1914 (see 722).

77. BEN HUR (1917). Ben Hur M. Co., Cleveland, 1917B.

78. BENNER (1908–*1910*). Benner M. C. Co., New York, 1908–*1910*.

79. BERG (1902–1904). Berg Auto. Co., New York, Cleveland, 1902–1904. (T) WORTHINGTON, 1904 (see 897).

80. BERGDOLL (1910–1913). Louis J. Bergdoll M. Co., Philadelphia, 1910–1913B.

81. BERKSHIRE (1905–1912). Berkshire (Auto.) M. C. Co., Pittsfield, Cambridge, Mass., 1905–1912B. (R) 1907.

82. BERLIET (1906–1909). American Locomotive Co., Providence, R.I., 1906–1913C. (N) ALCO, 1909 (see 15).

83. BERTOLET (1908–1912). Bertolet M. C. Co., Reading, Pa., 1908–1912.

84. BETHLEHEM (1907–1908). Bethlehem Auto. Co., Bethlehem, Pa., 1907–1908B.

85. BEVERLEY (1903–1907). Upton Machinery Co., Beverley, Mass., E1903–1905. (T) Beverley Mfg. Co., 1905–1907C. (T) CAMERON, 1908 (see 118).

86. BIDDLE (1915–1922). Biddle M. C. Co., Philadelphia, New York, 1915–1921R. (T) Biddle–Crane M. C. Co., 1922.

87. BIMEL (1916–1917). Bimel (Buggy) Auto. Co., Sydney, O., E1915–1917. (F) ELCO (see 270).

88. BIRCH (1916–1923). Birch M. Corp., Chicago, 1916–1923.

89. BLACK CROW (1907–1911). Black Mfg. Co., Chicago, 1907–1911. (T) Crow M. C. Co. (see 200).
Black Diamond Co. (see 106).

90. BLACK HAWK (1902–1903). Clark Mfg. Co., Moline, Ill., E1902–1903.

91. BLISS (1906). E. W. Bliss & Co., Brooklyn, N.Y., E1906C—presses.

92. B.L.M. (1906–1907). B.L.M. M. C. & Equipment Co., Brooklyn, N.Y., 1906–1907B.

93. BLOMSTROM (1907–1909). Blomstrom Mfg. Co., Detroit, 1907–1909.
    Blomstrom M. C. Co., C.H. (see 665).
    Blood Bros. Machine Co. (see 180).

94. BORLAND (1912–1914)(E). Borland–Grannis Co., Chicago, 1912–1914.

95. BOSS (1903–*1909*)(S). Boss Knitting Machine Wks., Reading, Pa., E1903–*1909*.

96. BOUR–DAVIS (1916–1923). Bour–Davis M. C. Co., Detroit, 1916–1918. (T) Louisiana M. C. Co., Shreveport, La., 1918. (R) 1921. (T) Ponder M. C. Co., Shreveport, 1923 (see 643).

97. BRAMWELL (1902–1904). Bramwell M. Co., Boston, Mass., E1902–1904. (T) SPRINGFIELD 1904 (see 771).

98. BRAZIER (1902–1904). H. Bartol Brazier, Philadelphia, 1902–1904.

99. BRECHT (1901–1902(S). Brecht Auto. Co., St. Louis, 1901–1902.

100. BREW–HATCHER (1904–1905). Brew–Hatcher Co., Cleveland, 1904–1905C.

101. BREWSTER (1915–1925). Brewster & Co., Long Island City, N.Y., E1915–1925C—bodies.

102. BRIGGS–DETROITER (1911–1915). Briggs–Detroiter Co., Detroit, 1911–1915B. (T) Detroiter M. C. Co., 1915 (see 236).

103. BRISCOE (1914–1921). Briscoe M. Co., Jackson, Mich., 1914–1921. (T) EARL, 1921 (see 263).

Bristol Engineering Co. (see 17).

104. BROC (1909–1917)(E). The Broc Car. & V. Co., Cleveland, 1909–1917.

Brown Machine Co., J. (see 117).

Brunn's E. V. Co. (see 149).

105. BRUSH (1907–1912). Brush Runabout Co., Detroit, 1907–1912B. (T) United States M. Co., 1910.

Buckeye Mfg. Co. (see 469).

106. BUCKMOBILE (1903–1905). Buckmobile Co., Utica, N.Y., 1903–1904. (N) Black Diamond Co., Geneva, N.Y., 1904–1905B.

Buffalo Auto. & Auto–Bi Co. (see 819).

107. BUFFALO (1900–1906)(E). Buffalo Elec. C. Co., Buffalo, N.Y., 1900–1906. (T) BABCOCK, 1906 (see 56).

108. BUFFUM (1900–1906). H. H. Buffum & Co., Abington, Mass., 1900–1906B.

109. BUGGYABOUT (1906–1908)(HW). Hatfield (Auto. Mfg.) M. V. Co., Cortland, N.Y., Miamisburg, O., 1906–1908. (T) KAUFFMAN (see 439).

110. BUGGYCAR (1908–1909)(HW). The Buggycar Co., Cincinnati, O., 1908–1909. (F) POSTAL (see 653).

111. BUGMOBILE (1907–*1909*). Bugmobile Co. of America, Chicago, 1907–*1909*.

112. BUICK (1903–to date). Buick M. Co., Flint, Mich., 1903–1917. (T) Gen. Ms., 1908. Gen. Ms., Division, 1917.

113. BURDICK (1909–1911). Burdick M. C. Co., Eau Claire, Wis., 1909–1911.

114. BURG (1910–*1913*). L. Burg Car. Co., Dallas City, Ill., 1910–*1913*.
    Burtt Mfg. Co. (see 121).
115. BYRIDER (1907–*1908*)(E). Byrider Elec. Auto. Co., Cleveland, 1907–*1908*.

C

116. CADILLAC (1902–to date). Cadillac Auto. Co., Detroit, 1902–1905. Cadillac M. C. Co., 1905–1917. (T) Gen. Ms. 1908; Gen. Ms. Division, 1917.
117. CAMERON (1902–1905). United M. Corp., Pawtucket, R.I., 1902–1904. (T) Brown Machine Co., 1904–1905C.
118. CAMERON (1907–1919). Cameron C. Co., Beverley, Mass., 1907. (A) Beverley Mfg. Co., 1908. (R) 1912. (Rg) Cameron Mfg. Co., New Haven, Conn., 1913–1914B. (Rg) Cameron Ms. Corp., Norwalk, Conn., 1916. (Rg) Cameron Corp., 1919C—engines.
119. CAMPBELL (1918–1919). Campbell M. C. Co., Kingston, N.Y., 1918–1919B. (F) EMERSON (see 276).
120. CANDA (1900–1901). Canda Mfg. Co., Carteret, N.J., 1900–1901D.
121. CANNON (1904–1905). Burtt Mfg. Co., Kalamazoo, Mich., E1904–1905C.
122. CARHARTT (1910–1912). Carhartt Auto. Corp., Detroit, 1910–1912.
123. CARNATION (1913–1914). American Voiturette Co., Detroit, 1913R. (N) Car–Nation M. C. Co., Detroit, 1914B.

Carpenter, M. H. (see 631).

Carter M. C. Co. (see 868).

124. CARTERCAR (1906–1915). Motorcar Co., Detroit, 1906–1908. (N) Cartercar Co., Pontiac, Mich., 1908. (T) Gen. Ms., 1910.

125. CASE (1910–1927). Case Threshing Machine Co., J. I., Racine, Wis., E1910–1927C. (A) PIERCE–RACINE, 1910 (see 635).

126. CENTAUR (1902–1903)(E). Centaur M. V. Co., Buffalo, N.Y., 1902–1903D.

127. CENTURY (1911–1914)(E). Century Elec. V. Co., Detroit, 1911–1914.

128. CENTURY (1900–1904)(S,E,G). Century M. V. Co., Syracuse, N.Y., 1900–1904B.

129. C–F (1907–*1909*). Cornish–Friedberg M. C. Co., Chicago, E1907–*1909*.

130. CHADWICK (1905–1917). Fairmont Engineering Co., Philadelphia, 1905–1907. (T) Chadwick Engineering Wks., Pottstown, Pa., 1907–1917.

131. CHALFANT (1906–1912). Chalfant M. C. Co., Lenover, Pa., 1906–1912.

132. CHALMERS–(DETROIT) (1908–1910); CHALMERS (1911–1923). Chalmers (Detroit) M. Co., 1908–1923. (T) Maxwell M. Corp., 1921. (F) THOMAS–DETROIT (see 820).

133. CHAMPION (1908–*1910*)(HW). Famous Mfg. Co., Chicago, 1908–*1910*.

134. CHANDLER (1913–1928). Chandler M. C. Co., Cleveland, 1913–1926. Chandler–Cleveland Ms. Corp. (merger with Cleveland Auto. Co.) 1926. (T) Hupp M. C. Corp., 1928.

135. CHECKER (1955–to date). Checker Cab Mfg. Co., Kalamazoo, Mich., E1955–to date.

Chelsea Mfg. Co. (see 874).

136. CHEVELLE (1964–to date). Gen. Ms. Corp., Chevrolet Division.

137. CHEVROLET (1911–to date). Chevrolet M. C. Co., Flint, Mich., 1911–1918. (A) Little M. C. Co., 1913. (A) Gen. Ms., 1916. (T) Gen. Ms., 1918: Gen. Ms. Division, 1918.

138. CHEVY II (1961–to date). Gen. Ms. Corp., Chevrolet Division. (N) NOVA, 1968.

139. CHICAGO (1917–1918). Pan–American Ms. Corp., Chicago, 1917–1921. (N) PAN–AMERICAN (see 616).

140. CHICAGO ELECTRIC (1913–1917). Chicago Elec. M. C. Co., Chicago, 1913–1917.

Chicago Coach & Car. Co. (see 253).

141. CHIEF (1908–1909). Chief Mfg. Co., Buffalo, N.Y., 1908–*1909*.

Christopher Bros. (see 832).

142. CHRYSLER (1924–to date). Chrysler (M.) Corp., Detroit, 1924–to date. (A) Maxwell M. Corp., 1925. (A) Dodge Bros., 1928. (See DE SOTO—232, DODGE—245, IMPERIAL—417, PLYMOUTH—640, VALIANT—846.)

143. CHURCH (1913). Church M. C. Co., Chicago, 1913.

144. CHURCH–ADRIAN (1902–1903). Church Mfg. Co., Adrian, Mich., 1902–1903D.

145. CHURCH–FIELD (1913)(E). Church–Field M. Co., Sibley, Mich., 1913B.

146. CINO (1909–1913). Haberer & Co., Cincinnati, 1909–1913C.

147. CLARK (1898–1910)(S). Edward S. Clark, Boston, Mass., 1898–1910C—trucks.

148. CLARK (1908–1909)(E). Allen & Clark Co., Toledo, 1908–1909.

149. CLARK (1906–1910)(E). Brunn's Elec. V. Co., Buffalo, N.Y., E1906–1910.

Clark Mfg. Co. (see 90).

150. CLARK (1909–1912). Clark M. C. Co., Shelbyville, Ind., 1909–1913. (R) 1912. (T) METEOR, 1913 (see 537).

Clarke–Carter Auto. Co. (see 209).

151. CLARK–HATFIELD (1908–1909). Clark--Hatfield Auto. Co., Oshkosh, Wis., 1908–1909.

152. CLARKMOBILE (1903–1906). Clarkmobile Co., Lansing, Mich., 1903–1906. (T) DEERE–CLARK, 1906 (see 222).

Cleburne M. C. Mfg. Co. (see 500).

153. CLEVELAND (1919–1926). Cleveland Auto. Co., Cleveland, 1919–1926. (T) CHANDLER, 1926 (see 134).

154. CLEVELAND (1908–1909). Cleveland Auto Cab Co., Geneva, O., 1908–1909. (T) Ewing Auto. Co., 1909 (see 288).

155. CLEVELAND (1902–1908). Cleveland M. C. Co., Cleveland, New York, 1902–1908D.

156. CLIMBER (1921–1923). Climber M. Corp., Little Rock, Ark., 1921–1923B.

157. CLUB CAR (1910–1911). Club Car Co. of America, New York, 1910–1911. Built by Merchant & Evans, Philadelphia.

158. COATES–GOSHEN (1908–1911). Coates–Goshen Auto. Co., Goshen, N.Y., 1908–1911B.

159. COLBURN (1907–1912). Colburn Auto. Co., Denver, 1907–1912C.

160. COLBY (1911–1914). Colby M. Co., Mason City, Ia., 1911–1914. (A) MIDLAND, 1913 (see 544).

161. COLE (1909–1924). Cole M. C. Co., Indianapolis, E1909–1924D.

162. COLT (1907). Colt Runabout Co., Yonkers, N.Y., 1907B.

Columbia Elec. Co. (see 480).

163. COLUMBIA (1895–1912). Pope Mfg. Co., Hartford, Conn., 1895–1899. (T) Elec. V. Co., 1899–1907B. (T) Columbia M. C. Co., 1909–1912B. (T) United States M. Co., 1910.

164. COLUMBIA (1916–1924). Columbia Ms. Co., Detroit, 1916–1924B. (A) LIBERTY, 1923 (see 486).

Columbus Buggy Co. (see 305).

Columbus M. V. Co. (see 725).

Commercial M. Co. (see 615).

165. COMET (1917–1922). Comet Auto. Co., Decatur, Ill., 1917–1922B.

166. COMET (1960–1966). Ford Motor Co.

167. COMMONWEALTH (1917–1922). Commonwealth Ms. Co., Chicago, 1917–1923B. (N) GOODSPEED, 1922 (see 350). (F) PARTIN–PALMER (see 618).

168. COMPOUND (1903–1907). Eisenhut Horseless Vehicle Co., Middletown, Conn., 1903–1907B.

Connecticut Auto Wks. (see 329).

169. CONOVER (1906–1908). Conover M. C. Co., Paterson, N.J., 1906–1908D.

170. CONRAD (1900–1903)(S,G). Conrad M. Car. Co., Buffalo, N.Y., 1900–1903B.

Consolidated Mfg. Co. (see 898).

Consolidated M. Co. (see 571).

Consolidated Ordnance Co. (see 33).

171. CONTINENTAL (1907–1908). University Auto. Co., New Haven, Conn., 1907. (T) Continental Auto. Mfg. Co., 1907–1908D.

172. CONTINENTAL (1909–1912). Indiana M. & Mfg. Co., Franklin, Ind., 1909–1912B.

173. CONTINENTAL (1939–1948; 1955–to date). Ford M. Co. Also called LINCOLN CONTINENTAL.

174. CONTINENTAL (1933–1934). Continental DeVaux Co., Detroit, 1933. (T) Continental Auto. Co., 1934. (F) DEVAUX (see 237).

Cook M. V. Co. (see 752).

175. COPPOCK (1907–1908). Coppock M. C. Co., Decatur, Ind., 1907–1909. (T) Decatur M. C. Co. 1909C— trucks.

176. CORBIN (1902–1912). Corbin M. V. Co., New Britain, Conn., 1902–1912C.

177. CORBITT (1912–1915). Corbitt Auto. Co., Henderson, N.C., 1912–1915C—trucks.

178. CORD (1929–1932; 1936–1937). Auburn Auto. Co., Auburn, Ind., 1903–1937 (see 46).

178A. CORD (1965–1966). Cord Auto. Co., Tulsa, Okla., 1965–1966B.

179. CORINTHIAN (1921–1922). Corinthian Ms., Inc., Philadelphia, 1921–1922.

180. CORNELIAN (1915). Blood Bros. Machine Co., Allegan, Mich., E1915C.

Cornish–Friedberg M. C. Co. (see 129).

181. CORREJA (1906–1913). Vanderwater & Co., Elizabeth, N.J., E1908–1913C.

Cortland Cart & Car. Co. (see 376).

182. CORVAIR (1959–1969). Gen. Ms. Corp., Chevrolet Division.

183. CORVETTE (1952–to date). Gen. Ms. Corp., Chevrolet Division.

Corwin Mfg. Co. (see 337).

184. COSMOPOLITAN (1907–1910)(HW). D. W. Haydock Auto. Mfg. Co., St. Louis, 1907–1910.

185. COUNTRY CLUB (1903–1904). Country Club Car Co., Boston, Mass., 1903–1904.

186. COURIER (1902–1904). Sandusky Auto. Co., Sandusky, O., 1902–1904B.

187. COURIER (1922–1923). Courier Ms. Co., Sandusky, O., 1922–1923B. (F) MAIBOHM (see 507).

188. COURIER (1909–1912). Courier M. C. Co., Dayton, O., 1909–1912B. (T) United States M. Co., 1910.

189. COVERT (1903–1907). Covert (& Co., B. V.) M. V. Co., Lockport, N.Y., E1903–1907C.

190. CRAIG–TOLEDO (1906–1907). Craig–Toledo M. Co., Dundee, Mich., 1906–1907B. (F) Maumee M. C. Wks., 1906 (see 894).

191. CRANE (1913–1915). Crane M. C. Co., Bayonne, N.J., 1913–1915. (T) CRANE–SIMPLEX (see 193).

192. CRANE & BREED (1912). Crane & Breed Mfg. Co., Cincinnati, O., E1912C—trucks.

193. CRANE–SIMPLEX (1916–1917; 1923–1924). Simplex Auto. Co., Long Island City, N.Y., 1907–1917. (A) Crane M. C. Co., 1915; Crane–Simplex Co. of N.Y.C., Inc., 1923–1924.

194. CRAWFORD (1905–1923). Crawford Auto. Co., Hagerstown, Md., 1905–1923. (T) M. P. Moller & Co., 1923 (see 211).

195. CRESCENT (1907–1908). Crescent M. C. Co., Detroit, 1907–1908D.
Crescent M. Co. (see 594).
Crescent M. C. Co. (see 812).

196. CRESTMOBILE (1900–1904). Crest Mfg. Co., Dorchester, Mass., E1900–1904. (T) Alden Sampson, 1905 (see 723).

197. CROMPTON (1903–1905). Crompton M. Wks., Worcester, Mass., 1903–1905.

198. CROSLEY (1939–1952). Crosley Corp., Cincinnati, 1939–1952. (T) Gen. Tire & Rubber Co., 1952.

199. CROUCH (1900). Crouch Auto. Mfg. & Trans. Co., Baltimore, Md., 1900.

200. CROW–ELKHART (1911–1922). Crow M. (Car) Co., Elkhart, Ind., 1911–1922B. (Rg) 1916. (F) Black Mfg. Co. (see 89).

201. CROWN (1904–1907)(HW). Detroit Auto. V. Co., Detroit, Romeo, Mich., 1904–1907B.

202. CROWN (1913–1914). Crown M. C. Co., Louisville, Ky., 1913–1914. (T) HERCULES (see 387). (F) JONZ (see 434).

203. CROWN (1908–1910). Crown M. V. Co., Amesbury, Mass., 1908–1910.

204. CROWTHER–DURYEA (1917). Crowther–Duryea M. Co., Rochester, N.Y., 1917B.

205. CROXTON (1911–1914). Croxton M. Co., Washington, Pa., 1911–1914. (A) Croxton–Keeton, 1911 (see 206).

206. CROXTON–KEETON (1909–1911). Croxton–Keeton M. C. Co., Massillon, O., 1909–1911. (T) Croxton, 1911. (F) JEWEL (see 429).

207. CULVER (1905–1909). Practical Auto Co., Genoa, Ill., 1905–1909.

Cummins Auto Sales Co. (see 562).

208. CUNNINGHAM (1910–1934). James Cunningham & Sons, Rochester, N.Y., E1910–1934C—bodies.

209. CUTTING (1910–1913). Clarke–Carter Auto. Co., Jackson, Mich., 1910–1912. (T) Cutting M. C. Co., 1912–1913B.

210. C.V.I. (1907–1908). C.V.I. M. C. Co., Jackson, Mich., 1907–1908D.

D

211. DAGMAR (1922–1926). Crawford Auto. Co., Hagerstown, Md., 1922–1923. (T) M. P. Moller M. Co., 1923 (see 292, 557).

Daimler Mfg. Co. (see 27).

212. DANIELS (1915–1923). Daniels M. (Car) Co., Reading, Pa., 1915–1923B.

213. DARBY (1909–1910). Darby M. C. Co., St. Louis, 1909–1910D.

214. DARLING (1900–1902). Beardsley & Hubbs Mfg. Co., Shelby, O., E1900–1902. (Rg) Shelby M. C. Co., 1902 (see 744).

215. DARROW (1903–1904). Stuart Darrow, Oswego, N.Y., 1903–1904.

216. DAVIS (1910–1928). Geo. W. Davis Car. Co., Richmond, Ind., 1910–1912. (Rg) Davis M. C. Co., 1912–1928.

217. DAWSON (1904). J. H. Dawson Machinery Co., Chicago, E1904B.

Dayton M. C. Co. (see 799).

218. DEAL (1908–1911). Deal (Buggy) M. V. Co., (The), Jonesville, Mich., 1908–1911.

219. DEARBORN (1910–1911). J & M M. C. Co., Lawrenceburg, Ind. 1909–1911B. (N) JAMES 1911 (see 424). (F) J & M (see 425).

220. DECKER (1902–1903). Decker Automatic Tel. Exchange Co., Oswego, N.Y., E1902–1903C.

221. DEDION BOUTON (1900–1904). DeDion Bouton Motorette Co., Brooklyn, N.Y., 1900–1904B.

222. DEERE–CLARK (1906–1907). Deere–Clark M. C. Co., Moline, Ill., 1906–1907B. (A) Clarkmobile Co., 1906 (see 152).

223. DEERING MAGNETIC (1918). Deering Magnetic M. Corp., Chicago, 1918.

224. DELLING (1924–1929)(S). Delling Ms. Corp., Collingswood, N.J., 1924–1929C—buses.

225. DELUXE (1906–1909). DeLuxe M. C. Co., Detroit, 1906–1909. (A) Blomstrom, 1906 (see 665). (T) E–M–F Co., 1909 (see 277).

226. DEMOTCAR (1909–1913). Demotcar Co., Detroit, 1909–1913B. (R) 1910.

227. DEMOTTE (1904). Demotte M. C. Co., Philadelphia, 1904.

228. DERAIN (1910). Derain M. Co., Cleveland, 1910.

229. DESBERON (1901). Desberon M. C. Co., New York, 1901.

DeSchaum M. Syndicate (see 739).

230. DE SHAW (1909). De Shaw M. Co., Evergreen, L.I., N.Y., 1909.

231. DE SOTO (1913–1916). De Soto M. C. Co., Auburn, Ind., 1913–1916. ZIMMERMAN car under De Soto nameplate (see 901).

232. DE SOTO (1928–1960). De Soto M. Corp., Detroit, Chrysler subsidiary.

233. DETAMBLE (1909–1912). Detamble M. Co., Anderson, Ind., 1909–1912B.

Detroit Auto. Mfg. Co. (see 473).

Detroit Auto. Vehicle Co. (see 201).

234. DETROIT–DEARBORN (1909–1910). Detroit–Dearborn M. C. Co., Detroit, 1909–1910B.

235. DETROIT ELECTRIC (1907–1923). Anderson Car. Co., Detroit, 1907–1923 (see 35).

Detroit–Oxford Mfg. Co. (see 608).

Detroit Steam Ms. Co. (see 244).

236. DETROITER (1915–1917). Detroiter M. C. Co., Detroit, 1915–1917B. (F) BRIGGS–DETROITER (see 102).

237. DEVAUX (1931–1933). DeVaux–Hall Ms., Inc., Oakland, Cal., 1931–1933. (A) Durant M. Co. of California, 1930. (R) 1932. (T) Continental-DeVaux Co., 1933. (see 174).

Diamond Auto. Co. (see 666).

238. DIAMOND T (1907–1911). Diamond T M. C. Co., Chicago, 1907–1911C—trucks.

239. DIANA (1925–1928). Moon M. C. Co., St. Louis, E1905–1931B (see 564).

240. DILE (1914–1916). Dile M. C. Co., Reading, Pa., 1914–1916B.

241. DISPATCH (1912–1916). Dispatch M. C. Co., Minneapolis, Minn., 1912–1916C—trucks.

242. DIXIE FLYER (1916–1923). Dixie M. C. Co., Louisville, Ky., 1916–1919. (T) Kentucky Wagon Mfg. Co., 1919–1922 (see 387). (T) Associated Ms. Corp., 1922B (see 581).

243. DIXIE TOURIST (1908–1910). Southern M. C. Co., Houston, Tex., 1908–*1910*.

244. DOBLE (1917; 1923–1924)(S). General Engineering Co., Detroit, 1917. Detroit Steam Ms. Co., Detroit; Doble Steam Ms. Corp., Emeryville, Cal., *1924*.

245. DODGE (1914–to date). Dodge Bros., Detroit, 1914–1928. (T) Dillon, Read & Co., 1925. (T) Chrysler Corp., 1928.

246. DOLSON (1904–1907). J. L. Dolson & Sons, Charlotte, Mich., E1904. (N) Dolson Auto. Co., 1905–1907B.

247. DORRIS (1905–1924). Dorris M. C. Co., St. Louis, 1905–1924D.

248. DORT (1915–1924). Dort M. C. Co., Flint, Mich., 1915–1924.

249. DOUGLAS (1917–1919). Douglas M. Corp., Omaha, Neb., 1917–1919C—trucks.

250. DRAGON (1906–1908). Dragon (Auto) M. Co., Philadelphia, 1906–1908B.

251. DREXEL (1917). Drexel M. C. Co., Chicago, 1917B. (F) FARMACK (see 297).

252. DRIGGS (1921–1923). Driggs Ordnance & Mfg. Co., New Haven, Conn., 1921–1923. (R) 1923.

253. DUER (1907–1909). Chicago Coach & Car. Co., Chicago, 1907–1909C—trucks.

254. DUESENBERG (1921–1937). Duesenberg Auto. & Ms.

Co., Indianapolis, 1921–1925. (R) 1923. (Rg) Duesenberg Ms. Co., 1925. (Rg) Duesenberg, Inc., 1926. (T) Auburn Auto. Co., 1927.

255. DUPLEX (1908–*1909*). Duplex M. C. Co., Chicago, 1908–*1909*.

256. DUPONT (1919–1933). DuPont Ms., Inc., Moore, Pa., Wilmington, Del., Springfield, Mass., 1919–1933B.

257. DUQUESNE (1903–1906). Duquesne Construction Co., Buffalo, Jamestown, N.Y., 1903–1906B.

Durant Ms., Inc., New York, 1921–1932 (see DURANT —258, FLINT—308, LOCOMOBILE—492, PRINCETON —661, SHERIDAN—745, STAR—784).

258. DURANT (1921–1926; 1928–1931). Durant M. Co. of Michigan, Lansing, 1921–1932R. Durant M. Co. of N.J., Elizabeth, 1928–1931R.

259. DUROCAR (1907–*1910*). Durocar Mfg. Co., Los Angeles, E1907–*1910*.

260. DURYEA (1896–1907). Duryea M. Wagon Co., Springfield, Mass., 1896–1897D. Duryea Mfg. Co., Peoria, Ill., 1897–1900. (T) Duryea Power Co., Reading, Pa., 1900–1907B.

261. DYKE (1903–1904). A. L. Dyke, St. Louis, E1903–1904C.

E

262. EARL (1906–1908). Earl M. C. Co., Kenosha, Wis., 1906–1908B.

263. EARL (1921–1923). Earl Ms., Inc., Jackson, Mich., 1921–1923B. (F) BRISCOE (see 103).

Easton Machine Co. (see 569).

264. ECLIPSE (1902–1903)(S). Eclipse Auto. Co., Boston, 1902–1903D.

265. ECONOMY (1908–*1909*)(IIW). Economy M. Buggy Co., Fort Wayne, Ind., 1908–*1909*.

266. ECONOMY (1916–1918). Economy M. Co., Tiffin, O., 1916–1918.

267. EDSEL (1957–1959). Ford M. Co.

268. EDWARDS–KNIGHT (1912–1913). Edwards M. C. Co., Long Island City, N.Y., 1912–1913. (T) Willys–Overland Co., 1913 (see 887).

   E. H. V. Co. (Eisenhut Horseless V. Co.), Middletown, Conn. (see 168).

269. ELCAR (1915–1931). Elkhart Car. & M. C. Co., Elkhart, Ind., 1915–1923. (N) Elcar M. Co., 1923–1931. (F) PRATT (see 654).

270. ELCO (1915–1916). Bimel (Buggy) Auto. Co., Sydney, O., E1915–1917. (N) BIMEL, 1916 (see 87).

271. ELDRIDGE (1903–1906). National Sewing Machine Co., Belvidere, Ill., E1902–1906C. (F) FRIEDMAN (see 321).

   Electric Vehicle Co. (see 163, 568, 699).

272. ELGIN (1915–1924). Elgin M. C. Co., Chicago, 1915–1923. (A) NEW ERA, 1916 (see 584). (R) 1922. (Rg) Elgin Ms., Inc., 1923–1924.

273. ELITE (1901). D. B. Smith & Co., Utica, N.Y., 1901.
   Elkhart Carriage & Harness Mfg. Co. (see 654, 655).
   Elkhart M. C. Co. (see 793).

274. ELMORE (1901–1912). Elmore Mfg. Co., Clyde, O., 1901–1912. (T) Gen. Ms. Corp., 1909.

275. EMANCIPATOR (1909). Emancipator Auto Co., Chicago, 1909.

276. EMERSON (1917–1918). Emerson M. Co., Kingston, N.Y., 1917R. (T) CAMPBELL (see 119).
277. E–M–F (1908–1912). Everitt–Metzger–Flanders Co., Detroit, 1908–1910. (A) Northern Mfg. Co., Wayne Auto. Co., 1908. (A) DeLuxe M. C. Co., 1909. Sold by Studebaker Bros., 1908–1909. (T) Studebaker, 1910. Also called STUDEBAKER E–M–F (see 802).
278. EMPIRE (1909–1918). Empire M. C. Co., Indianapolis, 1909–1918D.
279. ENGER (1909–1917). Enger M. C. Co., Cincinnati, 1909–1917B.
280. ERSKINE (1926–1930). Studebaker Corp. of America (see 802).
281. Essex (1906–1908)(S). Essex M. C. Co., Boston, 1906–1908D.
282. ESSEX (1918–1933). Essex Ms., Detroit, 1918–1926. (T) Hudson M. C. Co., 1922.
283. EUCLID (1907). Euclid M. C. Co., Cleveland, 1907.
284. EUREKA (1907–1909). Eureka M. Buggy Mfg. Co., St. Louis, 1907–1909.
285. EUREKA (1908). Eureka M. Buggy Co., Beavertown, Pa., 1908. (T) KEARNS 1908 (see 440).
Evansville Auto. Co. (see 751, 829).
286. EVERITT (1909–1912). Metzger M. Co., Detroit, 1909–1912. (Rg) Everitt M. C. Co., 1912. (T) FLANDERS 1912 (see 306).
287. EVERYBODY'S (1907–1909). Everybody's M. C. Mfg. Co., St. Louis, 1907–1909.
288. EWING (1909–1910). Ewing Auto. Co., Geneva, O.,

1909–1910. (T) Gen. Ms. Co., 1909. (F) CLEVE-
LAND (see 154).

288A. EXCALIBUR SSK (1965–to date). Brooks Stevens
Assoc., S.S. Automobiles, Inc., Milwaukee, 1965–
to date.

F

289. FAGEOL (1917). Fageol Ms. Co., Oakland, Cal., 1917C
—buses.

Fairmont Engineering Co. (see 130).

290. FAL (1909–1914). F.A.L. Motor Co., Chicago, 1909–
1914B. (F) RELIABLE–DAYTON (see 688).

291. FALCON (1908–1910). Larsen Machine Co., Chicago,
E1908. (T) Falcon Engineering Co., 1908–1910.

292. FALCON (1921–1922). M. P. Moller M. Co., Lewistown, Pa., 1920–1926. (F) MOLLER (see 211, 557).

293. FALCON (1921). Halladay Ms. Corp., Newark, O.,
1917–1922B. (F) HALLADAY (see 366). (N) HALLA-
DAY, 1922.

294. FALCON (1959–1969). Ford M. Co.

295. FALCON–KNIGHT (1927–1928). Falcon Ms. Corp., Detroit, 1927–1928. Famous Mfg. Co. (see 133).

296. FANNING (1902–1903)(E). F. J. Fanning Mfg. Co.,
Chicago, 1902–1903D.

297. FARMACK (1915–1916). Farmack M. C. Corp., Chicago, 1915–1916. (T) DREXEL (see 251).

298. FARMERS (1907–1912). International Harvester Co.,
Chicago, E1907–1912C—trucks. Also INTERNA-
TIONAL and I.H.C.

299. FEDERAL (1907–1908)(HW). Federal Auto. Co., Chi-

cago, 1907. (T) Rockford Auto. & Engineering Co., Rockford, Ill., 1908.

300. FEE (1908–1909). Fee M. C. Co., Detroit, 1908–1909.

301. FERGUS (1919–1921). Fergus Ms. of America, Inc., Newark, N.J., 1919–1922.

302. FERRIS (1920–1921). Ohio M. V. Co., Cleveland, 1920–1921B.

303. FIAT (1910–1915). Fiat Auto. Co., Poughkeepsie, N.Y., 1910–1915D.

304. FINDLAY (1910–1911). Findlay Car. Co., Findlay, O., 1910–1911B.

305. FIRESTONE–COLUMBUS (1903–1915)(E,G). Columbus Buggy Co., Columbus, O., 1903–1913. (R) 1913. (T) New Columbus Buggy Co., 1914–1915B.

306. FLANDERS (1912). Flanders M. Co., Detroit, 1912. (T) United States M. Co., 1912.

307. FLANDERS (1910–1912). Everitt–Metzger–Flanders Co., Detroit, 1908–1910. (T) Studebaker Bros. Mfg. Co., 1910 (see 802).

308. FLINT (1923–1927). Durant M. Co. of Mich., Flint, Mich., 1922–1932B.

309. FLINT (1902–1903). Flint Auto. Co., Flint, Mich., 1902–1903D.

310. FORD (1903–to date). Ford M. Co., Detroit, 1903–to date. (See COMET—166, CONTINENTAL—173, EDSEL—267, FALCON—294, LINCOLN—488, MAVERICK 522A, MERCURY—533, MUSTANG—576, THUNDERBIRD—821).

Forest City M. C. Co. (see 429).

Fort Pitt Mfg. Co. (see 639).

311. FOSTER (1900–1903)(S). Foster & Co., Rochester,

N.Y., 1900. (N) Foster Auto. Mfg. Co., 1900–1903B.

312. FOSTORIA (1916). Fostoria Light Car Co., Fostoria, O., 1916.

313. FOSTORIA (1906–1907). Fostoria M. C. Co., Fostoria, O., 1906–1907D. (F) OXFORD (see 608).

314. FOURNIER SEARCHMONT (1903). Fournier Searchmont Auto. Co., Philadelphia, 1903. (F) SEARCHMONT (see 732).

Four Traction Auto. Co. (see 438).

Four Wheel Drive Auto. Co. (see 330).

315. FOX (1922–1923). Fox M. Co., Philadelphia, 1922–1923B.

316. FRANKLIN (1901–1934). H. H. Franklin Mfg. Co., Syracuse, N.Y., E1901–1934B.

317. FRAYER–MILLER (1904–1910). Oscar Lear Auto. Co., Columbus, O., 1904–1910. (R) 1909. (T) Kelly–Springfield Co., 1910.

318. FRAZER (1946–1951). Kaiser–Frazer Co., Detroit, 1946–1953C (see 436).

319. FREDONIA (1902–1904). Fredonia Mfg. Co., Youngstown, O., 1902–1904B.

320. FREEMONT (1920–1922). Freemont M. Corp., Freemont, O., 1920–1922C—trucks.

321. FRIEDMAN (1900–1903). Friedman Auto. Co., Chicago, 1900–1903. Built by Nat. Sewing Machine Co., 1902–1903. (T) N. S. M. Co., 1903. (N) ELDRIDGE, 1903 (see 271).

322. FRIEND (1920–1922). Friend M. Corp., Pontiac, Mich., 1920–1922B. (R) 1921. (F) OLYMPIAN (see 598).

323. FRITCHLE (1907–1917; 1920)(E). Fritchle (Auto & Battery) Elec. Co., Denver, 1907–*1920*.

324. FRONTENAC (1906–1913). Abendroth & Root Mfg. Co., Newburg, N.Y., E1906–1913C—trucks.

325. F.R.P. (1914–1917). Findley Robertson Porter Co., Port Jefferson, L.I., N.Y., 1914–1917.

326. F–S (1911–1912). F–S Ms. Co., Milwaukee, 1911–1912C—trucks. (F) PETREL (see 629).

327. FULLER (1908–*1911*). Angus Auto. Co., Angus, Neb., 1908–*1911*.

328. FULLER (1909–1911). Fuller Buggy Co., Jackson, Mich., 1909–1911C—trucks.

329. FULTON (1908). Connecticut Auto Wks., New Haven, Conn., 1908.

330. F–W–D (1909–1911). Four Wheel Drive Auto Co., Clintonville, Wis., 1909–1911C—trucks.

G

331. GABRIEL (1910). Gabriel Car. Co., W. H., Cleveland, 1910C—trucks.

332. GADABOUT (1914–1915). Gadabout Corp., Detroit, 1914–1915.

333. GAETH (1903–1910). Gaeth Auto. Co., Cleveland, 1903–1910. (T) Stuyvesant (see 805).

334. GALE (1904–1910). Western Tool Wks., Galesburg, Ill., 1904–1908. (T) Robson Mfg. Co., 1908–1910D.

335. GARDNER (1920–1931). Gardner M. C. Co., St. Louis, 1920–1931.

336. GARFORD (1908–1913). Garford Auto. Co., Elyria, O., 1908–1912. Sold by Studebaker, 1910–1911. (T)

Willys–Overland Co., 1912. Also called STUDE-
BAKER GARFORD.

337. GAS–AU–LEC (1905–1907). Vaughn Machine Co.,
Peabody, Mass., 1905. (T) Corwin Mfg. Co., Peabody, 1905–1907D.

Gas Engine & Power Co. (see 406).

338. GASMOBILE (1898–1902). Auto. Co. of America,
Marion, N.J., 1898–1902B.

339. GAYLORD (1910–1913). Gaylord M. C. Co., Gaylord,
Mich., 1910–1913B.

340. GEARLESS (1907–1909). Gearless (Transmission)
M. C. Co., Rochester, N.Y., E1907–1909B.

341. GENERAL (1903–1904). Gen. Auto. & Mfg. Co., Cleveland, 1903–1904B.

342. GENERAL ELECTRIC (1898–1900). Gen. Elec. Auto.
Co., Philadelphia, 1898–1900D.

Gen. Engineering Co. (see 244).

Gen. Ms. Co., Detroit, 1908–1916. (T) Chevrolet M. C. Co., 1916. (Rg) Gen. Ms. Corp.,
1916–to date. (See BUICK—112, CADILLAC—116,
CARTERCAR—124, CHEVELLE—136, CHEVROLET—
137, CHEVY II—138, CORVAIR—182, CORVETTE—
183, ELMORE—274, HERTZ—391, INTER–STATE—
420, LA SALLE—475, MARQUETTE—513, OAK-
LAND—592, OLDSMOBILE—597, PONTIAC—644,
RAINIER—667, SCRIPPS–BOOTH—731, SHERIDAN
—745, TEMPEST—815, VIKING—852, WELCH—
874, WELCH–DETROIT—875.)

343. GENEVA (1901–1903). Geneva Auto & Mfg. Co.,
Geneva, O., 1901–1903B.

344. GERONIMO (1917–1919). Geronimo M. Co., Enid, Okla., 1917–1919B.

345. GIBBS (1903–1905). Gibbs Eng. & Mfg. Co., Glendale, N.Y., 1903–1905B.

346. G.J.G. (1909–1915). G.J.G. M. C. Co., White Plains, N.Y., 1909–1915.

347. GLEASON (1910–1914). Kansas City V. Co., Kansas City, Mo., 1910–1913. (N) Bauer Machine Wks., 1913. (N) BAUER 1914 (see 68).

348. GLIDE (1901–1917). Bartholomew Co., The, Peoria, Ill., E1901–1917.

349. GLOBE (1920–1921). Globe M. Co., Cleveland, 1920–1921.

350. GOODSPEED (1922). Commonwealth Ms. Corp., Chicago, 1917–1922B. (F) COMMONWEALTH (see 167).

351. GRAHAM (1930–1940). Graham–Paige Ms. Corp., Detroit, 1928–1940C. (F) GRAHAM–PAIGE.

352. GRAHAM–PAIGE (1928–1930). Graham–Paige Ms. Corp., Detroit, 1928–1940C. (F) PAIGE–DETROIT (see 612). (N) GRAHAM.

353. GRANT (1913–1921). Grant M. C. Co., Findlay, O., 1913–1922B. (A) Findlay (Car.) M. Co., 1913.

354. GRAY (1922–1926). Gray M. Corp., Detroit, 1922–1926B.

355. GREAT EAGLE (1911–*1914*). U.S. Car. Co., Columbus, O., 1911–*1914*).

356. GREAT SMITH (1909–1911). Smith Auto. Co., Topeka, Kan., 1904–1911B. (F) SMITH (see 759).

357. GREAT SOUTHERN (1910–1915). Great Southern Auto. Co., Birmingham, Ala., 1910–1915.

358. GREAT WESTERN (1907–1915). Model Auto. Co., Peru, Ind., 1907–1909. (Rg) Great Western Auto. Co., 1909–1915B.

359. GRINNELL (1910–1916)(E). Grinnell M. C. Co., Detroit, 1910–1916.

360. GROUT (1899–1914)(S). Grout Bros., Orange, Mass., 1899–1909. (R) 1907. (T) Grout Auto. Co., 1909–1914B. (R) 1912.

361. GUY VAUGHAN (1910–1913). W. A. Woods Co., Kingston, N.Y., 1910–1912. (T) Vaughan M. C. Co., 1912–1913B.

H

Haberer & Co. (see 146).

362. HACKETT (1916–1917). Hackett M. C. Co., Jackson, Mich., 1916–1919. (T) LORRAINE, 1919 (see 497). (F) ARGO (see 41).

363. HAL (1915–1918). H. A. Lozier M. C. Co., Cleveland, 1915. (Rg) Hal M. C. Co., 1916–1918B.

364. HALL (1903–1904). Hall M. V. Co., Dover, N.J., 1903–1904D.

365. HALLADAY (1906–1917). Streator M. C. Co., Streator, Ill., 1906–1915. (R) 1911. (T) Barley Mfg. Co., 1915. Halladay interests sold to Halladay Ms. Corp., 1917 (see 366, 702).

366. HALLADAY (1917–1920, 1922). Halladay Ms. Corp., Mansfield, Newark, O., 1917–1922B. (A) Halladay interests from Barley Mfg. Co., 1917 (see 293).

367. HAMMER (1905–1906). Hammer M. Co., Detroit, 1905–1906D.

368. HAMMER SOMMER (1903–1904). Hammer Sommer Auto. Car. Co., Detroit, 1903–1904D.

Handley Co., J. I. (see 25).

369. HANDLEY–KNIGHT (1920–1922). Handley–Knight Co., Kalamazoo, Mich., 1920–1922.

370. HANSON (1919–1923). Hanson M. Co., Atlanta, Ga., 1919–1923.

Hare's Ms. (see 492, 532).

371. HARPER (1907). Harper Buggy Co., Columbia City, Ind., 1907.

372. HARRISON (1906–1907). Harrison (Wagon) M. Co., Grand Rapids, Mich., E1906–1907B.

373. HARROUN (1917). Harroun Ms. Co., Detroit, Wayne, Mich., 1917–1918C.

374. HARVARD (1915). Pioneer M. C. Co., Troy, N.Y., 1915.

375. HASBROUCK (1899–1901). Hasbrouck M. Co., New York, 1899–1901B.

Hatfield (Auto. Mfg.) M. V. Co. (see 109).

376. HATFIELD (1916–1924)(HW). Cortland Cart & Car. Co., Sydney, N.Y., 1916–1924B.

377. HAVERS (1910–1914). Havers M. C. Co., Port Huron, Mich., 1910–1914B.

378. HAWLEY (1907). Hawley Auto. Co., Constantine, Mich., 1907.

379. HAY–BERG (1907–1908). Hay–Berg M. C. Co., Milwaukee, 1907–1908D.

Haydock Auto Mfg. Co., D. W. (see 184).

380. HAYNES (1904–1924). Haynes–Apperson Co., Kokomo, Ind., 1895–1905. (Rg) Haynes Auto. Co., 1906–1924B.

381. HAYNES–APPERSON (1895–1904). Haynes–Apperson Co., Kokomo, Ind., 1895–1905. (Rg) Haynes Auto. Co., 1906 (see 380).

382. H.C.S. (1920–1924). H.C.S. M. C. Co., Indianapolis, 1920–1924. (T) H.C.S. Cab Mfg. Co., 1924C —taxis.

383. HEINE VELOX (1906–1908). Heine Velox M. Co., San Francisco, 1906–1908D.

384. HENDERSON (1912–1914). Henderson M. C. Co., Indianapolis, 1912–1914B.

385. HENRY (1909–1912). Henry M. Sales Co., Muskegon, Mich., 1909–1912B. (R) 1911.

386. HENRY J (1950–1955). Kaiser–Frazer Co., Detroit (see 436).

387. HERCULES (1914–1915). Hercules M. C. Co., New Albany, Ind., 1914. (T) Kentucky Wagon Mfg. Co., Louisville, Ky., 1915. (N) DIXIE FLYER, 1916 (see 242). (F) CROWN (see 202).

388. HERFF–BROOKS (1914–1916). Herff–Brooks Corp., Indianapolis (sales), 1914–1916. Wayne Wks., Richmond, Ind. (manufacture), 1905–1916C (see 695).

389. HERRESHOFF (1909–1913). Herreshoff M. Co., Detroit, 1909–1913B.

390. HERTEL (1895–1900). Max Hertel, Chicago, 1895–1898. (T) Oakman M. V. Co., Springfield, Mass., 1898–1900B.

391. HERTZ (1924–1927). Yellow (Cab) Mfg. Co., Chicago, E1921–1926. (T) Gen. Ms. 1925. (N) Yellow Truck & Coach Mfg. Co., 1926. (F) AMBASSADOR (see 21).

392. HEWITT (1905–1909). Hewitt M. C. Co., New York, 1905–1909C—trucks. (F) STANDARD (see 777).

393. HILL (1907–1908). Hill M. C. Co., Haverhill, Mass., 1907–1908D.

     Hillsdale M. Co. (see 678).

394. HOBBIE (1909–1910)(HW). Hobbie Auto. Co., Hampton, Ia., 1909–1910C.

395. HOFFMAN (1902–1903)(S). Hoffman Auto. Mfg. Co., Cleveland, 1902–1903. (T) ROYAL TOURIST (see 715).

396. HOLLIER (1915–1918). Lewis Spring & Axle Co., Jackson, Mich., E1915–1918C.

397. HOLLEY (1900–1904). Holley M. Co., Bradford, Pa., E1900–1904B.

398. HOLLY (1913). Holly M. Co., Mt. Holly, N.J., 1913B.

399. HOLMES (1907). Holmes M. V. Co., East Boston, Mass., E1907B.

400. HOLMES (1918–1923). Holmes Auto. Co., Canton, O., 1918–1921. (Rg) Holmes M. C. Co., 1921–1923B.

401. HOLSMAN (1902–1910)(HW). Holsman Auto. Co., Chicago, 1902–1910B.

402. HOL–TAN (1907). Hollander & Tangman, New York, 1907. (Moon under H–T nameplate.)

403. HOLYOKE (1899–1903). Holyoke M. Wks., Holyoke, Mass., 1899–1903. (T) MATHESON, 1903 (see 522).

403A. HORNET (1969–to date). American Ms. Corp.

404. HOUPT (1909–1910). Harry S. Houpt Mfg. Co., Bristol, Conn., 1909–1910. (T) New Departure Mfg. Co. (N) HOUPT–ROCKWELL (see 405).

405. HOUPT–ROCKWELL (1910–1911). New Departure Mfg. Co., Bristol, Conn., E1909–1911C. (A) HOUPT, 1910. (F) ROCKWELL (see 706).

406. HOWARD (1903–1906). Howard Auto. Co., Yonkers, N.Y., 1903–1905. (T) Gas Eng. & Power Co., Morris Heights, N.Y., 1905–1906C.

407. HOWARD (1912–1914). Howard M. C. Co., Connersville, Ind., 1912–1913. (T) Lexington M. C. Co., Lexington, Ky., (Rg) Lexington–Howard Co., 1913 (see 485).

408. HUDSON (1909–1957). Hudson M. C. Co., Detroit, 1909–1954. (T) American Ms. Co., Kenosha, Wis., 1954. (N) RAMBLER, 1957 (see 670, 817).

409. HUFFMAN (1919–1926). Huffman Bros. M. Co., Elkhart, Ind., E1919–1926. (R) 1923.

410. HUNTINGTON (1907). Huntington Auto. Co., Huntington, N.Y., 1907B.

411. HUPMOBILE (1909–1936; 1938–1940). Hupp M. C. Co., Detroit, 1909–1940C. (A) Chandler–Cleveland Co., 1928.
    Hupp Corp. (see 679).

412. HUPP–YATES (1910–1916)(E). Hupp–Yates Elec. Car. Co., Detroit, 1910–1916.

413. HYDRO–CAR (1901). American Bicycle Co., New York, E1900–1902B. (T) International M. C. Co., Toledo, O., 1902 (see 823).

I

Ideal M. C. Co. (see 804).

414. ILLINOIS (1910–1912). The Overholt Co., Galesburg, Ill., 1909–1912. (F) OVERHOLT (see 604).

415. IMPERIAL (1903–1905). Imperial Auto. Co., Detroit, 1903–1905D.

416. IMPERIAL (1909–1915). Imperial Auto. Co., Jackson,

Mich., 1909–1914. (T) Mutual Ms., 1915 (see 511).

417. IMPERIAL (1929–to date). Chrysler Corp.

418. IMPERIAL (1907–1908). Imperial M. C. Co., Williamsport, Pa., 1907–1908B.

419. IMPERIAL (1903–1905). Rodgers & Co., Columbus, O., 1903–1905D.

Indiana M. & Mfg. Co. (see 172).

International Harvester Co. (see 298).

International M. C. Co. (see 413, 823, 870).

International M. C. Co., Stamford, Conn. (see 459).

420. INTER-STATE (1908–1918). Inter-State Auto. Co., Muncie, Ind., 1908–1919. (R) 1913.

421. IOWA (1908–*1909*). Iowa M. C. Co., Kellogg, Ia., 1908–*1909*.

422. IROQUOIS (1905–1908). Iroquois M. (C.) V. Co., Syracuse, Seneca Falls, N.Y., 1905–1908. (R) 1907.

J

423. JACKSON (1902–1923) (S,G). Jackson Auto Co., Jackson, Mich., 1902–1922. (T). Associated Ms. Corp., 1922. (Rg) National Ms. Corp., 1923B.

424. JAMES (1911). J & M M. C. Co., Lawrenceburg, Ind., 1909–1911B. (F) DEARBORN (see 219).

425. J & M (1909). J & M M. C. Co., Lawrenceburg, Ind., 1909–1911B. (N) DEARBORN (see 219).

425A. JAVELIN (1967–to date). American Ms. Corp.

426. JEEP (1941–to date); JEEPSTER (1949–1950; 1967). Willys–Overland Co., Toledo (see 887).

427. JEFFERY (1913–1917). Thomas B. Jeffery & Co., Kenosha, Wis., 1902–1916. (T) Nash Ms. Co., 1916. (N) NASH, 1917. (F) RAMBLER (see 669).

428. JENKINS (1907–1910). Jenkins M. C. Co., Rochester, N.Y., 1907–1910.

Jersey City Machine Co. (see 43).

429. JEWEL (1905–1909). Forest City M. C. Co., Massillon, O., 1905–1909. (Rg) Jewel M. C. Co., 1909. (T) CROXTON–KEETON (see 206).

430. JEWETT (1922–1926). Paige–Detroit M. C. Co., Detroit, 1919–1928 (see 612).

431. JOHNSON (1905–1912)(S). Johnson Service Co., Milwaukee, 1905–1912C.

432. JONES (1915–1920). Jones M. C. Co., Wichita, Kan., 1915–1920B.

433. JONES–CORBIN (1902–1907). Jones–Corbin Auto Co., Philadelphia, 1902–1907B.

434. JONZ (1909–1913). Jonz Auto. Co., Beatrice, Neb., 1909–1912. (T) American Auto. Mfg. Co., New Albany, Ind., 1912R. (T) CROWN, 1914 (see 202).

435. JORDAN (1916–1931). Jordan M. C. Co., Cleveland, 1916–1931B.

K

436. KAISER (1946–1954). Kaiser–Frazer Co., Detroit, 1946–1953. (A) Willys–Overland Ms. Co., 1953. (Rg) Kaiser Ms. Corp., 1953–1955C (see 318, 386).

437. KANSAS CITY (1905–1907). Kansas City M. V. Co., Kansas City, Mo., 1905–1907B.

Kansas City Vehicle Co. (see 347).

438. KATO (1907–*1909*). Four Traction Auto. Co., Mankato, Minn., 1907–*1909*.

439. KAUFFMAN (1908–1910). Advance M. V. Co., Miamis-

burg, O., 1908–1910. (T) Kauffman M. C. Co., 1910B. (F) Buggyabout (see 109).

440. Kearns (1908–1912). Kearns M. Buggy Co., Beavertown, Pa., 1908–1912C—trucks. (F) Eureka (see 285).

441. Keeton (1908). Keeton Town Car Wks., Detroit, 1908.

442. Keeton (1912–1914). Keeton M. Co., Detroit, 1912–1914B. (T) American Voiturette Co., 1914 (see 123).

Kelsey Mfg. Co., C. W. (see 570, 764).

443. Kelsey (1921–1924). Kelsey M. Co., Newark, N.J., 1921–1924C—taxis. (R) 1922. (Rg) 1924.

444. Kenmore (1909–1912). Kenmore Mfg. Co., Chicago, 1909–1912.

445. Kensington (1899–1903). Kensington (Bicycle Mfg.) Auto. Co., Buffalo, N.Y., E1899–1903B.

446. Kent (1916–1917). Kent Ms. Corp., Belleville, N.J., 1916–1917B.

Kentucky Wagon Mfg. Co. (see 242, 387).

447. Kenworthy (1920–1921). Kenworthy Ms. Corp., Mishawaka, Wis., 1920–1921B.

448. Kermath (1906–1907). Kermath M. C. Co., Detroit, 1906–1907.

449. Kessler (1921). Kessler M. Co., Detroit, 1921.

450. Keystone Six (1909–1910). Munch M. C. Co., Yonkers, N.Y., 1909. (Rg) Munch–Allen M. C. Co., DuBois, Pa., 1910.

451. Kiblinger (1907–1909). W. H. Kiblinger Co., Auburn, Ind., 1907–1909. (T) W. H. McIntyre Co., 1909 (see 529).

452. KIDDER (1900–1903)(S). Kidder M. V. Co., New Haven, Conn., 1900–1903. (T) SPRINGER (see 770).

453. KIMBALL (1910)(E). C. P. Kimball & Co., Chicago, 1910.

454. KING (1911–1923). King M. C. Co., Detroit, 1911–1923B. (R) 1912, 1920.
Kingston M. C. Co. (see 17).
Kirk Mfg. Co. (see 898).

455. KISSELKAR (1907–1931). Kissel M. C. Co., Hartford, Wis., 1907–1931B. (N) KISSEL, 1917.

456. KLEIBER (1925–1930). Kleiber M. (T) Co., San Francisco, 1925–1930C—trucks.

457. KLINE KAR (1909–1922). B. C. K. M. C. Co., York, Pa., 1909–1913R. (Rg) Kline M. C. Co., 1913–1922.

458. KLINK (1907–1909). Klink M. C. Co., Danville, N.Y., 1907–1909.

459. KLOCK (1900)(S). Percy L. Klock, Stamford, Conn., 1900. (T) International M. C. Co., Stamford, Conn., 1900.

460. KNICKERBOCKER (1901–1902). Ward–Leonard Elec. Co., Bronxville, N.Y., E1901–1903C (see 864).
Knight & Kilbourne (see 749).

461. KNOX (1900–1915). Knox Auto. Co., Springfield, Mass., 1900–1915B. (R) 1907.

462. KOBUSCH (1906). Kobusch Auto. Co., St. Louis, 1906. (T) St. Louis Car Co., 1906 (see 28).

463. KOEHLER (1909–1912). H. J. Koehler Co., New York, 1909–1912C—trucks.
Konigslow, Otto (see 603).

464. KRIT (1909–1914). Krit M. C. Co., Detroit, 1909–1914B.

465. KUNZ (1901–1902). J. L. Kunz Machine Co., Milwaukee, 1901–1902.

466. KURTZ AUTOMATIC (1902–1921). Kurtz M. C. Co., Cleveland, 1920–1921.

L

467. LAFAYETTE (1920–1924). Lafayette Ms. Co., Milwaukee, 1920–1924B.

468. LAFAYETTE (1934–1937). Nash Ms. Corp., Kenosha, Wis. Became Nash model.

469. LAMBERT (1905–1917). Buckeye Mfg. Co., Anderson, Ind., 1905–1917C—tractors. (F) UNION (see 838).

470. LANCASTER (1900–1901). J. H. Lancaster Co., New York, 1900–1901D.

471. LANE (1899–1910)(S). Lane (Bros.) M. V. Co., Poughkeepsie, N.Y., E1899–1910D.

472. LANSDEN (1904–1909)(E). Lansden Car Co., Newark, N.J., 1904–1909C—trucks.

473. LA PETITE (1905–1907). Detroit Auto. Mfg. Co., Detroit, 1905–1907. (T) MARVEL (see 518).

474. LARK (1958–1966). Studebaker Corp. (see 802). Larsen Machine Co. (see 291).

475. LA SALLE (1927–1940). Gen. Ms. Corp., Cadillac Division.

476. LAUREL (1916–1919). Laurel M. C. Co., Richmond, Ind., 1916. (Rg) Laurel Ms. Corp., 1917–1919.

477. LAUTH–JUERGENS (1907–1909). Lauth–Juergens M. C. Co., Chicago, 1907–1909C—trucks.

478. LEACH (1899). Leach M. V. Co., Everett, Mass., 1899.
479. LEACH–BILTWELL (1920–1923). Leach–Biltwell M. C. Co., Los Angeles, 1920–1923.
480. LEADER (1905–1912). Columbia Elec. Co., McCordsville, Noblesville, Knightstown, Ind., 1905–1912D.

Lear Auto. Co., Oscar (see 317).

Lebanon M. Wks. (see 845).

481. LENDE (1908–1909). Lende Auto. Mfg. Co., Minneapolis, 1908–1909.
482. LENOX (1911–1916). Lenox M. C. Co., Jamaica Plain, Hyde Park, Mass., 1911–1916. (F) MARTELL (see 516).
483. LEWIS (1899–1900). W. V. Lewis Co., Philadelphia, 1899–1900B.
484. LEWIS (1913–1915). L. P. C. M. Co., Racine, Wis., 1913–1915B.

Lewis Spring & Axle Co. (see 396).

485. LEXINGTON (1909–1926). Lexington M. C. Co., Lexington, Ky., Connersville, Ind., 1909–1913. Merged with Howard M. C. Co. (Rg) Lexington–Howard Co., 1913–1918. (Rg) Lexington M. Co., 1918–1926B. (R) 1923.
486. LIBERTY (1916–1923). Liberty M. C. Co., Detroit, 1916–1923B. (T) COLUMBIA, 1923 (see 164).
487. LINCOLN (1908–*1909*). Lincoln Auto. Co., Lincoln, Ill., 1908–*1909*.
488. LINCOLN (1920–1961). Lincoln M. Co., Detroit, 1920–1922. (R) 1921. (T) Ford M. Co., 1922. LINCOLN CONTINENTAL, 1961–to date.
489. LINDSLEY (1908)(HW). J. V. Lindsley Co., Indian-

apolis, 1908. (T) Dowagiac M. C. Co., 1909C—trucks.

490. LION (1909–1912). Lion M. C. Co., Adrian, Mich., 1909–1912. Burned out.

491. LITTLE (1911–1914). Little M. C. Co., Flint, Mich., 1911–1914. (T) CHEVROLET, 1913 (see 137).

492. LOCOMOBILE (1899–1929). Locomobile Co. of America, Bridgeport, Conn., 1899–1920. (A) Overman, 1902 (see 851). (Rg) Locomobile Co., 1920. Hare's Ms. control, 1920–1922. (T) Durant Ms., 1922.

493. LOGAN (1905–1908). Logan Construction Co., Chillicothe, O., 1905–1908B.

Long Co., R. H. (see 70).

494. LOOMIS (1901–1904). Loomis Autocar Co., Westfield, Mass., 1901–1904B.

495. LORD BALTIMORE (1913). Lord Baltimore M. C. Co., Baltimore, Md., 1913C—trucks.

496. LORRAINE (1907–1908). Lorraine Auto. Mfg. Co., Chicago, 1907–1908D.

497. LORRAINE (1919–1921). Lorraine Ms. Co., Detroit, Grand Rapids, Mich., 1919–1921B. (F) Hackett M. C. Co. (see 362).

Louisiana M. C. Co. (see 96).

498. LOWELL–AMERICAN (1908–1909). Lowell–American Auto. Co., Lowell, Mass., 1908–1909.

499. LOZIER (1904–1914). Lozier M. Co., Plattsburg, N.Y., Detroit, E1904–1914. (R) 1913.

Lozier M. C. Co., H. A. (see 363).

L.P.C. M. Co. (see 484).

500. LUCK–UTILITY (1912–1913). Cleburne M. C. Mfg. Co., Cleburne, Texas, 1912–1913.

501. LUVERNE (1906–1917). Luverne Auto. Co., Luverne, Minn., 1906–1917C—trucks.

502. LYMAN & BURNHAM (1903–1904). Lyman & Burnham, Boston, 1903–1904D.

503. LYONS–KNIGHT (1913–1915). Lyons–Atlas Co., Indianapolis, 1913–1915.

M

504. MACKLE–THOMPSON (1903). Mackle–Thompson Auto. Co., Elizabeth, N.J., 1903.

505. MADISON (1915–1918). Madison M. Co., Anderson, Ind., 1915. (Rg) Madison Ms. Co., 1916–1918.

506. MAHONING (1904–1905). Mahoning M. C. Co., Youngstown, O., 1904–1905D.

507. MAIBOHM (1916–1922). Maibohm Ms. Co., Racine, Wis., Sandusky, O., E1916–1922. (R) 1921. (T) COURIER (see 187).

508. MARATHON (1910–1914). Southern M. Wks., Jackson, Tenn., 1910. (N) Marathon M. Wks., 1911–1914B. (F) SOUTHERN (see 762).

509. MARBLE–SWIFT (1903–1905). Marble–Swift Auto. Co., Chicago, 1903–1905D.

510. MARION (1904–1913). Marion M. C. Co., Indianapolis, 1904–1913B.

511. MARION–HANDLEY (1915–1917). Mutual Ms. Co., Jackson, Mich., 1915–1917B. (F) IMPERIAL (see 416).

Marlboro Auto. & Car. Co. (see 858).

512. MARMON (1904–1933). Nordyke & Marmon, Indianapolis, E1904–1926. (N) Marmon M. C. Co., 1926–1933B.

513. MARQUETTE (1929–1930). Gen. Ms. Corp., Buick Division.

514. MARR (1903–1904). Marr Auto Car Co., Detroit, 1903–1904D.

515. MARSH (1899–1900, 1905). Marsh Bros., Brockton, Mass., 1899–1905. (T) American M. Co., 1905. (T) WALTHAM, 1905 (see 862).

516. MARTELL (1908–1910). Martell M. C. Co., Jamaica Plain, Mass., 1908–1910. (N) LENOX (see 482).

517. MARTIN–WASP (1920–1922). Martin–Wasp Corp., Bennington, Vt., 1920–1922B.

518. MARVEL (1907). Marvel M. C. Co., Detroit, 1907B. (F) LA PETITE (see 473).

519. MARYLAND (1901). Maryland Auto. Mfg. Co., Luke, Md., 1901B.

520. MARYLAND (1906–1910). Sinclair–Scott, Baltimore, 1906–1910C. (A) ARIEL, 1906 (see 44).

521. MASON (1906–1909; 1911–1916). Mason Auto. Co., Des Moines, Ia., 1906–1910. (Rg) Maytag–Mason M. C. Co., 1910. (Rg) Mason M. C. Co., 1911–1916B. (R) 1913.

522. MATHESON (1903–1913). Matheson M. C. Co., Holyoke, Mass., Wilkes–Barre, Pa., 1903–1910B. (T) Matheson Auto. Co., 1910–1913B. (R) 1912. (F) HOLYOKE (see 403).

Mathews M. Co. (see 763).

Maumee M. C. Wks. (see 190, 894).

522A. MAVERICK (1969–to date). Ford Motor Co.

523. MAXIM–GOODRIDGE (1908). Maxim–Goodridge Co., Hartford, Conn., 1908.

524. MAXWELL (1913–1925). Maxwell M. Co., Detroit, 1913–1921. (A) Chalmers M. Co., 1921. (Rg)

Maxwell M. Corp., 1921–1925. (T) Chrysler Corp., 1925. (F) Unit of United States M. Co.

525. MAXWELL–BRISCOE (1904–1912). Maxwell–Briscoe M. Co., Tarrytown, N.Y., 1904–1912B. (T) United States M. Co., 1910.

526. MAYTAG (1910). Maytag–Mason M. C. Co., Waterloo, Ia., 1910. (T) Mason M. C. Co., 1911 (see 521). (F) Mason Auto. Co. (see 521).

527. McCUE (1909–1910). The McCue Co., Hartford, Conn., E1909–1910C.

528. McFARLAN (1909–1928). McFarlan Car. Co., Connersville, Ind., E1909–1913. (Rg) McFarlan M. Co., 1913–1928B.

529. McINTYRE (1909–1916). W. H. McIntyre Co., Auburn, Ind., 1909–1916B. (F) KIBLINGER (see 451).

530. MECCA (1915–1916). Times Square Auto. Co. of New York & Chicago, E1915–1916C.

(Med–Bow) Medcraft Auto. Co. (see 772).

531. MENGES (1907–1908). Menges M. C. Co., Grand Rapids, Mich., 1907–1908.

532. MERCER (1909–1923). Mercer Auto. Co., Trenton, N.J., 1909–1919. (Rg) Mercer Ms. Co., 1919–1923B. Hare's Ms. control, 1920–1922. (F) Walter Auto. Co. (see 861).

533. MERCURY (1938–to date). Ford M. Co.

534. MERIT (1920–1922). Merit M. Co., Cleveland, 1920–1922.

535. METEOR (1902–1903)(S). Meteor Engineering Co., Reading, Pa., 1902–1903B. (F) READING STEAMER (see 683).

536. METEOR (1907–1909). Meteor M. C. Co., Bettendorf, Ia., 1907–1909. Burned out.

537. METEOR (1913–1915). Meteor M. C. Co., Shelbyville, Ind., Piqua, O., 1913–1915C. (F) CLARK (see 150).

538. METEOR (1919–1921). Meteor Ms. Corp., Philadelphia, 1919–1921D.

539. METEOR (1900–1901). Springfield Cornice Wks., Springfield, Mass., 1900–1901. (T) AUTOMOTOR (see 54).

540. METZ (1909–1921). C. H. Metz Co., Waltham, Mass., 1909–1921. (T) Waltham M. Mfrs., Inc., 1921 (see 863). (F) Waltham Mfg. Co. (see 862).

Metzger M. Co. (see 286).

541. MICHIGAN (1903–1907). Michigan Auto Co., Ltd., Kalamazoo, Mich., 1903–1907.

542. MICHIGAN (1910–1913). Michigan M. C. Co., Kalamazoo, Mich., 1910–1913B. Owned by Michigan Buggy Co.

543. MIDDLEBY (1908–1912). Middleby Auto. Co., Reading, Pa., 1908–1912 (see 681).

544. MIDLAND (1908–1912). Midland M. C. Co., Moline, Ill., 1908–1912B. (T) COLBY, 1913 (see 160).

545. MIER (1908–*1909*)(HW). Mier Car. & Buggy Co., Ligonier, Ind., 1908–*1909*.

546. MILBURN (1914–1923)(E). Milburn Wagon Co., Toledo, 1914–1923.

547. MILLER (1912–1913). Miller C. Co., Detroit, 1912–1913C—trucks.

548. MILLER (1907–1908). Miller M. C. Co., Bridgeport, Conn., 1907–1908D.

549. MILWAUKEE (1900–1902)(S). Milwaukee Auto. Co., Milwaukee, 1900–1902B.

550. MITCHELL (1903–1923). Mitchell M. C. Co., Racine, Wis., E1903–1910. (Rg) Mitchell–Lewis M. Co., 1910–1916. (Rg) Mitchell Ms. Co., Inc., 1916–1923B.

551. MOBILE (1899–1903)(S). Mobile Co. of America, Tarrytown, N.Y., 1899–1903D.

Model Auto. Co. (see 358).

552. MODEL (1903–1906). Model Gas Engine Wks., Auburn, Ind., 1903–1906. (R) 1904.

Modern Tool Co. (see 622).

553. MOHAWK (1903–1904). Mohawk Auto & Cycle Co., N. Indianapolis, 1903–1904D.

554. MOHLER & DEGRESS (1901–1905). Mohler & Degress, Astoria, L.I., N.Y., 1901–1905D.

555. MOLINE (1904–1913). Moline Auto. Co., East Moline, Ill., E1904–1919. (N) MOLINE–KNIGHT, 1913.

556. MOLINE–KNIGHT (1913–1919). Moline Auto. Co., East Moline, Ill., E1904–1919. (T) R & V Motor Co., 1919 (see 676). (F) MOLINE.

557. MOLLER (1920). M. P. Moller M. Co., Lewistown, Pa., 1920–1926. (N) FALCON, 1921 (see 211, 292).

558. MONARCH (1899–1905). Chicago M. V. Co., 1899–1903. (Rg) Monarch M. V. Co., 1903–1905D.

559. MONARCH (1905–1909). Monarch M. C. Co., N. Aurora, Ill., 1905–1909B.

560. MONARCH (1907–1909). Monarch Machine Co., Des Moines, Ia., 1907–1909.

561. MONARCH (1913–1916). Monarch M. C. Co., Detroit, 1913–1916B.

562. MONITOR (1915–1921). Cummins Auto Sales Co., Columbus, O., 1915. (T) Monitor M. C. Co., 1916–1921B.

563. MONROE (1914–1920). Monroe M. C. Co., Flint, Mich., 1914–1920B. Wm. Small & Co., sales agent, 1917. (R) 1918—bought by Small.

564. MOON (1905–1929). Moon M. C. Co., St. Louis, E1905–1931B (see DIANA—239, WINDSOR—889).

565. MOORE (1906–1907). Moore Auto. Co., New York, 1906–1907D.

Moore Mfg. Co., Charles J. (see 877).

566. MOORE (1918–1920). Moore M. V. Co., Danville, Ill., 1918–1920B.

567. MORA (1905–1910). Mora M. C. Co., Newark, N.J., 1905–1910B.

568. MORRIS & SALEM (1895–1899)(E). Morris & Salem, Philadelphia, 1895–1897. (T) Elec. Car. & Wagon Co., 1897. (T) Elec. V. Co., Hartford, Conn., 1897–1909. (N) COLUMBIA, 1899 (see 163).

569. MORSE (1907–1915). Easton Machine Co., S. Brockton, Mass., 1907–1915C.

Motorcar Co. (see 124).

Motor Car Co. of New York (see 22).

Motor Car Mfg. Co. (see 620).

570. MOTORETTE (1910–1911). C. W. Kelsey Mfg. Co., Hartford, Conn., 1910–1911.

571. MOYEA (1903–1904). Moyea Auto. Co., New York, 1903. (T) Consolidated M. Co., 1904. (T) SAMPSON, 1905 (see 723).

572. MOYER (1910–1915). H. A. Moyer, Syracuse, N.Y., E1910–1915C.

573. MULTIPLEX (1913). Multiplex Mfg. Co., Berwick, Pa., 1913C.

Munch M. C. Co. (see 450).

Munch–Allen M. C. Co. (see 450).

574. MUNTZ (1950–1951). Muntz T. V., Inc., Chicago, 1950. (N) Muntz M. Co., 1951.

575. MURRAY (1916–1920). Murray M. C. Co., Pittsburgh, Pa., Newark, N.J., 1916–1920B.

576. MUSTANG (1964–to date). Ford M. Co.

Mutual Ms. Co. (see 416, 511).

N

577. NANCE (1910–1913). Nance M. C. Co., Philadelphia, 1910–1913. (T) TOURAINE (see 825).

578. NAPIER (1904–1909). Napier M. Co. of America, Jamaica Plain, Mass., 1904–1909B. (R) 1907.

579. NAPOLEON (1916–1920). Napoleon Auto. Mfg. Co., Napoleon, O., 1916–1918. (Rg) Napoleon Ms. Co., 1918–1920C—trucks.

580. NASH (1917–1957). Nash Ms. Co., Kenosha, Wis., 1916–1936. Nash–Kelvinator Corp., 1936–1954. (T) American Ms. Co., 1954. (F) JEFFERY (see 13, 427, 468, 670).

581. NATIONAL (1900–1923). National Auto. & Elec. Co., Indianapolis, 1900–1902. (Rg) National M. V. Co., 1902–1916. (Rg) National M. C. & V. Co., 1916–1922. (T) Associated Ms. Corp., 1922. (A) DIXIE FLYER, JACKSON, 1922. (Rg) National Ms. Corp., 1923B.

National Sewing Machine Co. (see 271).

582. NEILSON (1907). Neilson M. C. Co., Detroit, 1907.

583. NELSON (1916–1920). E. A. Nelson M. C. Co., De-

troit, 1916–1919. (Rg) Nelson M. C. Co., 1919–1920B.

New Columbus Buggy Co. (see 305).

New Departure Mfg. Co. (see 405, 706).

584. NEW ERA (1915–1916). New Era Engineering Co., Joliet, Ill., 1915. (T) Elgin M. C. Co., 1916 (see 272).

585. NEW PARRY (1911). M. C. Mfg. Co., Indianapolis, 1911–1917. (N) PATHFINDER, 1911 (see 620). (F) PARRY (see 617).

586. NIAGARA (1915–1916). Mutual M. C. Co., Buffalo, N.Y., 1915–1916.

587. NIAGARA (1903–1905). Wilson Auto. Mfg. Co., Wilson, N.Y., 1903–1905D.

588. NOMA (1919–1923). Noma M. Corp., New York, 1919–1923.

Nordyke & Marmon (see 512).

589. NORTHERN (1902–1908). Northern Mfg. Co., Detroit, 1902–1906. (Rg) Northern M. C. Co., 1906–1908. (T) E-M-F, 1908.

590. NORWALK (1910–1922). Norwalk M. C. Co., Norwalk, O., Martinsburg, W. Va., 1910–1922. (R) 1911, 1914. (F) AUTO–BUG (see 51).

591. NYBERG (1911–1913). Nyberg Auto. Wks., Anderson, Ind., 1911–1913B. (F) RIDER–LEWIS (see 698).

O

592. OAKLAND (1907–1932). Oakland M. C. Co., Pontiac, Mich., 1907–1917. (T) Gen. Ms. Co., 1909; Division, 1917.

Oakman M. V. Co. (see 390).

593. OGREN (1914–1922). Ogren M. C. Co., Chicago, 1914–1916. (Rg) Ogren M. Wks., 1916. (Rg) Ogren M. C. Co., Milwaukee, 1917–1922B.

Ohio Auto. Co. (see 609).

594. OHIO (1909–1915). Ohio M. C. Co., Cincinnati, 1909–1912B. (T) Crescent M. Co., 1912–1915. (R) 1914.

595. OHIO ELECTRIC (1909–1915). Ohio Elec. Car. Co., Toledo, 1909–1915.

Ohio M. V. Co. (see 302).

596. OKEY (1906–1908). Okey M. C. Co., Columbus, O., 1906–1908. (R) 1907.

Olds Co., R. E. (see 691).

597. OLDSMOBILE (1901–to date). Olds M. Wks., Detroit, Lansing, Mich., E1901–1917. (T) Gen. Ms. Co. 1908; Division, 1917.

598. OLYMPIAN (1916–1920). Olympian Ms. Co., Pontiac, Mich., 1916–1920B. (T) Friend M. Corp. (see 322).

599. ONLY (1910–1913). Only Car Co., Port Jefferson, L.I., N.Y., 1910–1913B.

600. ORIENT (1900–1905). Waltham Mfg. Co., Waltham, Mass., 1900–1909. (A) American M. Co., Brockton, 1905. (N) WALTHAM, 1905 (see 862).

601. ORSON (1910–1913). Orson Auto. Co., New York, 1910–1913. Built by Brightwood M. Mfg. Co., Springfield, Mass.

602. OTTO (1900–1912). Otto Gas Engine Wks., Philadelphia, E1909–1912C.

603. OTTOCAR (1903–1904). Otto Konigslow, Cleveland, E1903–1904.

604. OVERHOLT (1909–1910). The Overholt Co., Gales-

burg, Ill., 1909–1912. (N) Illinois, 1910 (see 414).

605. Overland (1903–1908). Standard Wheel Co., Terre Haute, Indianapolis, 1903–1905. (T) Overland Auto. Co., Indianapolis, 1906–1908. (T) Willys–Overland, 1908 (see 887).

Overman Auto. Co. (see 851).

606. Owen (1909–1911). Owen M. C. Co., Lansing, Mich., 1909–1911. (T) Reo 1910 (see 691).

607. Owen–Magnetic (1914–1920). R. M. Owen & Co., New York, 1914–1920B. (T) Baker, R & L Co., 1915.

608. Oxford (1905–1906). Detroit–Oxford Mfg. Co., Oxford, Mich., 1905–1906. (T) Fostoria (see 313).

P

609. Packard (1900–1958). Ohio Auto. Co., Warren, O., 1900–1902. (T) Packard M. C. Co., Detroit, 1902–1954. (T) Studebaker–Packard Corp., 1954–1958 (see 802).

610. Page (1907–1909). Page Gas Engine Co., Adrian, Mich., 1907–1909.

611. Page (1906–1907). Page M. V. Co., Providence, R.I., 1906–1907.

612. Paige–Detroit (1919–1928). Paige–Detroit M. C. Co., Detroit, 1919–1928. (T) Graham–Paige Ms. Corp., 1928 (see 430, 352).

613. Palmer & Singer (1907–1914). Palmer & Singer Mfg. Co., New York, E1907–1914B.

614. Pan (1918–1921). Pan Ms. Co., St. Cloud, Minn., 1918–1921B.

615. Pan–American (1902–1903). Pan–American M. Co.,

Mamaroneck, N.Y., 1902–1903. (T) Commercial M. Co., 1903.

616. PAN–AMERICAN (1918–1921). Pan–American Ms. Corp., Decatur, Ill., 1917–1921B. (F) CHICAGO (see 139).

617. PARRY (1909–1911). Parry Auto. Co., Indianapolis, 1909–1911. (R) 1910. (T) NEW PARRY (see 585).

618. PARTIN–PALMER (1913–1917). Partin Mfg. Co., Chicago (Sales); Palmer M. C. Co. (Mfrs.), 1913–1915B. (T) Commonwealth Ms. Co., 1915–1917. (N) COMMONWEALTH, 1917 (see 167). (F) SUBURBAN (see 806).

619. PATERSON (1908–1923). W. A. Paterson Co., Flint, Mich., 1909–1923D.

620. PATHFINDER (1911–1917). Motor Car Mfg. Co., Indianapolis, 1911–1917. (Rg) Pathfinder M. C. Co. of America, 1917B.

621. PAWTUCKET (1901–1902)(S). Pawtucket Steamboat Co., Pawtucket, R.I., 1901–1902.

622. PAYNE–MODERN (1907–1910). Modern Tool Co., Erie, Pa., E1907–1910C.

Peets Mfg. Co., The C.S. (see 641).

623. PEERLESS (1900–1933). Peerless Mfg. Co., Cleveland, E1900–1903. (Rg) Peerless M.C. Co., 1903–1933. (Rg) Peerless Corp., 1933C.

624. PENN (1910–1913). Penn M. C. Co., New Castle, Pa., 1910–1913B.

625. PENNSY (1916–1917). Pennsy Ms. Co., Pittsburgh, Pa., 1916–1917.

626. PENNSYLVANIA (1907–1911). Pennsylvania Auto–M. Co., Bryn Mawr, Pa., 1907–1911B.

627. PERFECTION (1906–1908). Perfection Auto. Wks., South Bend, Ind., 1906–1908B.

628. PERFEX (1912–*1914*). Perfex Co., Los Angeles, 1912–*1914*.

629. PETREL (1908–1910). Petrel M. C. Co., Milwaukee, 1908–1910B. (T) F–S Ms. Co., 1911 (see 326).

630. PHELPS (1903–1905). Phelps M. V. Co., Stoneham, Mass., 1903–1905. (T) SHAWMUT, 1905 (see 743).

631. PHIANNA (1916–1921). Phianna M. Co., Newark, N.J., 1916–1918B. (T) M. H. Carpenter, Long Island City, N.Y., 1918–1921.

632. PICKARD (1908–*1912*). Pickard Bros., Brockton, Mass., E1908–*1912*.

633. PIEDMONT (1919–1922). Piedmont M. C. Co., Lynchburg, Va., 1919–1922B.

634. PIERCE–ARROW (1901–1938). Geo. N. Pierce Co., Buffalo, N.Y., E1901–1908. (Rg) Pierce–Arrow M. C. Co., 1908–1916. (Rg) Pierce–Arrow M. C. Corp., 1916–1938B. (R) 1921. Studebaker control, 1928–1933.

635. PIERCE–RACINE (1903–1910). Pierce M. Co., Racine, Wis., E1903–1910. (T) CASE (see 125).

636. PILOT (1910–1923). Pilot M. C. Co., Richmond, Ind., 1910–1923B.

637. PIONEER (1906–1909). Pioneer Car Co., Inc., El Reno, Okla., 1906–1909.
Pioneer M. C. Co. (see 374).

638. PITTSBURGH (1896–1899). Pittsburgh M. V. Co., Pittsburgh, Pa., 1896–1899. (T) AUTOCAR (see 52).

639. PITTSBURG SIX (1905–1910). Fort Pitt Mfg. Co., New Kensington, Pa., 1905–1910.

640. PLYMOUTH (1928–to date). Plymouth M. Corp., Chrysler Division.

641. P.M.C. (1908). The C. S. Peets Mfg. Co., New York, 1908.

642. POMEROY (1902). Pomeroy M. V. Co., Brooklyn, N.Y., 1902.

643. PONDER (1923). Ponder M. C. Co., Shreveport, La., 1923. (F) BOUR–DAVIS (see 96).

644. PONTIAC (1925–to date). Oakland M. C. Co., Pontiac, Mich., 1907–1932. (T) Gen. Ms. Co., 1909; Pontiac Division, 1932.

645. PONTIAC (1907–1908). Pontiac Spring & Wagon Wks., Pontiac, Mich., 1907–1908. (T) Motorcar Co., 1908 (see 124).

646. POPE–HARTFORD (1903–1914). Pope Mfg. Co., Hartford, Conn., E1895–1914B. (R) 1913 (see 163).

647. POPE–ROBINSON (1900–1904). Robinson M. V. Co., Hyde Park, Mass., 1900–1902. (Rg) Pope–Robinson Co., 1902–1904.

648. POPE–TOLEDO (1903–1909). Pope M. C. Co., Toledo, 1903–1909. (R) 1907. (T) Willys–Overland, 1909. (F) TOLEDO (see 823).

649. POPE–TRIBUNE (1903–1907). Pope Mfg. Co., Hagerstown, Md., 1903–1907B.

650. POPE–WAVERLEY (1903–1908)(E). Pope M. C. Co., Indianapolis, 1903–1908. (R) 1907. (T) Waverley Co., 1908 (see 871). (F) WAVERLEY (see 870).

651. POPULAIRE (1904). American Auto. & Power Co., Boston, 1904.

652. PORTER (1919–1922). American & British Mfg. Co., Bridgeport, Conn., 1919–1922B. (R) 1921.

Porter Co., Findley Robinson (see 325).

653. POSTAL (1907–1908)(HW). Postal Auto. & Engine Co., Bedford, Ind., 1907–1908. (T) BUGGYCAR (see 110).

Practical Auto. Co. (see 207).

654. PRATT (1911–1915). Elkhart Car. & Harness Mfg. Co., Elkhart, Ind., E1909–1915. (T) Elkhart Car. & M. C. Co., 1915 (see 269).

655. PRATT–ELKHART (1909–1911). Elkhart Car. & Harness Mfg. Co., Elkhart, Ind., E1909–1915. (N) PRATT (see 654).

656. PREMIER (1903–1924). Premier M. Mfg. Co., Indianapolis, 1903–1915. (R) 1913. (Rg) Premier M. C. Co., 1915–1923. (R) 1920. (Rg) Premier Ms., Inc., 1923–1924C—taxis.

657. PREMOCAR (1918–1923). Preston M. C. Co., Birmingham, Ala., 1918–1921. (Rg) Preston Ms. Corp., 1921–1923B.

658. PRESCOTT (1901–1905). Prescott Auto. Mfg. Co., Passaic, N.J., 1901–1905D.

Preston Ms. Corp. (see 657).

659. PRIMO (1911). Primo M. C. Co., Atlanta, Ga., 1911.

660. PRINCESS (1916). Princess M. C. Corp., Detroit, E1916.

661. PRINCETON (1924–1925). Durant M. Co. of Indiana, Muncie, Ind., 1924–1925.

662. PULLMAN (1905–1917). York M. C. Co., York, Pa., 1905–1910. (Rg) Pullman M. C. Co., 1910–1917B.

663. PULLMAN (1907–1908). Pullman (Auto.) M. C. Co., Chicago, 1907–1908.

664. PUNGS–FINCH (1904–1910). Pungs–Finch Auto. & Gas

Engine Co., Detroit, 1904–1910C. (F) SINTZ (see 755).

Q

665. QUEEN (1903–1906). C. H. Blomstrom M. C. Co., Detroit, 1903–1906. (T) DELUXE (see 225).

R

666. R.A.C. (1911–1912). Diamond Auto. Co., South Bend, Ind., 1911–1912. (F) RICKETTS (see 697).

667. RAINIER (1905–1911). Rainier M. C. Co., Saginaw, Mich., 1905–1911. (R) 1908. (T) Gen. Ms. Co., 1909.

668. RALEIGH (1921). Raleigh Ms. Corp., Bridgeton, N.J., 1921.

669. RAMBLER (1902–1913). Thomas B. Jeffery & Co., Kenosha, Wis., 1902–1916. (N) JEFFERY (see 427).

670. RAMBLER (1950–1969). Nash–Kelvinator Corp., 1936–1954. (T) American Ms. Corp., 1954–to date. Rand Mfg. Co. (see 865).

671. RANDALL (1903–1906). J. V. & C. Randall & Co., Newton, Pa., 1903–1906D.

672. RANGER (1907). Ranger M. Wks., Chicago, 1907.

673. RANGER (1920–1922). Southern Ms. Mfg. Ass'n, Ltd., Houston, Texas, 1920–1922B.

674. RAUCH & LANG (1906–1916)(E). Rauch & Lang Car. Co., Cleveland, 1905–1915. (T) Baker M. V. Co. (Rg) Baker, Rauch & Lang, 1915–1919. (Rg) Rauch & Lang, Inc., 1919 (see 675).

675. RAULANG (1919–1924)(E). Rauch & Lang, Inc., Chicopee Falls, Mass., 1919–1924C—taxis (see 674).

676. R & V KNIGHT (1919–1923). Root & Vandervoort M. Co., East Moline, Ill., 1919–1923B. (F) MOLINE–KNIGHT (see 556).

677. RAYFIELD (1911–1915). Rayfield M. C. Co., Springfield, Ill., 1911–1915B.

678. RAYMOND (1908). Hillsdale M. Co., Hillsdale, Mich., 1908.

679. R.C.H. (1911–1916). Hupp Corp., Detroit, 1911 (R) 1912. (Rg) R.C.H. Corp., 1912–1916.

680. READ (1913). Read M. C. Co., Detroit, 1913B.

681. READING (1910–1912). Middleby Auto. Co., Reading, Pa., 1908–1912 (see 543).

682. READING–DURYEA (1904–1905). Waterloo M. Wks., Waterloo, Ia., 1904–1905D.

683. READING STEAMER (1900–1902). Steam V. Co. of America, Reading, Pa., 1900–1902B. (T) Meteor Engineering Co., 1902 (see 535).

683A. REBEL (1968–to date). American Ms. Corp. RAMBLER model 1957–1960; 1966–1967.

684. REBER (1902–1903). Reber Mfg. Co., Reading, Pa., 1902–1903. (T) Acme M. C. Co., 1903 (see 5).

685. REEVES (1908–1909)(HW). Reeves Pulley Co., Columbus, Ind., E1908–1909.

686. REGAL (1908–1918). Regal M. C. Co., Detroit, 1908–1918B.
Reid Mfg. Co. (see 894).

687. REGAS (1903–1905). Regas Auto. Co., Rochester, N.Y., 1903–1905D.

688. RELIABLE DAYTON (1906–1909). Reliable Dayton M. C. (& Mfg.) Co. Chicago, 1906–1909. (T) FAL (see 290).

689. RELIANCE (1903–1907). Reliance M. C. Co., Detroit,

1903–1907. (Rg) Reliance M. T. Co., 1907C—trucks.

690. REMINGTON (1901–1904). Remington Auto. & M. Co., Utica, N.Y., 1901–1907D.

691. REO (1904–1936). R. E. Olds Co., Lansing, Mich., 1904. (N) Reo Car Co., 1904–1936C—trucks. (A) Owen M. C. Co., 1910 (see 606).

692. REPUBLIC (1910–1916). Republic M. C. Co., Hamilton, O., 1910–1916D.

693. REVERE (1918–1925). Revere M. C. Corp., Logansport, Ind., 1918–1923. (T) Revere Ms. Co., 1923–1925. (R) 1921.

694. RICHELIEU (1921–1923). Richelieu M. C. Corp., Asbury Park, Rahway, N.J., 1921–1923B.

Richmond Iron Wks. Corp. (see 853).

695. RICHMOND (1905–1916). Wayne Wks., Richmond, Ind., E1905–1916C (see 388).

696. RICKENBACKER (1922–1926). Rickenbacker M. C. Co., Detroit, 1922–1926B.

697. RICKETTS (1909–1911). Ricketts Auto. Wks., South Bend, Ind., 1909–1911. (T) R.A.C. (see 666).

698. RIDER–LEWIS (1908–1910). Rider-Lewis M. C. Co., Anderson, Ind., 1908–1910B. (T) NYBERG (see 591).

699. RIKER (1898–1901)(E). Riker Elec. M. Co., Brooklyn, N.Y., 1898–1901. (T) Elec. V. Co. (see 163).

700. RIVIERA (1907). Milton H. Schnader, Reading, Pa., 1907.

701. ROADER (1910–1911). Roader Car Co., Brockton, Mass., 1910–1911.

702. ROAMER (1916–1923). Barley Mfg. Co., Kalamazoo,

Mich., 1916–1918. (Rg) Barley M. C. Co., 1918–1923. (Rg) Roamer M. C. Co., 1923 (see 65, 365).

Roamer M. C. Co. (see 65).

Robinson M. V. Co. (see 647).

Robson Mfg. Co. (see 334).

703. ROCKAWAY (1902–1903). Charles D. Shain, Rockaway, N.Y., 1902–1903C.

Rockford Auto. & Engine Co. (see 299).

704. ROCK HILL (1910–1915). Rock Hill Buggy Co., Rock Hill, S.C., 1910–1915. (T) ANDERSON (see 36).

705. ROCKNE (1931–1933). Studebaker Corp. of America (see 802).

706. ROCKWELL (1909). New Departure Mfg. Co., Bristol, Conn., E1909–1911C. (N) HOUPT–ROCKWELL, 1910 (see 405).

Rodgers & Co. (see 419).

707. ROEBLING–PLANCHE (1906–1909). Walter Auto. Co., Trenton, N.J., 1905–1909. (T) MERCER, 1909 (see 532). (F) WALTER (see 861).

708. ROGERS (1909–*1912*). Rogers M. C. Co., Omaha, Neb., 1909–*1912*.

709. ROLLIN (1924–1925). Rollin M. Co., Cleveland, 1924–1925B.

710. ROOSEVELT (1929–1930). Marmon M. C. Co., Indianapolis, 1904–1933B.

Root & Vandervoort M. Co. (see 676).

711. ROSS (1915–1917). Ross & Young Machine Co., Detroit, E1915. (N) Ross Auto. Co., 1915–1917B.

712. ROSS (1906–1910)(S). Louis S. Ross, Newtonville, Mass., 1906–1910D.

713. ROSSLER (1907). Rossler Mfg. Co., Buffalo, N.Y., 1907.

714. ROYAL (1904–1905)(E). Royal Auto. Co., Chicago, 1904–1905B.

715. ROYAL TOURIST (1903–1911). Royal M. C. Co., Cleveland, 1903–1905. (Rg) Royal Tourist Car Co., 1905–1910B. (R) 1909. (F) HOFFMAN (see 395).

716. RUBAY (1922–1923). The Rubay Co., Cleveland, E1922–1923C.

717. RUSSELL (1903). Russell M. C. Co., Cleveland, 1903.

S

Saginaw M. C. Co. (see 899).

718. ST. JOE (1908–1909). St. Joe M. C. Co., Elkhart, Ind., 1908–1909. (T) SELLERS (see 736).

St. Louis Car Co. (see 28, 779).

719. ST. LOUIS (1899–1900). St. Louis Gasoline M. Co., St. Louis, 1899–1900D.

720. ST. LOUIS (1899–1907). St. Louis M. C. Co., St. Louis, Peoria, Ill., 1899–1907B.

721. SALTER (1909). Wm. A. Salter M. Co., Kansas City, Mo., 1909.

722. S & M (1913–1914). S & M M. Co., Detroit, 1913–1914B. (T) Benham Mfg. Co., 1914 (see 76).

723. SAMPSON (1904–1912). Alden Sampson Mfg. Co., Pittsfield, Mass., E1904–1912B. (A) MOYEA—571, CRESTMOBILE—196, 1905. (T) United States M. Co., 1910.

724. S & M SIMPLEX (1904–1907). Smith & Mabley Mfg.

Co., New York, E1904–1907. (T) Simplex (see 750).

Sandusky Auto. Co. (see 186).

725. Santos–Dumont (1902–1904). Columbus M. V. Co., Columbus, O., 1902–1904B.

726. Saxon (1913–1922). Saxon M. Co., Detroit, 1913–1915. (Rg) Saxon M. C. Corp., 1915–1922B.

727. Sayers & Scovil (1917–1924). Sayers & Scovil Co., Cincinnati, E1917–1924C.

728. Schacht (1905–1914). Schacht Mfg. Co., Cincinnati, 1905–1914C—trucks.

729. Schaum (1901). Schaum Auto. Mfg. Co., Baltimore, Md., 1901.

Schnader, Milton H. (see 700).

730. Scioto (1910–1911). Scioto M. C. Co., Chillicothe, O., 1910–1911. (T) Arbenz (see 39).

731. Scripps–Booth (1913–1922). Scripps–Booth Co., Detroit, E1913–1922. (T) Gen. Ms. Corp., 1917.

732. Searchmont (1900–1901, 1903). Searchmont Auto. Co., Philadelphia, 1900–1901, 1903B. (T) Fournier–Searchmont Auto. Co., 1903 (see 314).

733. Sears (1908–1909)(HW). Sears, Roebuck & Co., Chicago (see 18).

734. Sebring (1910). Sebring M. C. Co., Sebring, O., 1910.

735. Selden (1905–1914). Selden M. V. Co., Rochester, N.Y., 1905–1914C—trucks.

736. Sellers (1910–1911). Sellers Auto. Co., Elkhart, Ind., 1910–1911. (F) St. Joe (see 718).

737. Senator (1906–1910). The Victor Auto. Co., Ridgeville, Ind., 1906–1910.

738. SENECA (1918–1922). Seneca M. C. Co., Fostoria, O., 1918–1922.

739. SEVEN LITTLE BUFFALOES (1908)(HW). DeSchaum M. Syndicate, Buffalo, N.Y., 1908C—trucks.

740. SEVERIN (1920–1921). Severin M. Co., Kansas City, Mo., 1920–1921B.

741. S.G.V. (1909–1915). Acme M. C. Co., Reading, Pa., 1903–1911. (Rg) S.G.V. M. C. Co., 1911–1915. (R) 1914. (F) ACME (see 5).

Shain, Charles D. (see 703).

742. SHARP–ARROW (1908–1911). Sharp Arrow M. Co., Trenton, N.J., 1908–1910. (Rg) Sharp Arrow Auto. Co., East Stroudsburg, Pa., 1910–1911.

743. SHAWMUT (1905–1909). Shawmut M. C. Co., Stoneham, Mass., 1905–1909D. (F) PHELPS (see 630).

744. SHELBY (1902–1903). Shelby M. C. Co., Shelby, O., 1902–1903B. (F) Beardsley & Hubbs (see 214).

745. SHERIDAN (1920–1921). Sheridan M. C. Co., Muncie, Ind. (Gen. Ms. Corp. subsidiary), 1920–1921. (T) Durant M. Co. of Indiana, 1921. (N) DURANT, 1922.

746. SHOEMAKER (1907–1908). Shoemaker Auto. Co., Freeport, Ill., 1907–1908. (R) 1907.

747. SIBLEY (1910). Sibley M. C. Co., Detroit, 1910. (T) Sibley–Curtiss, 1911 (see 748).

748. SIBLEY–CURTISS (1911–1912). Sibley–Curtiss M. Co., Simsbury, Conn., 1911–1912. (F) SIBLEY (see 747).

749. SILENT KNIGHT (1906–1910). Knight & Kilbourne, Chicago, 1906–1910.

750. SIMPLEX (1907–1915). Simplex Auto. Co., New York, 1907–1917. (A) Crane M. C. Co., 1915. (N) Crane–

Simplex Co. of N.Y.C., Long Island City, N.Y.
(see 193). (F) Smith & Mabley Mfg. Co. (see 724).
Simplex M. Co. (see 29).

751. SIMPLICITY (1906–1910). Evansville Auto. Co., Evansville, Ind., 1906–1910D (see 829).

752. SIMPLO (1908–1909). Cook M. V. Co., St. Louis, 1908–1909.

Sinclair–Scott Co. (see 520).

753. SINGER (1914–1920). Singer M. Co., New York, Mt. Vernon, N.Y., 1914–1920B. (A) Palmer & Singer asscts, 1914.

754. SINGLE CENTER (1907–1909)(IIW). Single Center Buggy Co., Evansville, Ind., 1907–1909.

755. SINTZ (1903–1904). Sintz Auto Gas Engine Co., Grand Rapids, Mich., E1903–1904. (T) Pungs–Finch (see 664).

756. S.J.R. (1915–1916). S.J.R. M. Co., Boston, Mass., 1915–1916.

757. SKELTON (1920–1921). Skelton Ms. Corp., St. Louis, 1920–1921B.

758. SKENE (1900–1901)(S). Skene Auto. Co., Lewiston, Me., 1900–1901D.

759. SMITH (1904–1909). Smith Auto. Co., Topeka, Kan., 1904–1911B. (N) GREAT SMITH, 1909 (see 356).

Smith & Co., D. B. (see 273).

760. SNYDER (1908–1909). D. D. Snyder, Danville, Ill., E1908–1909.

761. SOULES (1905–1908). Soules M. C. Co., Grand Rapids, Mich., 1905–1908D.

Southern M. C. Co. (see 243).
Southern Ms. Mfg. Ass'n, Ltd. (see 673).

762. SOUTHERN (1908–1910). Southern M. Wks., Jackson, Tenn., 1908–1911. (N) MARATHON, 1910. (T) Marathon M. Wks., 1911 (see 508).

763. SOVEREIGN (1907). Mathews M. Co., Camden, N.J., 1907.

764. SPARTAN (1910). C. W. Kelsey Mfg. Co., Hartford, Conn., 1910C.

765. SPAULDING (1902–1903). Spaulding Auto. & M. Co., Buffalo, N.Y., 1902–1903B.

766. SPAULDING (1909–1917). Spaulding Mfg. Co., Grinnell, Ia., 1909–1917C—bodies.

767. SPEEDWELL (1907–1915). Speedwell M. C. Co., Dayton, O., 1907–1915B.

768. SPHINX (1915–1916). Sphinx M. C. Co., York, Pa., 1915–1916.

769. SPOERER (1908–1912). Carl Spoerer's Son's Co., Baltimore, Md., 1908–1912C.

770. SPRINGER (1903–1906). Springer M. V. Co., New York, 1903–1906D. (A) Kidder M. V. Co., 1903 (see 452).

771. SPRINGFIELD (1903–1904). Springfield Auto. Co., Springfield, O., 1903–1904D. (F) Bramwell M. Co. (see 97).

772. SPRINGFIELD (1907–1908). Medcraft Auto. Co., Springfield, Mass., 1907–1908D.

773. SPRINGFIELD (1908–1910). Springfield M. C. Co., Springfield, Ill., 1908–1910D.

774. SPRINGFIELD (1901). Springfield M. V. Co., Springfield, Mass., 1901.

775. STAFFORD (1909–1914). Stafford M. C. Co., Kansas City, Mo., 1909–1914C.

776. STANDARD (1902). Standard Auto. Co., Indianapolis, Ind., 1902.
777. STANDARD (1904–1905). Standard M. Construction Co., Jersey City, N.J., 1904–1905. (T) HEWITT, 1905 (see 392). (F) U.S. Long Distance (see 841).
778. STANDARD (1915–1923). Steel Car Co., Butler, Pa., E1915–1923C.
779. STANDARD SIX (1909–1911). St. Louis Car Co., St. Louis, E1906–1911C. (F) AMERICAN MORS (see 28). Standard Wheel Co. (see 605).
780. STANLEY (1907–1909)(HW). Stanley Auto. Mfg. Co., Mooreland, Ind., 1907–1908. (T) Troy Auto. & Buggy Co., Troy, O., 1908–1909.
781. STANLEY (1896–1899; 1901–1924)(S). Stanley Bros., Newton, Mass., 1896–1917. (Rg) Stanley M. Car. Co., 1917–1924. (R) 1923. (T) Steam V. Corp. of America, Syracuse, N.Y., Allentown, Pa., 1924D.
782. STANLEY–WHITNEY (1899–1902)(S). Stanley Mfg. Co., Lawrence, Mass., 1899–1902. (F) WHITNEY (see 882).
783. STANWOOD (1921–1923). Stanwood M. C. Co., St. Louis, 1921–1923.
784. STAR (1922–1928). Durant M. Co. of N.J., Elizabeth, N.J., 1921–1929.
785. STATES (1916–1917). States M. C. Mfg. Co., Kalamazoo, Mich., 1916–1917.
786. STAVER (1907–1914). Staver Car. Co., Chicago, 1907–1914.
787. STEAMOBILE (1900–1902)(S). Keene Steamobile Co., Keene, N.H., 1900. (T) Steamobile Co. of America, Reading, Pa., 1901–1902D.

S. Corp. of America (see 782).

788. STEARNS (1900)(E); (1901–1904)(S). E. C. Stearns & Co., Syracuse, N.Y., 1900. (N) Stearns Steam Car. Co., 1901–1904D.

789. STEARNS (1898–1929). F. B. Stearns Co., Cleveland, 1898–1929D.

Steel Car Co. (see 778).

790. STEELE SWALLOW (1907–1908). Steele Swallow Auto. Co., Jackson, Mich., 1907–1908D.

791. STEPHENS (1917–1924). Stephens M. C. Co. (Division, Moline Plow Co.), Freeport, Ill., E1917–1924C.

792. STERLING (1915). Sterling Auto. Mfg. Co., New York, 1915–1916. (T) Consolidated Ordnance Co., 1916 (see 33).

793. STERLING (1908–1911). Elkhart M. C. Co., Elkhart, Ind., 1908–1911B.

794. STERLING–KNIGHT (1924–1925). Sterling–Knight Co., Warren, O., 1924–1925.

795. STEVENS–DURYEA (1902–1915; 1919–1924). J. Stevens Arms & Tool Co., Stevens–Duryea Co., Chicopee Falls, Mass., E1902–1919. (Rg) Stevens–Duryea, Inc., 1919–1922B. (Rg) Stevens–Duryea M., Inc., 1923–1924B.

796. STEWART (1914–1916). Stewart Ms. Corp., Buffalo, N.Y., 1914–1916C—trucks.

797. STILSON (1907–1911). Stilson M. C. Co., Pittsfield, Mass., 1907–1911B.

798. STODDARD (1904). Stoddard Mfg. Co., Dayton, O., E1904. (T) Dayton M. C. Co., 1904 (see 799).

799. STODDARD–DAYTON (1904–1912). Dayton M. C. Co.,

Dayton, O., 1904–1912B. (T) United States M. Co., 1910.

800. STRATHMORE (1900–1901)(S). Strathmore Auto. Co., Boston, 1900–1901D.

801. STRATTON (1908–1909). Stratton Car. Co., Muncie, Ind., E1908–1909.

Streator M. C. Co. (see 365).

802. STUDEBAKER (1902–1963)(E,G). Studebaker Bros. Mfg. Co., South Bend, Ind., E1902–1911. (N) Studebaker Corp. of America, 1911–1954. (R) 1933. (T) Studebaker–Packard Corp., 1954–1958. (Rg) Studebaker Corp., 1962. Production moved to Canada, 1963–1966C. (Agent) E–M–F, 1908–1910, FLANDERS, 1910; GARFORD, 1910–1911. (A) E–M–F, 1910. (See AVANTI—55, E–M–F—277, ERSKINE—280, GARFORD—336, LARK—474, PACKARD—609, ROCKNE—705.)

803. STURTEVANT (1904–1907). Sturtevant Blower Wks., Hyde Park, Mass., E1904–1907C.

804. STUTZ (1911–1937). Ideal M. C. Co., Indianapolis, 1911–1913. (N) Stutz M. C. Co., 1913–1916. (N) Stutz M. C. Co. of America, Inc., 1916–1937B.

805. STUYVESANT (1910–1913). Stuyvesant M. C. Co., Cleveland, 1910–1913. (F) GAETH (see 333).

806. SUBURBAN (1911–1913). Suburban M. C. Co., Detroit, 1911. (T) Palmer M. C. Co., Chicago, 1912–1913. (N) PARTIN–PALMER, 1913 (see 618).

807. SUCCESS (1906–1909)(HW). Success Auto Buggy Mfg. Co., St. Louis, 1906–1909.

808. SULTAN (1906–1912). Sultan M. Co., Springfield, Mass., 1906–1912D.

809. SUN (1915–1917). Sun M. C. Co., Elkhart, Ind., 1915–1917B.

810. SUNSET (1905–1907). Sunset Auto. Co., San Francisco, 1905–1907D.

811. SUNSET (1907–1909). Victory M. C. Co., San Jose, Cal., 1907–1909.

812. SUPERIOR (1914). Crescent M. C. Co., St. Louis, 1914B.

813. SYNNESTVEDT (1904–1908). Synnestvedt Machine Co., Pittsburgh, 1904–1908D.

T

814. TAUNTON (1901–1904). Taunton M. C. Co., Taunton, Mass., 1901–1904D.

815. TEMPEST (1960–to date). Gen. Ms. Corp.

816. TEMPLAR (1917–1924). Templar Ms. Corp., Cleveland, 1917–1924B. (R) 1922. (Rg) 1923.

817. TERRAPLANE (1932–1938). Hudson M. C. Co., Detroit (see 408).

818. TEXAN (1918–1921). Texas M. C. Ass'n, Fort Worth, Tex., 1918–1921B.

819. THOMAS FLYER (1901–1914). E. R. Thomas M. Co., Buffalo, N.Y., E1901–1915. (R) 1912. (Rg) 1913. (F) Buffalo Auto & Auto–Bi Co.

820. THOMAS–DETROIT (1906–1908). E. R. Thomas–Detroit Co., Detroit, 1906–1908. (N) Chalmers–Detroit M. Co. (see 132).

821. THUNDERBIRD (1954–to date). Ford M. Co.

822. TINCHER (1904–1909). Tincher M. C. Co., South Bend, Ind., 1904–1909B.

823. TOLEDO (1900–1902)(S). American Bicycle Co., New York, E1900–1902B. (T) International M. C. Co., Toledo, 1902. (T) Pope M. C. Co., Toledo, 1903. (N) POPE–TOLEDO (see 648).

824. TOURAINE (1906–*1907*). Auto. Parts & Equip. Co., Chicago, 1906–*1907*.

825. TOURAINE (1913–1914). Touraine Co., Philadelphia, 1913–1914C—trucks. (F) NANCE (see 577).

826. TOURIST (1903–1909). Auto V. Co., Los Angeles, 1903–1909D.

827. TRAVELER (1913–1914). Traveler M. C. Co., Detroit, 1913–1914.

828. TRAVELER (1907). Bellefontaine Auto. Co., Bellefontaine, O., 1907. (F) ZENT (see 900).

829. TRAVELER (1906–1910). Evansville Auto. Co., Evansville, Ind., 1906–1910D (see 751).

830. TREBERT (1907). Trebert Gas Engine Co., Rochester, N.Y., E1907C.

831. TRIBUNE (1913–*1914*). Tribune M. Co., Detroit, 1913–*1914*.

832. TRIUMPH (1908–1910). Christopher Bros., Chicago, 1908–1910.

833. TRIUMPH (1906–1907). Triumph M. C. Co., Chicago, 1906–1907. (T) BENDIX (see 75).

834. TRIUMPH (1900–1901). Triumph M. V. Co., Chicago, 1900–1901D.

Troy Auto & Buggy Co. (see 780).

835. TULSA (1917–1922). Tulsa Auto. Mfg. Co., Tulsa, Okla., 1917–1920. (Rg) 1920. (T) Witt–Thompson M. Co., 1921–1922.

836. TWOMBLEY (1904). Twombley M. Car. Co., New York, 1904.

837. TWYFORD (1902–1908). Twyford M. C. Co., Brookville, Pa., 1902–1908D.

U

838. UNION (1902–1905). Union Auto. Co., Anderson, Ind., 1902–1905. (T) LAMBERT (see 469).

839. UNION (1908–1909)(HW). Union Car. Co., St. Louis, E1908–1909.

United M. Corp. (see 117).

840. UNITED STATES (1899–1901). (E) United States Auto. Co., Attleboro, Mass., 1899–1901B.

United States M. Co., New York, 1910–1912B (see BRUSH—105, COLUMBIA—163, COURIER—188, MAXWELL—525, SAMPSON—723, STODDARD–DAYTON—799). (T) Maxwell M. Co., 1913 (see 524).

U.S. Car. Co. (see 355).

841. U.S. LONG DISTANCE (1900–1904). U.S. Long Distance Auto. Co., New York, 1900–1904. (T) Standard M. Construction Co. (see 777).

842. U.S. (1908). U.S. M. C. Co., Upper Sandusky, O., 1908.

843. U.S. (1899–1900). U.S. M. V. Co., New York, 1899–1900.

University Auto. Co. (see 171).

844. UPTON (1903–1905). Upton Machinery Co., Beverley, Mass., E1903–1905. (T) Beverley Mfg. Co. (see 85).

845. UPTON (1904–1907). Upton M. Co., Lebanon, Pa., 1904–1906. (T) Lebanon M. Wks., 1906–1907D.

V

846. VALIANT (1959–to date). Chrysler Corp.

Vanderwater & Co. (see 181).

Vaughan M. C. Co. (see 361).

Vaughn Machine Co. (see 337).

847. VELIE (1908–1928). Velie M. V. Co., Moline, Ill., 1908–1928C.

848. VERNON (1910). Vernon M. C. Co., Detroit, 1910.

Victor Auto Co., The (see 737).

849. VICTOR (1907–1909)(HW). Victor Auto. Mfg. Co., St. Louis, 1907–1909.

850. VICTOR (1907–1911). Victor M. C. Co., St. Louis, 1907–1911.

851. VICTOR (1899–1902)(S). Overman Auto. Co., New York, 1899–1902. (T) Locomobile Co. of America, 1902.

Victory M. C. Co. (see 811).

852. VIKING (1929–1930). Gen. Ms. Corp.

853. VIRGINIAN (1910–1912). Richmond Iron Wks. Corp., Richmond, Va., 1910–1912B.

854. VOGUE (1916–1923). Vogue M. C. Co., Tiffin, O., 1916–1923B.

855. VULCAN (1913–1915). Vulcan Mfg. Co., Painesville, O., 1913–1915B.

W

856. WAHL (1913). Wahl M. Co., Detroit, 1913B.

857. WALDRON (1910)(HW). Waldron Runabout Mfg. Co., Waldron, Ill., 1910.

858. WALKER (1900–1902)(S). Marlboro Auto. & Car. Co., Marlboro, Mass., 1900–1902D.

859. WALKER (1905–1906). Walker M. C. Co., Detroit, 1905–1906D.

860. WALL (1901–1904). Wall Mfg. Co., Philadelphia, E1901–1904C.

861. WALTER (1903–1909). American Chocolate Machinery Co., New York, E1903–1905. (N) Walter Auto. Co., Trenton, N.J., 1905–1909. (T) Mercer Auto. Co. (see 532).

862. WALTHAM (1905–1909). Waltham Mfg. Co., Waltham, Mass., 1900–1909. (A) American M. Co., 1905 (see 515). (T) C. H. Metz, 1909 (see 540). (F) ORIENT (see 600).

863. WALTHAM (1921–1922). Waltham M. Mfrs., Inc., Waltham, Mass., 1921–1922B. (F) C. H. Metz (see 540).

864. WARD LEONARD (1902–1903). Ward–Leonard Electrical Co., Bronxville, N.Y., 1901–1903C. (F) Knickerbocker (see 460).

Warren Auto. Co. (see 66).

865. WARREN (1913–1914). Rand Mfg. Co., Detroit, 1913–1914. (F) WARREN–DETROIT (see 866).

866. WARREN–DETROIT (1909–1913). Warren–Detroit M. C. Co., Detroit, 1909–1913. (R) 1912. (T) Rand Mfg. Co., 1913 (see 865).

867. WARWICK (1901–1904). Warwick Cycle & Auto. Co., Springfield, Mass., 1901–1904D.

868. WASHINGTON (1907–1924). Carter M. C. Co., Hyattsville, Md., 1907–1912B. (T) Washington M. C. Co., Washington, D.C., 1912–1924.

869. WASHINGTON (1920–1924). Washington M. Co., Eaton, O., 1920–1924.

Waterloo M. Wks. (see 682).

870. WAVERLEY (1900–1903)(E). American Bicycle Co., New York, 1900–1902B. (T) International M. C. Co., Toledo, 1902. (T) Pope M. C. Co., 1903 (see 650).

871. WAVERLEY (1908–1915)(E). Waverley Co., Indianapolis, 1908–1915. (F) POPE–WAVERLEY (see 650).

872. WAYNE (1904–1908). Wayne Auto. Co., Detroit, 1904–1908. (T) E–M–F Co., 1908 (see 277).

Wayne Wks. (see 388, 695).

873. WEBB JAY (1907–1909)(S). Webb Jay M. Co., Chicago, 1907–1909.

874. WELCH (1901–1909). Chelsea Mfg. Co., Chelsea, Mich., 1901–1904B. (Rg) Welch M. C. Co., Pontiac, Mich., 1904–1909. (T) Gen. Ms. Co., 1909.

875. WELCH–DETROIT (1909–1911). Welch Co. of Detroit, Detroit, 1909–1911. (T) Gen. Ms. Co., 1909.

876. WESTCOTT (1910–1925). Westcott M. C. Co., Richmond, Ind., Springfield, O., 1910–1925B.

Western Tool Wks. (see 334).

877. WESTFIELD (1902–1903). Charles J. Moore Mfg. Co., Westfield, Mass., 1902–1903D.

878. WHIPPET (1926–1931). Willys–Overland Co. (see 887).

879. WHITE (1901–1918)(S,G). White Sewing Machine Co., Cleveland, E1901–1906. (N) The White Co., 1906–1918C—trucks.

880. WHITE STAR (1909–1911). Atlanta M. C. Co., Atlanta, Ga., 1909–1911B.

881. WHITNEY (1902–1903). Whitney Auto. Co., Whitney Pt., N.Y., 1902–1903.

882. WHITNEY (1898–1899)(S). Whitney M. Wagon Co., Boston, Mass., 1898–1899. (T) Stanley Mfg. Co., 1899 (see 782).

883. WILCOX (1910–1912). H. E. Wilcox M. C. Co., Minneapolis, 1907–1912C—trucks. (F) WOLFE (see 893).

884. WILLS ST. CLAIRE (1922–1927). C. H. Wills & Co., Marysville, Mich., 1922–1923R. (Rg) Wills St. Claire M. Co., 1923–1927B.

885. WILLYS (1929–1941; 1951–1955). Willys–Overland Co. (see 887).

886. WILLYS–KNIGHT (1915–1931). Willys–Overland Co. (see 887).

887. WILLYS–OVERLAND (1908–1927). Willys–Overland Co., Toledo, 1908–1953. (A) POPE–TOLEDO 1909, GARFORD 1912, EDWARDS–KNIGHT, 1913. (R) 1933. (Rg) 1936. (T) Kaiser–Frazer Co., 1953. (Rg) Willys Ms., Inc., 1953. (N) Kaiser–Jeep Corp., 1963. (F) Overland Auto. Co. (see 30, 605, 878, 885, 886).

Wilson Auto. Mfg. Co. (see 587).

888. WINDSOR (1906). Windsor Auto. Co., Evansville, Ind., 1906.

889. WINDSOR (1929–1930). Moon M. C. Co., St. Louis, E1905–1931 (see 239). (F) MOON (see 564).

890. WINTHER (1921–1923). Winther Ms., Inc., Kenosha, Wis., E1921–1923B.

891. WINTON (1897–1924). Winton M. (Car.) C. Co., Cleveland, 1897–1924C—engines.

892. WISCO (1909–1910). Wisconsin Car. Co., Milwaukee, 1909–1910.

Witt–Thompson M. Co. (see 835).

893. WOLFE (1907–1910). H. E. Wilcox M. C. Co., Minneapolis, 1907–1912C—trucks. (N) WILCOX, 1910 (see 883).

894. WOLVERINE (1903–1906). Reid Mfg. Co., Detroit, 1903–1905. (T) Wolverine Auto. & Comm. V. Co., Dundee, Detroit, 1906B. (T) Maumee M. C. Wks., 1906. (T) Craig–Toledo M. Co., 1906 (see 190).

895. WOODS (1899–1917)(E,G). Woods M. V. Co., Chicago, 1899–1917.

Woods Co., W. A. (see 361).

896. WORTH (1907–1908)(HW). Worth M. C. Mfg. Co., Evansville, Ind., 1907–1908D.

897. WORTHINGTON (1904–1906). Worthington Auto. Co., New York, 1904–1906D. (F) Berg Auto. Co. (see 79).

Y

898. YALE (1903–1906). Kirk Mfg. Co., Toledo, E1903–1905. (T) Consolidated Mfg. Co., 1905–1906B.

899. YALE (1916–1917). Saginaw M. C. Co., Saginaw, Mich., 1916–1917B.

Yellow Cab Mfg. Co. (see 21, 391).

York M. C. Co. (see 662).

Z

900. ZENT (1905–1907). Zent M. C. Co., Bellefontaine, O., 1905–1907. (N) TRAVELER, 1907 (see 828).

901. ZIMMERMAN (1908–1916). Zimmerman Mfg. Co., Auburn, Ind., 1908–1917D (see 231).

cars and companies— supplementary list B

A

1. ADRIA (1921). Adria M. C. Co., Batavia, N.Y.
2. AERO TYPE FOUR (1921). Victor Page Ms. Corp., New York.
3. AKRON (1901). Akron M. Car. Co., Akron, O.
4. AMERICAN (1907). American Auto. V. Co., Detroit.
5. AMERICAN STEAMER (1921)(S). American Steam Truck Co., Chicago.
6. ANCHOR (1906). Anchor M. C. Co., Cincinnati, O.
7. APOLLO (1907). Chicago Recording Scale Co., Chicago.
8. Auto. & Marine Power Co., Camden, N.J. (1901).

B

9. BAKER (1921)(S). The Baker Steam M. C. & Mfg. Co., Pueblo, Colo.

10. BARBARINO (1925). Barbarino M. Co., Brooklyn, N.Y.
11. BELL (1907). W. L. Bell, Kansas City, Mo.
12. BILLY FOUR (1910). McNabb Iron Wks., Atlanta, Ga.
13. BIRMINGHAM (1922). Birmingham Ms., Jamestown, N.Y.
14. BOLTE, T. H., Kearney, Neb. (1901).
15. Boston High Wheel Mfg. Co., Boston, Mass. (1908).
16. BOWMAN (1921). Bowman M. C. Co., Covington, Ky.
17. BRADLEY (1920). Bradley M. Co., Cicero, Ill.
18. BROWN (1916). Brown Car. Co., Cincinnati, O.
19. BURNS (1908). Burns Bros., Havre de Grace, Md.
20. BUSH (1919). Bush M. Co., Chicago.

C

21. CARROLL (1920). Carroll Auto. Co., Lorain, O.
22. CARROLL (1913). Carroll M. C. Co., Strasburg, Pa.
23. CAVAC (1910). Small M. C. Co., Detroit.
24. C DE L (1913). C de L Engineering Wks., Nutley, N.J.
25. CHAMPION (1916). Champion Auto Equip. Co., Wabash, Ind.
26. CHAMPION (1919). Champion Ms. Corp., Philadelphia.
27. CHICAGO (1905). Chicago Auto. Mfg. Co., Chicago.
28. CLASSIC (1917). Classic M. C. Corp., Chicago.
29. CLERMONT STEAMER (1922). Clermont Steamer, Inc., New York.
30. COATS (1921)(S). Coats Steamers, Inc., Indianapolis.
31. COEY FLYER (1912). Coey–Mitchell Auto. Co., Chicago.
32. COLONIAL (1922). Colonial Ms. Corp., Boston.

33. COMMANDOR (1922). Commandor Ms. Corp., New York, Milwaukee.
34. CRUSADER (1923). Crusaders Ms. Corp., York, Pa.

D

35. D.A.C. (1922). Detroit Air Cooled Car Co., Detroit.
36. DARLING (1917). Darling M. Co., Dayton, O.
37. DAVIS (1947–1948). Davis M. C. Co., Van Nuys, Cal.
38. DISBROW (1917). Disbrow Ms. Co., Cleveland.
39. DORCHESTER (1907). Hub Auto. Co., Boston.
40. DUESENBERG (1966). Duesenberg Corp., Indianapolis.
41. DUQUESNE (1913). Duquesne M. C. Co., Pittsburgh.
42. DYMAXION (1933). Buckminster Fuller.

E

43. EAGLE (1924). Durant Ms., Inc.
44. ECONOMY (1919). Economy M. Co., The, Tiffin, O.
45. EUREKA (1907). Eureka M. Co., Seattle, Wash.

F

46. FARNER (1922). Farner M. C. Co., Streator, Ill.
47. FLYER (1913). Flyer M. C. Co., Detroit.
48. FRONTENAC (1922). Frontenac M. Co. of America, Indianapolis.
49. FRONTMOBILE (1917). Safety M. Co., Grenloch, N.J.
50. FULTON (1908). Fulton M. C. Co., New York.

G

51. GEARLESS (1921)(S). Gearless Ms. Corp., Pittsburgh.
52. GEM (1917). Gem M. C. Co., Grand Rapids, Mich.
53. GENESEE (1912). Genesee M. Co., Batavia, N.Y.

54. GHENT (1919). Ghent M. Co., Ottawa, Ill.
55. Gurley, T. W., Meyersdale, Pa. (1901).

H
56. HAASE (1904). Northwestern Furniture Co., Milwaukee.
57. HANOVER (1921). Hanover M. Co., Inc., Hanover, Pa.
58. HARDING (1916). Harding M. C. Co., Cleveland.

I
59. INGRAHAM–HATCH (1917). Ingraham–Hatch M. Corp., Staten Island, N.Y.

J
60. JARVIS–HUNTINGTON (1912). Jarvis Machy. & Supply Co., Huntington, W.Va.

K
61. KELLER (1949). Keller Ms. Corp., Huntsville, Ala.

L
62. LA MARNE (1920). La Marne M. C. Co., Cleveland.
63. LANPHER (1910). Lanpher M. Buggy Co., Carthage, Mo.
64. LESCINA (1915). Lescina Auto. Co., Newark, N.J.
65. LINCOLN (1914). Lincoln M. C. Co., Detroit.
66. LONE STAR (1917). Lone Star M. Truck & Tractor Ass'n, San Antonio, Tex.

M

67. MAJESTIC (1916). Majestic M. Co., New York.
68. MALCOLM (1915). Malcolm M. Co., Detroit.
69. MERCURY (1904). Mercury Machine Co., Philadelphia.
70. MERCURY (1918). Mercury Cars, Inc., Hollis, Long Island, N.Y.
71. MESSERER (1901). Messerer Auto. Co., Newark, N.J.
72. METROPOL (1913). Metropol M. Corp., New York.
73. MONDEX–MAGIC (1913). Aristos Co., New York.
74. MORSE–RADIO (1910). Morse–Radio Auto. Co., Springfield, Mass.
75. M.P. (1915). Mt. Pleasant M. C. Co., Mt. Pleasant, Mich.
76. MURDAUGH (1900). Murdaugh Auto. Co., Oxford, Pa.
77. MURRAY–MAC (1921). Murray–Mac Ms. Co., Boston.

N

78. NORTHWAY (1921). Northway M. Sales Co., Natick, Mass.

O

79. OMAHA (1913). Omaha M. Co., Omaha, Neb.

P

80. PARENTI (1920). Parenti M. Corp., Buffalo, N.Y.
81. PILGRIM (1916). Pilgrim M. C. Co., Detroit.
82. PLAYBOY (1948). Playboy M. C. Corp., Tonawanda, N.Y.
83. PURITAN (1917). Puritan Ms. Co., Framingham, Mass.

R

84. REMINGTON (1915). Remington M. Co., New York.
85. RICHARD (1915). Richard Auto. Mfg. Co., Cleveland.
86. ROBERTS (1904). O. G. Roberts, Columbus, O.
87. ROGERS & HANFORD (1902). Rogers & Hanford, Cleveland.
88. ROMER (1921). Romer Ms. Corp., Boston.
89. ROTARIAN (1921). Bournonville Rotary Valve M. Co., Hoboken, N.J.
90. RUXTON (1929). New Era Ms. Co., Inc., New York.

S

91. SCARAB (1935). William Stout, Detroit.
92. SCOTT–NEWCOMB (1921)(S). Standard Engineering Co., St. Louis.
93. SERRIFILE (1921). Serrifile M. C. Co., Hollis, N.Y.
94. SERVITOR (1907). Barnes Mfg. Co., Sandusky, O.
95. SPERLING (1921). Associated Ms. Corp., New York.
96. Strong & Rogers, Cleveland (1900).

T

97. TRASK–DETROIT (1922)(S). Detroit Steam M. Corp., Detroit.
98. TRUMBULL (1902). Trumbull Mfg. Co., Warren, O.
99. TUCKER (1947). Tucker Corp., Detroit.

U

100. UNION (1911). Union Sales Co., Columbus, O.

V
101. VARSITY (1910). University M. C. Co., Detroit.
102. VERA (1912). Vera M. C. Co., Providence, R.I.
103. VERNON (1919). Vernon Auto. Co., Mt. Vernon, N.Y.

W
104. WATT (1910). Watt M. Co., Detroit.
105. W.F.S. (1911). W.F.S. M. C. Co., Philadelphia.
106. WHITE (1909). Geo. White Buggy Co., Rock Island, Ill.
107. Wildman, Alfred F., Morrisville, Pa. (1902).

number of companies versus production

The number of companies declined after 1909, but production continued to rise. While the logarithmic scales used are not identical, they serve to show the relationship.

Output records were established as World War I broke out, after World Wars I and II, at the close of the booming 1920's, and in the late 1960's.

Declines in production were caused by World War I, the recession of 1921, the depression of the 1930's, the recessions of 1938, 1952, and 1958. Production ceased during World War II.

Economic depression and recession, not wars, are the enemy of the industry.

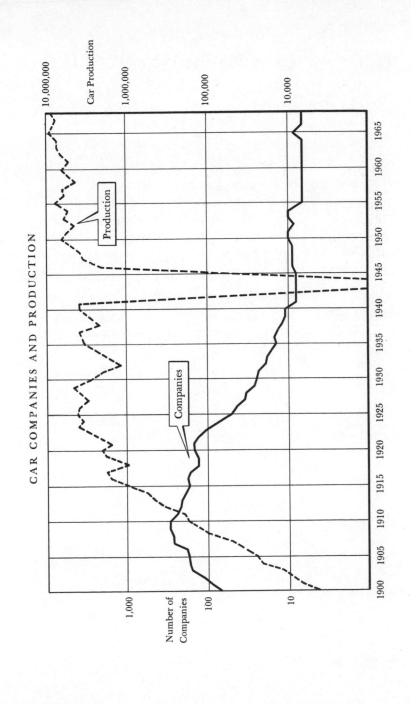

CAR COMPANIES AND PRODUCTION

table of factory location

Automobile Factories Have Been Located in 270 Different
Cities in 33 States, As Follows:

New York	38	California	5	Colorado	1
Ohio	34	Minnesota	4	Delaware	1
Massachusetts	32	Kansas	3	Georgia	1
Indiana	30	Nebraska	3	Louisiana	1
Michigan	28	Oklahoma	3	Maine	1
Pennsylvania	27	Texas	3	North Carolina	1
Illinois	18	Kentucky	2	New Hampshire	1
New Jersey	18	Missouri	2	South Carolina	1
Connecticut	9	Rhode Island	2	Virginia	1
Iowa	8	Alabama	1	Vermont	1
Wisconsin	8	Arkansas	1	West Virginia	1

genealogies

Family trees of important companies are presented on the following pages. Under "Cars Manufactured" are listed all the makes produced by companies composing the family. The names of cars no longer being built are italicized. The years during which the cars were manufactured can be found by turning to the "A" list.

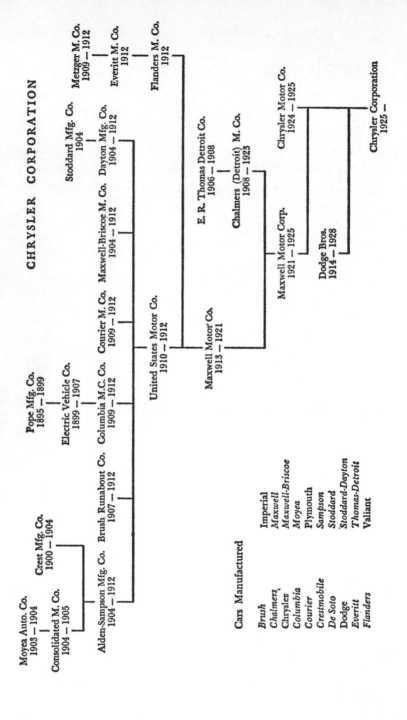

CHRYSLER CORPORATION

Moyea Auto. Co. 1903 — 1904
Crest Mfg. Co. 1900 — 1904
Consolidated M. Co. 1904 — 1905
Alden-Sampson Mfg. Co. 1904 — 1912
Brush Runabout Co. 1907 — 1912

Pope Mfg. Co. 1895 — 1899
Electric Vehicle Co. 1899 — 1907
Columbia M.C. Co. 1909 — 1912
Courier M. Co. 1909 — 1912
Maxwell-Briscoe M. Co. 1904 — 1912
Dayton Mfg. Co. 1904 — 1912

Stoddard Mfg. Co. 1904
Metzger M. Co. 1909 — 1912
Everitt M. Co. 1912
Flanders M. Co. 1912

United States Motor Co. 1910 — 1912
Maxwell Motor Co. 1913 — 1921
Maxwell Motor Corp. 1921 — 1925

E. R. Thomas Detroit Co. 1906 — 1908
Chalmers (Detroit) M. Co. 1908 — 1923

Dodge Bros. 1914 — 1928

Chrysler Motor Co. 1924 — 1925

Chrysler Corporation 1925 —

Cars Manufactured

Brush
Chalmers
Chrysler
Columbia
Courier
Crestmobile
De Soto
Dodge
Everitt
Flanders

Imperial
Maxwell
Maxwell-Briscoe
Moyea
Plymouth
Sampson
Stoddard
Stoddard-Dayton
Thomas-Detroit
Valiant

GENERAL MOTORS CORPORATION

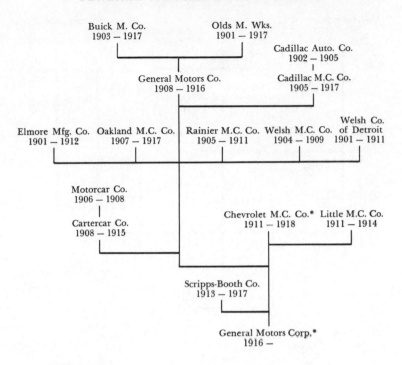

Cars Manufactured

Buick	Corvette	
Cadillac	*Elmore*	*Rainier*
Cartercar	*LaSalle*	*Scripps-Booth*
Chevelle	*Little*	*Sheridan*
Chevrolet	*Marquette*	Tempest
Chevy II	*Oakland*	*Viking*
(Nova)	Oldsmobile	*Welsh*
Corvair	Pontiac	*Welsh-Detroit*

*Chevrolet acquired control of General Motors Co. in 1916. General Motors Corp. organized in 1916. Buick, Cadillac, Oakland, and Oldsmobile made divisions in 1917. Chevrolet made division in 1918.

STUDEBAKER CORPORATION

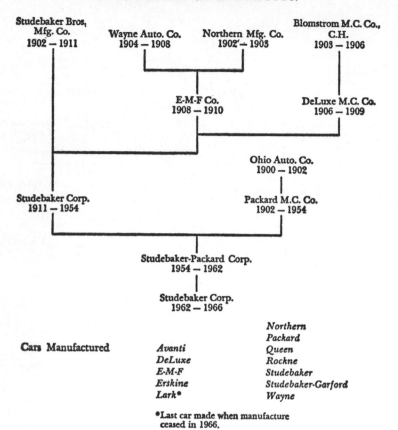

Studebaker Bros, Mfg. Co. 1902 — 1911	Wayne Auto. Co. 1904 — 1908	Northern Mfg. Co. 1902 — 1903	Blomstrom M.C. Co., C.H. 1903 — 1906

E-M-F Co. 1908 — 1910

DeLuxe M.C. Co. 1906 — 1909

Ohio Auto. Co. 1900 — 1902

Studebaker Corp. 1911 — 1954

Packard M.C. Co. 1902 — 1954

Studebaker-Packard Corp. 1954 — 1962

Studebaker Corp. 1962 — 1966

Cars Manufactured

Avanti
DeLuxe
E-M-F
Erskine
*Lark**

Northern
Packard
Queen
Rockne
Studebaker
Studebaker-Garford
Wayne

*Last car made when manufacture ceased in 1966.

AMERICAN MOTORS CORPORATION

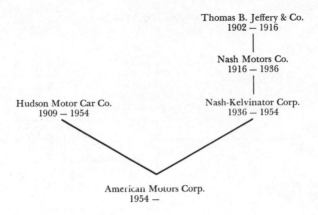

Thomas B. Jeffery & Co.
1902 — 1916

Nash Motors Co.
1916 — 1936

Hudson Motor Car Co.
1909 — 1954

Nash-Kelvinator Corp.
1936 — 1954

American Motors Corp.
1954 —

Cars Manufactured

Ajax
Ambassador
AMK
Hornet
Hudson
Javelin

Jeffery
Lafayette
Nash
Rambler
Rebel

FORD MOTOR COMPANY

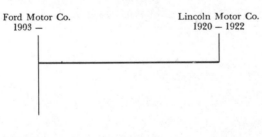

Ford Motor Co.
1903 —

Lincoln Motor Co.
1920 — 1922

Cars Manufactured

Comet
Continental
Edsel
Falcon
Ford

Lincoln
Maverick
Mercury
Mustang
Thunderbird

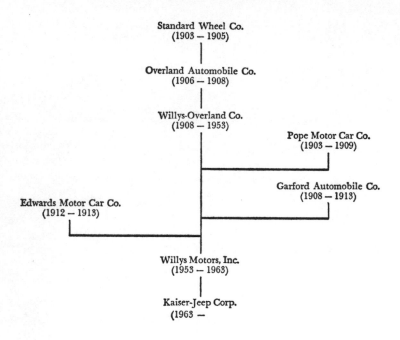

Standard Wheel Co.
(1903 — 1905)

Overland Automobile Co.
(1906 — 1908)

Willys-Overland Co.
(1908 — 1953)

Pope Motor Car Co.
(1903 — 1909)

Garford Automobile Co.
(1908 — 1913)

Edwards Motor Car Co.
(1912 — 1913)

Willys Motors, Inc.
(1953 — 1963)

Kaiser-Jeep Corp.
(1963 —

Cars Manufactured

Americar	*Whippet*
Garford	*Willys*
Jeep	*Willys-Knight*
Jeepster	*Willys-Overland*
Overland	

index